# John Godber

## Plays: 4

## Our House, Christmas Crackers, Crown Prince, Sold

*Our House*: 'It scores in every area that it tackles. Its portrait of a comfortable, disputatious marriage is so subtle it looks as easy as telly comedy, [while] its politics are more precise than those of any debate play: they touch, of course, on the miners' strike but also on the sale of council houses and the relocation of 'problem families'. Its historical snapshots are graphic and swift. It twists unpredictably between the wistful and the caustic.' *Observer*

*Christmas Crackers*: 'A festive fairy-tale for grown ups. The quick, one-line questions and answers, tart comments capped with tarter responses are very funny. Godber has always been able to introduce characters with deft, almost cartoon-like precision, and here he gives us a succession of them, increasingly bizarre yet remaining lifelike.' *The Times*

*Crown Prince*: 'An environmental satire . . . set in a not-too-distant future in which it is 30C at Christmas, most of Hull is under water, and bungalows on high ground are changing hands for £5m. The most radical drama he has produced for some time.' *Guardian*

*Sold*: '*Sold* is a bleak indictment of a troubling phenomenon. Estimates indicate that between 4,000 and 8,000 women are sold into the sex trade in Britain every year . . . Godber and Thornton opt to concentrate on the story of just one . . . it is testament to Godber's determination to break new ground.' *Guardian*

**John Godber** was born in Upton, near Pontefract, in 1956. He trained as a teacher at Bretton Hall College, in Wakefield, did an MA in Drama and an MPhil/PhD in Drama at Leeds University. Since 1984 he has been Artistic Director of Hull Truck Theatre Company. His plays include: *Happy Jack*; *September in the Rain*; *Bouncers* (winner of seven Los Angeles Critics Circle awards); *Up 'n' Under* (Olivier Comedy of the Year Award, 1984); *Shakers* and *Shakers Restirred* (both with Jane Thornton); *Up 'n' Under 2*; *Blood, Sweat and Tears*; *Teechers*; *Salt of the Earth*; *On the Piste*; *Happy Families*; *The Office Party*; *April in Paris*; *Passion Killers* and *Lucky Sods*; *Perfect Pitch*; *Seasons in the Sun*; *Departures*; *Men of the World*; *Reunion*; *Fly Me to the Moon*; *Beef and Yorkshire Pudding*; *Going Dutch*; *Wrestle Mad*; *Christmas Crackers*; *Crown Prince*; *Sold* (with Jane Thornton), and *Horrid Henry*. Television and film work includes: *The Ritz*; *The Continental*; *My Kingdom for a Horse*; *Chalkface* (all BBC2), episodes of *Crown Court*; *Grange Hill* and *Brookside* and screenplays for *On the Piste* and *Up 'n' Under*. He is a D.Litt. of Hull and Lincoln Universities. He is Professor of Contemporary Theatre at Liverpool Hope University, and Professor of Drama at Hull University. In 2005 he won two BAFTAs for writing and directing *Odd Squad*.

# JOHN GODBER

## Plays: 4

**Our House**
**Christmas Crackers**
**Crown Prince**
**Sold**

*with an introduction by the author*

**Methuen Drama**

## METHUEN CONTEMPORARY DRAMATISTS

1 3 5 7 9 10 8 6 4 2

This collection first published in Great Britain in 2009 by Methuen Drama

Methuen Drama
A & C Black Publishers Limited
36 Soho Square
London W1D 3QY
www.methuendrama.com

*Our House, Christmas Crackers, Crown Prince* and *Sold* all first published by Methuen
Drama in 2009
*Our House, Christmas Crackers, Crown Prince*: Copyright © 2009 John Godber
*Sold* Copyright © 2009 John Godber and Jane Thornton

Introduction © 2009 John Godber

John Godber has asserted his rights under the Copyright, Designs and Patents
Act, 1988, to be identified as the author of these works

ISBN: 978 1 4081 1205 2

A CIP catalogue record for this book is available from the British Library

Typeset by SX Composing DTP, Rayleigh, Essex
Printed and bound in Great Britain by
CPI Cox & Wyman, Reading, RG1 8EX

# Contents

# A Chronology

1977  *Bouncers*, Edinburgh Festival; revived by Hull Truck
      Theatre Company at the Donmar Warehouse in
      1984
1981  *Cry Wolf*, Yorkshire Actors company
1981  *Cramp*, Edinburgh Festival; revived at Bloomsbury
      Theatre in 1987
1982  *EPA* (Minsthorpe High School)
1983  *Young Hearts Run Free* (Bretton Hall)
1984  *A Christmas Carol* (adaptation, Hull Truck)
      *September in the Rain* (Hull Truck)
      *Up 'n' Under 1* (Hull Truck, Edinburgh Festival;
      transferred to Donmar Warehouse)
      *Shakers* (with Jane Thornton, Hull Truck)
1982  *Happy Jack* (Hull Truck)
      *Up 'n' Under 2* (Hull Truck)
1985  *Blood, Sweat and Tears* (Hull Truck; then Tricycle
      Theatre)
1986  *Cramp* (Musical. Hull Truck)
1987  *Oliver Twist* (Hull Truck)
      *Teechers* (Hull Truck, Edinburgh Festival; revived at
      the Arts Theatre, 1988)
1988  *Salt of the Earth* (Wakefield Centenary; then Hull
      Truck, Edinburgh Festival; then Donmar Warehouse)
1989  *Office Party* (Nottingham Playhouse)
1990  *On the Piste* (Hull Truck, Derby Playhouse; then
      Garrick, 1993)
1991  *Everyday Heroes* (with Jane Thornton, Community
      Play, Bassetlaw)
      *Bouncers, 1990s Re-mix* (Hull Truck)
      *Shakers Re-stirred* (with Jane Thornton, Hull Truck)
      *Happy Families* (Little Theatre Guild, then West
      Yorkshire Playhouse, 1992)
1992  *April in Paris* (Hull Truck; then Ambassadors, 1994)

1994  *Passion Killers* (Hull Truck, Derby Playhouse)
1995  *Lucky Sods* (Hull Truck; then Hampstead Theatre)
      *Dracula* (with Jane Thornton, Hull Truck)
1996  *Gym and Tonic* (Hull Truck, Derby Playhouse)
1997  *Weekend Breaks* (Hull Truck, Alhambra, Bradford)
      *It Started with a Kiss* (Hull Truck)
1998  *Unleashed* (Hull Truck, Edinburgh Festival; then
      Bloomsbury, 1999)
      *Hooray for Hollywood* (Hull Truck)
      *Perfect Pitch* (Stephen Joseph Theatre, Scarborough)
      *Seasons in the Sun* (Hull Truck, West Yorkshire
      Playhouse)
1999  *Big Trouble in the Little Bedroom* (Hull Truck)
2000  *Thick as a Brick* (Hull Truck)
2001  *Our House* (Hull Truck)
      *Departures* (Bolton Octagon Theatre, then Hull Truck)
2002  *Moby Dick* (with Nick Lane, Hull Truck)
      *Young Hearts* (co-production with Bransholme
      Kingswood Secondary School, Ferens Art Gallery,
      Hull Truck then Edinburgh Fringe Festival)
      *Men of the World* (Sheffield Crucible Theatre, then
      Hull Truck)
      *Reunion* (Hull Truck)
2003  *Screaming Blue Murder* (Hull Truck)
      *Fly Me to the Moon* (Chester Gateway Theatre)
      *Black Tie and Tales* (Hull Truck)
2004  *Beef and Yorkshire Pudding* (Theatre Royal and Opera
      House, Wakefield)
      *Going Dutch* (Hull Truck)
2005  *Wrestling Mad* (Hull Truck)
2006  *Christmas Crackers* (Hull Truck)
2007  *Crown Prince* (Hull Truck)
      *Sold* (with Jane Thornton, Hull Truck)
2008  *Horrid Henry* (Lyceum Theatre, Sheffield)

Further information can be found at *www.johngodber.co.uk*

# Introduction

The four plays in this collection are interrelated in many ways, perhaps primarily because they were all written for Hull Truck's Spring Street Theatre, where I have been premiering my work for almost half my adult life. As I write this introduction however, a new purpose-built theatre is being completed in Hull's city centre two hundred and fifty yards from the former Methodist church the company has called home for twenty-seven years. Indeed the next play I write will be premiered at a new four-hundred-and-forty-seat theatre, with a studio, rehearsal room, two bars, roof terraces and an education suite; a theatre that is naturally water-cooled, drawing on a spring nearly ninety metres beneath its footprint.

I am taking some time here to talk about the new Hull Truck theatre because it is only when I look at this most recent clutch of plays to be published that I am reminded what Hull Truck's magical space is all about. Indeed without such moments of reflection it is probable that I wouldn't have committed my feelings about Spring Street Theatre to paper at all. I am very fond of the theatre space and will miss the building perhaps more than I am prepared to admit to myself. I do hope however that we will be able to take the best of Hull Truck with us.

Indeed the new £15-million theatre has been built around the dimensions of the current auditorium; it reflects the shape and size of the space, has the same points of entrance for the audience and even has a mock proscenium which in the current space is only a means of holding up the roof. Over time various theatre consultants have constantly told us that the current theatre space should not work; it clearly has done for three decades. Hull Truck's genesis from its origins in 1971 with Mike Bradwell's carefully observed improvised plays, through Pam Brighton's political reign, to my own early experiments with popular physical theatre have all used this imperfect space to great effect. In the beginning Hull Truck didn't need the physical constraints of a theatre building, the name said it all, the actors rehearsed in Hull and toured in a truck. When Mike Bradwell left the company Hull Truck moved into what had been Humberside Theatre. It was famously reported that no one locally felt that the theatre would ever be a going concern. Pam Brighton ran the company for over a year and I left my job as Head of Drama at Minsthorpe High School at Christmas 1983 to run a company that was insolvent, a fact that wasn't mentioned in the job interview. Danny Boyle, the film director, was interviewed on the same day as me. He pulled the short straw and went to Hollywood, I came to Hull.

What has happened over the last twenty-five years or so is nothing short of extraordinary in the annals of British theatre history and someone somewhere will one day write the full history of the company.

When I consider our imminent relocation I wonder where those years have gone and remain convinced that we have one of the most play-friendly theatre spaces in the world. Almost everyone who has played at Hull Truck has become enraptured by the magic of the space. It is quite extraordinary that a theatre which is neither in the round, nor proscenium arch, nor a true thrust, but a fusion of these, should be such a great location for performing plays; but even this in a way exemplifies what theatre is all about, in that it is not an exact science.

Maybe we had this in mind when the opportunity to build a new theatre presented itself, for right from the start one thing was clear: we didn't want to change the performance space. The entire design for the new theatre works from the main auditorium outwards. Spring Street is a space that puts actors in a primary position, it is a space that demands the audience's attention, it is a space which is slightly irregular, has poor wing facilities, requires a raised stage to make the sightlines better and it is quite uncomfortable to sit in for long periods – hence the brevity of some of my early work – and yet it has worked as a functioning theatre for great plays, new plays, big bands, bad bands, stand-up comics and jazz festivals.

It is sometimes easy to forget that the old Hull Truck
theatre space was not designed. It did not have consultants
to measure the acoustics and it was not scrutinised for hours
by architects looking over drawings. It is, I am told by
experts, what they call a 'found space'; simply a room, a
room with a low ceiling, black walls, no depth, no height,
eleven foot to the rig, a room which is hot in the summer
and cold in the winter. I can hardly believe it but in a year's
time it will be a site for affordable housing. It may seem
crazy to some but this was the starting point for the new
theatre: we wanted to attempt to re-create something that
had evolved over time. We were starting with a blank sheet
of paper but what we knew instinctively was that what we
had worked, there was/is no reason why it shouldn't work
just down the road. However, when local theatre enthusiasts
ask if the new theatre will have hydraulics, a revolve, or
even a fly tower, they look crestfallen and disappointed
when I reply in the negative. How could we build a new
theatre that was just like the old one, some of them enquire?

There will of course be plenty to shout about that is new
in the new Hull Truck Theatre, but essentially the
relationship between the actor and the audience will and
should remain the same. There will of course be some
differences since we have more seats to fill and clearly the
issue of volume will be very much at the forefront of our
minds as we struggle to come to terms with our new space,
but we have constantly focused on the heartbeat of any
theatre building, the auditorium itself. By the time this
introduction is read the new theatre will be open and the
proof of the pudding will be in the eating – though some
things will inevitably, I dare say, have been lost in
translation.

So what will change if not the relationship between the
actor and the audience in the new Hull Truck Theatre?
Well, hopefully the theatre will not leak when it rains, it will
be cooler in the summer and warmer in the winter, the seats
will have more leg room having been designed around my
not-inconsiderable frame, and the actors will not contract
some dreaded bug every time they shower down after a

show, since the showers will be state-of-the-art and clean.
We will serve decent coffee and I'm told you will be able to
buy food throughout the day.

As for what happens on stage, however, I am fairly
adamant that at least where my own work is concerned,
very little will change. I have always been a fan of Berkoff
and Brecht, of physical theatre, political theatre and of
poetic theatre, and have constantly tested the notion as to
whether these forms can work alongside a desire to make
popular theatre. I'm bound to say that I think they can and
perhaps the early plays leading up to and including *Bouncers*
demonstrates this.

Theatre can be many things, in many shapes and sizes,
but the speed at which an audience can decode what is
happening on stage, the signals of performance, has a
relationship with the intensity of that shared experience. In
simple terms, the smaller the space potentially the more
intense the dramatic experience. We currently have 295
seats, 291 on a bad rainy day, and an impossibly low roof; it
is this low roof which makes the information on stage travel
to the back of the house quickly. Thus everyone in the
audience gets the information at more or less the same time.
Obviously for comedy this is very useful since no one is
waiting to hear a funny line, as is often the case in larger
venues. We have tried to compress the height of the new
theatre but, alas, the 440 seats bring an inevitably larger
volume, though we have tried to avoid an ocean of black
serge above the stage.

There will of course be changes in the new Hull Truck
but I can only hope that we have managed to transport that
certain magic which makes the space what it is. So why
build a theatre that doesn't have hydraulics, a revolve,
digital cameras and a fly tower? Why bother to spend fifteen
million pounds on a space that is so like the old one – surely
some folly?

It is absolutely clear that there is hardly space in this
introduction to develop a really strong argument for why we
have taken these steps, and it just might not be enough to
say that having written fifty-four plays for the current space

I think I know what I'm taking about. It might even be that
the reason we haven't changed the space has a more
fundamental core.

Consider the following: we are completely surrounded
now by the digital world; I even have a BlackBerry phone
myself and will watch out for football results and breaking
news. I will scan my ninety channels for something to watch,
a story to follow, a human tale to respond to, but I refuse to
subscribe to the seven hundred available channels on TV,
having experienced on holiday six hundred of them
peddling either porn or home shopping. In a world that
prides itself on getting the human story to you fast, it seems
that more often than not these stories are hidden away
somewhere in the edit, the commentary, the fog of media
coverage. In an effort to communicate across the airwaves
we have bleached out or somehow annexed what is human
about these narratives. This essence of a human story being
told transparently is entirely what I understand Peter Brook
to be about in his life's work. In some small way when we
present *Bouncers* through what Nick Hornby calls 'clear glass'
we are attempting to present the human form in the raw, no
set, no props, nothing to get in the way of actors and words.
We are searching for this purity of human emotion in the
theatre we produce and the digital world cannot compete
with the power of it. The problem, by its very nature, is that
it is evasive; nevertheless we have to build the conditions in
which it might thrive. When running a theatre it is all too
easy to forget why you got involved in it in the first place. I
am partly reminding myself here: it is simple and it is
human.

Some time ago a journalist wag described *Bouncers* as an
evening of poetry and mime. I was flattered; these are
entirely the fundamentals of theatre. I have seen helicopters,
trains, motor cars and pirate galleons come and go on stages
up and down the country. Most of the rest of those shows I
have forgotten by the time I've had my second tub of
Cornish Cream, but those plays where I have had to engage
my imagination I can still bring to my mind even now:
Berkoff's *Hamlet* in Edinburgh, Kantor's *Dead Class*, and his

final *Today is my Birthday*, Peter Brook's *The Man Who . . .*,
Theatre de Complicite's Kantor-influenced, *Street of
Crocodiles*. I remember these shows very well because I was a
part of the show. I was intelligently part of the action. The
play took place in my own head. The space on stage and the
space in our imaginations is of crucial importance for a
significant act of theatre to take place. I hope we will pack
this potential up with us when we leave our Spring Street
site and I hope I have left space for the audience's
imagination in my own work. Please forgive this brief
journey into the old Hull Truck Theatre and its artistic
rationale. The philosophy and the success of the company is
worth one book at least. For the time being however it may
have to settle with the above.

## Our House

The first play in this volume, *Our House*, was presented at
Hull Truck Theatre in 2001. It used the existing space and a
milk-shed which we rented at the side of the theatre to store
old sets and props. Act One took place in the milk-shed,
which we re-created as the parents' back garden and Act
Two took place in the living room of the mother's house.
The play assumes the father has died. In reality I was to lose
my mother in 2005 and as I had predicted in the play, life
was never the same again.

It was interesting working in the milk-shed since we had
real grass and real pigeons – the pigeons weren't designed,
they lived in the milk-shed – it logically followed that all the
acting had to have a sense of authenticity. The actors had to
play their parts as real as the grass they were acting on.

In some ways *Our House* is very different to *Bouncers* and
those other early physical plays, and yet in other ways it still
deals with the primacy of the actor in a space. There is a
cross-cutting structure of time-jumps in the play but the
essential truth of situation and character is once again the
thing that makes the play work.

It may be of some interest but, despite my physical build,

I have never been a night-club bouncer and while commentators claim that many of my plays are autobiographical I can correct those notions here by confirming that most of my plays aren't. *Our House*, however, is and has as many autobiographical elements as *Happy Families*, an earlier clearly stated autobiographical play.

   I had never written about the miners' strike when I left Upton, the mining village I grew up in, for Hull in 1984. It felt very close to me, it had created a schism in my family and it felt wrong to write about it at that time. Almost twenty years later I was able to look at the mining community I had left with clearer eyes, though I had visited that territory in 1988 with *Salt of the Earth*, a play commissioned by Wakefield Theatre Royal. I wanted to see the miners' strike of 1984 in a wider historical context. Appropriately in *Our House* the scenes after the miners' strike are all tinged with sadness. Indeed in many ways the reason the community begins to dismantle itself is because the glue of that society has been eroded by job losses. It could be argued that when the neighbours move in next door and make May's life a nightmare it is a corollary of the miners' strike. Whichever way you look at *Our House* you see the shroud of the miners' strike hanging over it and affecting the characters. Interestingly as time moves away from 1984 the fall-out of that huge event takes on more significance, as it did in the community the play reflects.

   The published version of *Our House* in this volume differs from the original in that I have rewritten the play into one location. Clearly it would be prohibitive to have two spaces, and would limit the potential to produce the play elsewhere. I have transposed Act One which took place in the garden to the living room, so the play in a sense has become much more traditional in its style. All other things in the play remain the same as the original, however, the cross-cutting, the developing story of a young man's life, his inability to please his parents and the conceited revenge theme. The final action of the play, when the writer son has secretly sought out a brutal snake breeder to buy his mother's house for a discounted price is indeed pure fiction. What we have therefore at the curtain is the revenge of the author in a play about his life wherein he changes the final outcome. In a way this could be seen as an extension of the notion of Kantor the artist, rearranging the presentation of his life's work in front of the audience's eyes.

I see a clear relationship between plays and dreams, between memory and history. Kantor's work has fascinated me for years and when I watch a production of *Our House* it is for me a cross between experiencing living history and distant memory.

## Christmas Crackers

One of the impossible things to strike a balance with when you are writing for a theatre that you have a hand in running is that you can't always write the plays that you really want to. No matter how much you try and divorce yourself from the issue you always have the box-office figure at the back of your mind. Now, some people might say that this is no bad thing because it means you have one eye on the size of the cast, the running costs of the play and the potential for it to attract an audience, any audience. Others might say that because of this you are limited in the scope and range of what you can do, and I suspect somewhere between the two arguments lies the truth. It is obvious and perhaps naive to admit because I have been doing it for so long but I know that my ideas are going to be compromised the moment I put pen to paper. Perhaps this is one of the reasons why I write another play – maybe the next one will not be so compromised – and yet there is a little bit of me that accepts that the mere act of writing down the play you have in your head is a compromise in itself. What I think I have become quite adept at is writing one play for the audience and another play for myself. In a way this allows me to write crowd-pleasing work that also has a theme and some artistic integrity; in fact I think I would say that was true of all the plays in this volume.

In *Christmas Crackers* I wanted to look at the chaos that is
an A & E department of a large city hospital. Over the last
ten years I have had personal experience of these
departments, if not with my mother then with myself or my
children. I have sat for hours wondering whether I would
ever be seen or wondering if the NHS would finally break
under the strain. Ironically some thirty odd years ago I was
asked by Jeremy Brock if I was interested in helping him
write a television drama set in a Bristol A & E department. I
turned down the offer suggesting that I didn't think it would
work. *Casualty* was the programme he was developing, so
much for what I know.

I have written in previous volumes about the role of the
outsider, the ever-watchful bouncers, the stand-up comic in
*Weekend Breaks*, the waitresses in the *Shakers* bar, the coach
drivers in *Men of the World*. In *Christmas Crackers* I chose the
watchful eyes of a security guard.  A security guard who, like
a playwright, will watch life come and go and will choose to
remember or forget various events as he sees fit, depending
on his world picture and whether it suits him. To that extent
we are all playwrights. With this conceit in mind I set out to
investigate quite how we project ourselves in our
imagination and how we would rearrange life if ever we had
the opportunity. Once again some might comment that the
similarities with Kantor's work are quite striking. This
convention also gave me the opportunity to play with my
interest in expressionist theatre, especially around the
mystical and fantastic elements of Prague and the Charles
Bridge at Christmas. Keith, the security guard, projects
himself into a world in which he can be whoever he chooses.
In order to impress the nurse with whom he has no real
relationship at the hospital he re-creates himself as an
urbane university lecturer showing students around Prague's
beautiful historic sights. When Kath meets the new Keith
she understandably melts: well, who wouldn't?

Here is another recurring theme in my work: the outsider
as unlikely hero. Keith, it transpires at the end of the play,
has not only fantasised about being someone else, but is also
the reason why Kath and Holly, the two nurses who are

going to Prague, have surprise tickets to go there in the first place. He is a Mr Scrooge who cannot melt from his security guard image and yet has a sensitive and loving soul. Would all security guards were the same!

The bleak realities of binge drinking, especially at Christmas, and the banner headline that field hospitals were to be set up in Hull city centre to deal with the casualties all helped shape the ideas behind the play. The madness of a night on the town was pitched against the imagined madness of expressionism in Prague. Maybe there are more similarities in these two worlds than we might first think.

*Christmas Crackers* was interesting to me in a number of ways: firstly it was a risk to see if an audience would be prepared to believe in one reality, the exterior of an A & E department, and then shift gear as the play takes the same characters into another time space and brings them back to the A & E department as if nothing had happened. Would adults go with such a fabulous notion? Well I'm delighted to report that they certainly appeared to, and I'm delighted to report that *Christmas Crackers* did the best business of any play at Hull Truck ever. Some members of the audience clearly got the switch in realities, some got the switch in styles, some I dare say got neither, but it confirmed what I had believed for years, that the popular imagination is much more receptive to new ideas than people often give it credit for. If they know the rules, they are quite happy to go with the narrative as long as it rings true from moment to moment. While *Christmas Crackers* deals with the harsh realities of life on an A & E unit it also demonstrates that we all have poetic interior worlds: this for me is one of the fascinating things about the human condition.

## Crown Prince

I have written fairly extensively about sport and have spoken at length about the event of theatre and the similarities between sport and theatre. I suppose it was inevitable as I got older that I would stop writing about

physical sports and I would start to look at more gentle
sports. Well, they don't come much more gentle than the
sport of Crown Green bowls. It was however with a concern
for the future and a real issue concerning my eldest
daughter Elizabeth, that I started to look seriously into the
phenomenon of global warming. I spent many weeks
reading books, searching articles and watching films and
videos about climate change. I have become convinced by
these learned men that something is happening to our
planet. We are, I believe, in denial and it was from this
starting point that I began to jot notes, which became *Crown
Prince*. What if we are all in denial, what if we are blind to
the missives from science? What will happen in the future?
These were the premises behind writing the play.

I have lived and worked in Hull and East Yorkshire since
1984 and it is well known for many things, not all of them
laudable, but what is perhaps less well known is that the
region is incredibly flat and would be vulnerable to flooding
should the ice-caps melt at any significant rate. Indeed an
exhibition at the local tourist attraction, the Deep,
demonstrates that Amsterdam and Hull would very soon be
lost should the waters rise to any great degree. For many
years I lived two hundred yards from the river Humber so
the issue of flooding had become a concern to my children.
Eventually we moved and by the time I came to write *Crown
Prince* we lived up the only hill in the region.

Writing about global warming in a way which would not
feel like political tub-thumping became the real challenge. I
had all the relevant facts but if an audience wanted facts
they could read the science available. So I set about penning
a piece of work that could present a political theme within a
comedy within a sport. It was something that I had admired
in Dario Fo's work for some years: how he could
communicate a number of things at the same time.

Even the location of Beech Hill Bowling Club, high on
the edge of the Yorkshire Wolds, has significance for all of
us who live here. Indeed, ironically two days after the play
had closed Hull and East Yorkshire experienced the worst
flooding for a generation. In the play Hull eventually floods

and people have to make for the only hill in the region. It
was more than spooky as I saw roads become impassable,
houses flooded, and the phrase that Hull had become a
'swimming pool' was a constant reference in the play. When
I wrote *Lucky Sods* many years ago it premiered two days
before Hull and the nation's first big lottery win of twenty-
five million. They say writing reflects a society but this was
more than strange.

*Crown Prince* is another character-based play which uses
time jumps to make a point. To that extent it has more in
common with *Our House* than *Bouncers*. It moves forward in
time while remaining in the same location. This gives the
play some architecture and vision. It also means that as a
writer I could exercise my imagination in projecting towards
a bleak water-logged future for this region. I hope that I am
wrong in this but, given the evidence, I fear that I may be
right.

The play also celebrates friendship in the bleaker
moments of life and is a testament to the never-dying spirit
of the human condition no matter how futile the future may
look. To this degree it borrows heavily from Beckett but
there is the dangerous whiff of individualism in the play as
the members of the bowling club vet who may join them in
their haven once Hull is under water. There is a fascistic
self-protective streak in these conservative bowlers.

One of the intentions with this play was to deliver a
curve ball to the audience, so that they, like the characters,
don't see the issue of global warming coming, and even
when they do, they feel that it really has nothing to do with
them. I was reminded of a quote from Arthur Miller when I
was researching the play where he said something like,
'Politics doesn't affect people until it affects them
personally'. He knew a thing or two. This is entirely the
driving theme in *Crown Prince*. It is not until the green
of the bowling club is being scorched by the severe
weather and they cannot find other clubs to play because
they are water-logged, that the conservative-minded
members of the club realise that things are happening
that are beyond their control. Like many of us, the

members of Beech Hill Bowling Club are in denial about changes to our climate.

## Sold

In so many ways *Sold* is the odd one out in this collection of plays. Not only with regard to the subject matter but also with regard to how the play works on stage. The play was written as a companion piece to Hull's Wilberforce celebrations and formed part of a year-long event which investigated the plight of modern-day slavery in all its forms. Hull Truck wanted to respond to this event and as a consequence Jane Thornton and I set about exploring areas of modern-day slavery that we found interesting. There had been a number of films and articles about sex slavery and we were both struck by the savagery of some of these stories, in many ways they wrote themselves.

Clearly, portraying this subject matter on stage became problematic, and researching the play was in itself troublesome. We both felt that we could not present the brutality we had come across on stage since it would not only be extremely difficult to do convincingly, but also we both felt that to 'pretend' to re-create that kind of brutality would be nothing short of exhibitionism. Personally I have always had a knee-jerk reaction to voyeuristic theatre. We, the audience, know what is happening on stage is artificial, yet it is trying to be brutal and real to convince us that the world is a brutal and real place. I have always felt that this kind of event in the theatre is frankly laughable since it can never communicate the brutality of the acts it is trying to re-create as the audience by their very presence are suspending their disbelief and secretly know the acts of brutality are not real. There will be an act of brutality again at tomorrow's matinee: this some how feels like a lie to me.

Brecht deals with this brilliantly in *Arturo Ui*. Ui is a character not unlike Hitler, he is not trying to be Hitler but he is saying to the audience that there is man in the real world called Hitler and here we have a character who is similar, look at his actions. The philosophy of this is simply communicated in a poem of Brecht's, 'Showing has to be shown' in which he says, 'An actor is not King Lear but he is always showing King Lear'. Jane and I both felt that this was the way to deal with the subject matter of bonded sex slavery in *Sold*.

We started with the premise of a question of the audience: if you could help get a girl out of bonded sex slavery would you? And if you did and she grew to have a relationship with you what would you do then? We deliberately created the central character, Ray, as a journalist looking for a story to sell to make money since he has fallen on hard times. With the knowledge that sex sells he visits a London brothel and comes across a mysterious and attractive eastern European girl. This in itself offered up a paradox. Ray has fallen on a story and a girl to tell it and he is prepared to use her for her story in order for him to regain his position as a cutting-edge journalist. This dilemma has a Brechtian feel to me.

However we wanted to make his dilemma more complicated, he was not only trying to help Anja but he also found her sexually attractive. Ray is in denial, he thinks he is helping the girl and to some extent he is, but he is also caught by her mysterious spell and would love to have sex with her were he in a different time, in a different world. He is trapped by the good intentions of his own actions. His denial is similar to the denial of the bowlers in *Crown Prince*.

The question for the audience is: would it have been better just to have left Anja and not tried to help her? How can we help these girls, isn't the situation hopeless? The play asks us: what the hell can we do to make this situation better? In every way it bounces the problem back into the audience. It does what theatre can only do in my view, it says to the audience: 'Have you seen this, what do you think about it, what are you going to do about it, where do you stand on it? Was he right or wrong to do what he did? Please discuss!'

It may be the teacher in me but I feel very strongly that it is not simply a matter of entertaining an audience, there has to be a moral dilemma in the play lurking at some level. Some members of the audience will see it within the architecture of the play and others may not, but it has to be there for me in order for the play to work as good theatre.

I hope that there are a number of moral dilemmas lurking beneath the surface of these four plays.

John Godber
October 2008

# Our House

*Our House* was first performed by Hull Truck Theatre Company in July 2001 at Spring Street Theatre, Hull. This revised version of the play was first performed by Hull Truck Theatre Company in January 2008 at Theatre Royal, Wakefield with the following cast:

| | |
|---|---|
| **May** | Jackie Naylor |
| **Ted** | Dicken Ashworth |
| **Jack** | Matt Booth |
| **Sharon** | Fiona Wass |
| **Steve** | Lewis Linford |
| **Sonja** | Anne-Marie Hosell |
| **Les** | Lewis Linford |
| **Candace** | Anne-Marie Hosell |
| **Sylvia** | Fiona Wass |
| **Lance** | Dicken Ashworth |

*Directed by* John Godber
*Designed* by Pip Leckenby

The action takes place in the living room of a council house between the years 1958 and 2001. The play is set in a West Yorkshire pit village.

# Act One

## Scene One

*The present.*

*The set is a cut-away of a council house built in the 1950s. It is spotlessly clean, though has seen many decades. Two large sofas occupy centre stage. Upstage there are doors through to a kitchen, and a door to the front door stage right. We are able to see through the cut-away wall to the front door, stage right, and to the dustbin, the fence and the next-door garden area. Upstage centre is a false wall where we will be able to see the next-door action when we need to. The living room is full of boxes and furniture ready for removal.*

*House lights. Music.* **May**, *a woman in her early seventies using a Eubank sweeper to tidy her living room. She is unsteady on her feet. As she works,* **Steve**, *a young man dressed in work clothes, appears at the back door. He reads from a small piece of paper. But* **May** *cannot hear him until he shouts.*

**Steve**  Hello? Hello? Is there anyone there? Hello!

**May**  Hello!

**Steve**  Hello! Are you there? Is this 102?

**May** *turns, moves to the back door.*

*Silence.*

**May**  What are you looking for, love?

**Steve**  102.

**May**  This is it!

**Steve**  I thought . . .

**May**  Are you from Mason's?

**Steve**  That's us . . .

**May**  I thought you weren't coming . . .

**Steve** (*defensive*)  No I . . .

**May**   I thought you weren't coming . . .

**Steve** (*defensive*)   Oh no, we . . .

**May**   I've just been to phone up . . .

**Steve**   No, we had a bit of a problem this morning . . .

**May**   I've phoned up twice . . .

**Steve**   The van wouldn't start.

**May**   The woman said you'd overlaid . . .

**Steve**   First time it's let me down and all . . .

**May**   She said you'd overlaid!

**Steve** (*obviously lying*)   No . . . Don't worry about that.

**May**   I mean I could have got Ken Swale, you know?

**Steve** (*looking around*)   I'm parked on the corner, can't get any closer for that skip . . .

**May**   Our Jack's arranged it . . .

**Steve** (*still looking around*)   A bit of a carry but . . .

**May**   I told him to use Ken Swale.

**Steve**   You'll be all right with me . . .

**May**   I thought it was going to be Mason's?

**Steve**   This is Mason's . . .

**May**   You're not a Mason, are you?

**Steve**   Not me no!

**May**   I mean, I went to school with Barry Mason . . .

**Steve**   I bought it off him . . .

**May**   I was going to say! I mean I know a Mason when I see one!

**Steve**   We've kept the name.

**May**    You'll be here all day if it's just you!

**Steve**    Is there much to go?

**May**    A house full, what do you think? Come on!

**Steve**    I thought there might be.

**May** *brings* **Steve** *into the house.*

**May**    And I can't help you, you know, so you can forget that!

**Steve**    Don't worry about that.

**May** (*louder*)    I say I can't help you.

**Steve**    I'll manage, no problem . . .

**Steve** *looks around at the distance between the van and the house.*

Probably break my bloody neck but . . .

**May**    I don't know how you're going to manage the wardrobe.

**Steve**    Piece of cake!

**May**    There's a dining table and all and three beds.

**Steve**    Smashing!

**Steve** *makes to move and is stopped as* **May** *speaks. She seems slightly disassociated.*

**May**    . . . I mean our Jack said he was going to do it but . . . He's bloody late and all.

**Steve**    I'll get you sorted . . .

**May**    I don't know how you're going to shift half of it. I mean, I've seen more fat on a chip!

**Steve** (*eagerly*)    I'm all power me!

**May**    You'll need to be. I mean, he's full of good intentions our Jack . . .

**Steve** *reads a note he has in his hand.*

**Steve**   Is it Mrs Willis?

**May**   Did my son speak to you? He's dealing with it. Done the exchange, moving me out, everything. I haven't had anything to do with it. So it's no good asking me owt!

**Steve**   Doing it all for you is he?

**May**   I thought you weren't coming. I'd have been in a right mess then!

**Steve**   You're not related to Jack Willis are you?

**May**   I'm his mother.

**Steve**   I thought it was him when he phoned up!

**May**   Do you know him?

**Steve**   I did.

**May**   He said it was going to be Mason's.

**Steve**   He used to be my English teacher.

**May**   That's going back!

**Steve**   That's right!

*A ball appears on the stage at the front door, it bounces off the wall.*

*Silence.*

**Steve**   What's that?

**May**   Them, next door.

**Steve**   Shall I throw it back?

**Steve** *moves to get the ball.*

**May** (*sharply*)   No! Leave it!

**Sonja**, *a young woman in her early twenties, enters over the small fence. She is wearing a mini skirt, looks slatternly and smokes. She says nothing, just comes and gets the ball, puts her chewing gum in **May**'s bin and exits.* **Steve** *feels tension.*

*A beat.*

**Steve**    So are you moving anywhere nice?

**May**    Eh?

**Steve**    They reckon them new bungalows in Badsworth are smashing. My mother's just gone into Ashgrove. She's eighty-four now like. I never thought I'd see her in there, but she seems happy enough.

**May**    I'm going to Spain.

**Steve**    Oh!

**May**    Los Boliches.

**Steve**    You don't want me to take all this down there, do you?

**May**    It's going in storage most of it!

**Steve**    I was going to say . . .

**May**    He's rigged me up with an apartment . . .

**Steve**    Sounds just right.

**May**    I'm not that bothered about going to be honest, but he says I'll get used to it . . .

**Steve**    It's all right for some, isn't it?

**May**    He's insisted on me being by the sea . . .

**Steve**    Couldn't you have gone to Cleethorpes?

**May**    I hate Cleethorpes . . . We used to go on the club trip. Hate it! I mean, I wouldn't have minded Scarborough, but it's all them hills. But he said, at least it's somewhere for him and the kids to come . . .

**Steve**    Lovely!

**May**    Only my cousin's been out there five years . . . and he said he'd get it sorted . . .

**Steve**    He doesn't fancy getting me sorted, does he?

**May**    He'll be here this morning so you can ask him.

*A beat.*

**Steve**    So how long have you lived here then?

**May**    Forty-five years . . .

**Steve**    Ooooph . . . !

**May**    Forty-five years!

**Steve** *looks around at the house and garden.*

**Steve**    Kept it looking good . . .

**May** (*tearful*)    I feel a bit . . .

**Steve**    Well you're bound to, aren't you?

**May**    I mean, I've got some fond memories of this house.

**May** *begins to get quite upset.*

I mean I know it's daft, I know it's only a house but, you know . . . I brought my lad up here and . . .

**Steve**    I know . . .

**May** (*upset*)    I mean . . . it's the only house we've ever had . . .

**Steve**    Oh dear . . .

**May**    I'm sorry . . .

**Steve**    Don't worry about it.

**May** (*crying*)    I mean, it's my home! And things change, don't they . . .

**Steve**    They do.

**May**    And there's nowt we can do about it, is there . . . ?

**Steve**    No . . . no, there's nowt you can do!

*The ball comes back onto the stage.*

*Silence. Tension.*

**Sonja** *enters again over the wall. This time she is fuming, and shouts as she enters.*

**Sonja** (*entering*)   What have I told you? Stop kicking it over, you little twat! What do you think I am?

**Sonja** *grabs the ball and exits.*

**May** *moves to start cleaning once more.*

*Silence.*

**Steve**   You don't have to do that, do you?

**May**   I want to keep it tidy . . . I mean it's only fair! I mean I've kept it tidy since my husband . . .

**Steve**   Oh dear!

**May**   Six months . . .

**Steve**   I'm sorry about that!

**May**   Seventy-one.

**Steve**   It's no age these days, is it?

**May**   Seventy-one.

**Steve** (*hopeful*)   Well, Spain sounds good.

**May**   He loved this house . . .

**Steve**   Aye well . . .

**May**   Worked all his life down t' pit; that's why he liked this house and his garden.

**Steve**   Right! I'll start, shall I? Or we'll never get you to Spain, will we?

**May** *goes back to the Eubank and starts cleaning once more. As she stands and works, the ball comes into the garden a third time but she does not see it or hear it.* **Steve** *exits with a box from the kitchen. He sees* **Sonja** *come for the ball. As she does, she flashes him a shot of her rear. He shakes his head, and exits.* **May** *is oblivious and continues. After a while* **May** *stops.*

**Scene Two**

*1958.*

**Ted** *is a memory. He is a large happy man who pushes a Silver Cross pram into the middle of the living room.* **May** *is still looking at the carpet and doesn't really notice him.* **Ted** *is dressed in a costume of the 1950s. He has been working outdoors.*

**Ted**    I'm going to bring him in here, May! Can you keep an eye on him, it's boiling out there! All the plaster's sweating in t' kitchen it's that bloody new! I thought he might get a cough or sommat. I didn't want it to go to his chest. I don't know how long it's going to be before it dries out. I mean I know it's a new house but . . . Anyway that's the bloody bathroom sorted!

**May**    Always swearing, he was!

**Ted**    Bloody warm out there and all!

**May** (*to herself*)    Always swearing.

*A beat.*

**Ted**    I can't believe we've got our own house!

**May**    It's not ours, is it, it's council's!

**Ted**    Betty Smeaton's still waiting for one, and they put their name down before us.

*As they stand,* **Sylvia** *comes to the front door. She is smoking.* **May** *has still not totally engaged in the scene.*

**Sylvia**    Morning! Can I come in?

**Sylvia** *enters.*

**Ted**    Morning.

**Sylvia**    I'm Sylvia . . . just thought I'd come and . . .

**May** (*abstracted*)    Bloody Sylvia . . . ?

**Sylvia**    Just came to say hello.

**May**    I'm May, this is Ted . . .

**Ted**    Is your plaster still sweating?

**Sylvia**    Oh you're all right asking me, Frank's just papered over it. I don't know if it was dry or what.

**Ted**    Sweating like bloody hell ours.

**Sylvia** *moves towards the pram.*

**Sylvia**    I say, her next door is having the coal house knocked out. She's making her coal house into another room.

**Ted**    Don't give her any ideas, Sylvia love, for God's sake!

**Sylvia**    I mean they've only been in there two weeks.

**Ted**    Well if she wants it doing she'll have to wait until I get round to it.

**Sylvia** *looks into the pram.*

**Sylvia**    Oh he's asleep, look.

**Ted**    Aye for a change.

**Sylvia**    Where do you work then?

**Ted**    Upton pit!

**Sylvia**    Same as Frank. (*Into the pram.*) Oh look at him! I think they're all colliers on this estate. And here's another one. (*Into the pram.*) How old is he?

**May**    Eighteen months.

**Sylvia**    Oh! What do you call him?

**May**    Jack. After my dad!

**Sylvia**    Jack, oh lovely. I've three, our Kenny four, Angela and Denise two and six . . . Anyway I shan't keep you, just came to say . . . you know . . .

**Sylvia** *exits in a cloud of cigarette smoke.*

*Silence.*

**May** (*abstracted*)   Bloody Sylvia!

**Ted**   I thought she was going to offer him a smoke!

**May** (*abstracted*)   Bloody Sylvia!

**Ted**   We can have a garage put on, you know? There's just about room.

**May**   What do you want a garage for, we haven't even got a bloody car?

**Ted** *grabs* **May** *tenderly*.

**Ted**   We'll get one . . . Ha ha, a Rolls Royce.

**May**   Oh bloody hell!

**Ted** *and* **May** *are tender and comfortable together*.

**Ted**   I bet you . . .

**May**   You'll waken him . . .

**Ted**   I won't.

**May**   Don't waken him, Ted, I'll be up all night with him.

**Ted**   I'm up all night anyway . . .

**Ted** *looks into the pram*.

Oh I think he's trumped or sommat . . .

**May**   Like father like son.

**Ted**   He's a bugger isn't he, he's awake all night and he's bloody asleep all day . . .

*A beat*.

**May**   Take him in the shade, it's too warm for him in here.

**Ted**   He's right . . .

**May**   Take him outside and do what you're told . . .

*The word 'hey' is used as both affection and a threat*.

**Ted**    'Hey . . .'

**May**    Don't you bloody 'hey' me . . .

**Ted** (*an idiosyncratic word*)    'Hey!'

**May**    'Hey!'

**Ted**    Come here . . .

**May**    What?

**Ted**    Give us a kiss.

**Ted** *kisses* **May**.

**May**    'Hey!'

**Ted**    'Hey!'

**Ted** *treats* **May** *warmly*.

**May**    You know what that leads to.

**Ted**    With a bit of luck!

**May**    Aye and one's a bloody enough at the minute!

*As* **Ted** *prepares to take the pram off stage he investigates the baby more closely. There is a clear stink.*

**Ted**    Oh hell . . .

**May**    Has he done one?

**Ted**    Aye he has, trumped and worse . . .

**May**    Well, go and change him then . . .

**Ted**    I think it's one of them that's gone right up to the back of his neck.

**May**    Oh lovely.

**Ted** *takes the pram and as he exits:*

**Ted**    How the bloody hell do they do that?

**May** *watches* **Ted** *take the baby and the pram off stage. She turns around and looks at the room. The memory has gone. She is back in the present.*

### Scene Three

*The present.*

**May** *walks over to her sofa and is about to start her work once more when* **Steve** *enters and picks up a small box.*

**Steve**    You've got some stuff in there!

**May** *tries to get the Eubank to work, but she then stops.*

**Steve**    I should leave that!

**May**    Just tidying up . . .

**Steve**    Get your Jack to do it . . . He'll be all right with that, wain't he? Bloody hell what have you got in this . . .

**May**    China . . .

**Steve** (*struggling*)    Hell . . .

**May**    Can you manage . . . ?

**Steve**    Oh aye, no problem . . . I'm fine. It'll keep me fit.

**May**    It will that . . .

**Steve**    Or kill me.

**Steve** *struggles off stage with the box.* **May** *returns to the back door and looks at the 'For Sale' sign in the corner of her garden off stage.*

**Scene Four**

*1960.*

**Ted** *enters. He is dressed in shirtsleeves and casual trousers. He carries a small garden tray full of bulbs.* **May** *is still not entirely within the memory scene.*

**Ted**    Kettle's on, so I'll make a cup of tea when I've planted these. Have you seen them privets? I've straightened them out, nice and private in them backs now. I was just telling your mam; she's sat knitting another balaclava by the way. Why he needs one in weather like this I don't know!

**May**    Where's my dad?

**Ted**    Taking our Jack around the block.

**May**    Again?

**Ted**    Well you know your dad, he can't get enough of him. I had to tell him that he was my son, but I don't think that went down too well. I thought he was going to paste me.

*A beat.*

**May**    Do you think my dad looks all right?

**Ted**    Aye why?

**May**    He does too much . . .

**Ted**    He's a good worker is your dad. They don't make 'em like that any more. He can pick two rings up at once.

**May**    That's what I mean.

**Ted**    A bloody cart horse couldn't do that.

*Silence.*

**May**    Have you seen owt of Sylvia?

**Ted**    I've heard 'em . . .

**May**    Noisy.

**Ted**    Allus shouting!

**May**    Not like us . . .

**Ted**    Not much . . .

**May**    They don't know how to argue, do they?

**Ted**    I heard her shouting at him yesterday, I thought there was a bloody fire or sommat . . .

**May**    Aye, I think he's a bit slack.

**Ted**    I was going to run out with a bucket!

**May**    I think he's a slate loose.

**Ted**    No, he hasn't a lot to think with! But he's only a button man.

**May**    A what?

**Ted**    He presses a button when a green light comes on. It's only light work, a right bloke wouldn't have it!

**Sylvia** *enters via the back door. She is smoking, and is worried.*

**Sylvia** (*off*)    May. (*Enters.*) Are you there, May?

**Ted**    We were just talking about you . . .

**Sylvia**    I'm sorry to bother you . . .

**Ted**    Not heard owt of you this week.

**Sylvia**    Will Ted come and have a look at Frank?

**Ted**    Why, what's up wi' him, love?

**Sylvia**    He's laid out on the bed.

**Ted**    He'll be tired out, Sylvia, it's horse work pushing that button you know!

**Sylvia**    I don't know if he's dead, drunk or what.

*A beat.*

**Ted**    Well I'll come and have a look, love, but . . .

**Sylvia**    I mean he's just laid there, he's not breathing.

*A beat.*

**Ted**    What shift is he on?

**Sylvia**    Days regular . . .

**Ted**    Are you sure he's not been down in t' Social, Sylvia?

**Sylvia**    He hardly ever goes in!

*A beat.*

**Ted**    Right . . . I'd better have a look at him then. I mean I'm not a bloody doctor but . . .

**Ted** *exits.*

**Sylvia**    I mean, I'm sorry to have to bother you . . .

**May**    Ted'll have a look at him.

**Sylvia**    I mean, I'm sorry to come around but . . .

**May**    Oh don't worry about that . . .

**Sylvia**    Only I've got the kids going mad, and now my bloody washer's playing me up! The mangle's knackered . . .

**May**    Oh hell!

**Sylvia**    It all happens at once, doesn't it? And now him! I'm mean, he's just laid there . . . must have collapsed or sommat. I mean it's pit work, isn't it? It's killing him!

**May**    Well let's hope he's all right, love!

**Sylvia**    If he's not dead I'll chuffin' kill him! I will honest!

**May**    Do you want a drink, he's just put the kettle on . . .

**Sylvia**    Oh no, I don't want to trouble you . . .

**May**    Don't be daft, have a drink.

**Sylvia**    No, I don't like coming in your house . . .

**May**    Why not?

**Sylvia**   Well it's all nice and clean, isn't it? I mean mine's a bloody shit heap, and I mean look at yours . . .

**May**   Don't be daft.

**Ted** *re-enters. He has vomit over one of his slippers.*

**Ted**   Well he's not dead, Sylvia love.

**Sylvia**   Are you sure?

**Ted**   Why, do you want him to be?

**Sylvia**   No I didn't mean that.

**Ted**   I mean, he's just been sick all over me so . . .

**Sylvia**   Oh the bloody swine him . . . !

**Ted**   All over my slippers!

**Sylvia**   Oh I'm sorry about that!

**Ted**   So he's definitely still alive.

**Sylvia**   I mean . . . I thought . . .

**Ted**   And he says he wants some chips making . . . so you'd better go and put a pan on he says.

**Sylvia**   I'm sorry to have to ask you.

**Ted**   In fact when I sat on the bed he started to get fresh with me, Sylvia, so . . .

**Sylvia**   Oh hell!

**Ted**   I should be very careful if you go in that bedroom.

**Sylvia**   He's like that when he's had a drink!

**Ted**   Aye well, tell him to keep his distance, when he sees me!

**Sylvia**   Oh I'm sorry about that, I mean sometimes I can't control him!

**Ted**   I thought my luck had changed!

**Sylvia** (*to* **May**)   Is he drunk then?

**Ted**   Well, he stinks of Whitbread's, Sylvia, so I think it's a safe bet.

**Sylvia**   He's a bloody lying swine is our Frank.

**Ted**   He must have drunk the club dry.

**Sylvia**   And do you know what? He tells me he never goes in that bloody club! He must think I've dropped off a bus!

**Sylvia** *exits.* **Ted** *picks up his bulbs. He stands with the tray.*

**Ted**   Oh!

**May**   What's up?

**Ted**   Their house . . .

**May**   Chip fat?

**Ted**   Good as gold but . . .

**May**   Nowt a bar of soap wouldn't sort out!

**Ted** *considers his slippers.*

**Ted**   Well I'd better leave this and go and wash my slippers.

**May**   Do you want a sandwich making . . . ?

**Ted**   I was gunna make myself one with that dripping!

**May**   Well don't put so much salt on.

**Ted**   I like salt on.

**May**   You can eat two tatties more than a pig!

**Ted**   'Hey you!'

**May**   Never mind 'hey you', it's true. And see where my dad is with our Jack.

**Ted**   He'll be on his way to bloody Blackpool by now!

**May**   And what have I said about swearing . . .

**Ted** *hobbles off looking at his slipper.*

**Ted**   Look at this . . .

**May**   Go on hop-a-long . . .

**Ted**   Bloody new slippers and all . . .

**Ted** *exits.* **May** *watches him hobble away and laughs very volubly to herself.*


## Scene Five

*The present.*

**Steve** *enters from the house entrance. He has another box with him, and also carries a small bedside cabinet which is clearly home-made. We have assumed that he has made a number trips to his van during the previous memory scene.*

**Steve**   It's going to be another warm 'un by the looks of it!

**May**   That cabinet can go in the skip! Our Jack made me it in woodwork.

**Steve** (*looks at the cabinet*)   I can see why he taught English then!

**May**   I didn't have the heart to tell him . . .

**Steve** *hovers a while to talk.*

**Steve**   He's done all right, hasn't he?

**May**   I suppose so . . .

**Steve**   Proud on him are you?

**May**   He's just our Jack.

**Steve**   Work's for BBC doesn't he?

**May**   He writes books now!

**Steve**   Oh right then.

**May**   They making 'em into films and God knows what . . .

**Steve**   I can remember him at school. Bloody hell, who'd've have thought it?

**May**   Go steady with that stuff, won't you?

**Steve**   Oh aye, don't worry about that! I'll take care of everything.

**Steve** *exits and bangs into the door with his leg.*

Sorry. Oh my bloody knee!

**May** *watches him go.*


**Scene Six**

*1964.*

**May** *stands in the middle of the room.* **Ted** *enters. He is dressed in slacks and an open-necked shirt, and is carrying an old-style bike. The scooter has the front wheel twisted around.*

**Ted**   Have you seen what he's done with this?

**May**   How's he done that . . . ?

**Ted**   He's all over the bloody shop!

**May**   Where is he?

**Ted**   I've sent him upstairs.

**May**   What for?

**Ted**   Because he's gets up my arse.

**May**   Eh?

**Ted**   He gets up my arse!

**May**   Why what's he done?

**Ted**   He can't stay on the damn thing.

**May**    Well he's learning isn't he?

**Ted**    He's like a fairy on it, he says his legs hurt him.

**May**    Well don't send him to bed for that.

**Ted**    I didn't send him for that, I sent him because he's chalked all over next door's wall. He can't ride a bike, but he can write on a wall and draw daft pictures!

**May**    Well, who's let him do that?

**Ted**    He's just bloody done it.

**May**    I thought you were watching him.

**Ted**    I was bloody watching him but I nipped across to have a word with Bill Fletcher and when I came back he'd chalked all over Sylvia's wall 'This house smells'.

**May**    Where's he got that from?

**Ted**    And that's why he's in bed.

**Sylvia** *enters straight into* **May**'s *house. She is furious.*

**Sylvia**    I say, are you there? I say, I'm not having this you know . . .

**Ted**    I know. I know.

**Sylvia**    I'm not having this . . .

**Ted**    Listen Sylvia, I've brought him in, love . . . He shouldn't have done it . . . I went over to Bill Fletcher's . . .

**Sylvia**    I mean have you seen my front wall . . . ?

**Ted**    Hey Sylvia. he's a good lad, he's never done owt like it before, love. He's all right. Now don't let's fall out about this.

**Sylvia**    I don't want to be falling out . . .

**Ted**    I don't want to be falling out . . .

**Sylvia**    But have you seen the state of my wall . . . ?

**Ted**    I'll get a bucket and sort it out for you.

**Sylvia**    I mean, he's ten and he's writing on walls.

**Ted**    Nay nay, hang on . . .

**Sylvia**    Bloody sly if you ask me . . .

**May** *has been watching this as if remembering.*

**May**    Hey now, he's not sly . . .

**Sylvia**    Why doesn't he write on your wall if he wants to write?

**May**    Now hang on, Ted's brought him in . . . he's in bed, and that's the end of it.

**Sylvia**    May, the lad's sly! He's sly! He poked our Angela in the eye last week and I never said owt!

**May**    Sylvia, Sylvia, listen to me, he's been brought up to know what's right and wrong. I mean we don't drink. We don't smoke, he goes to bed early every night, he's never done owt wrong!

**Ted**    Now May, hang on!

**May**    It's your Angela who's sly . . .

**Sylvia**    Well what's he done it for then?

**May**    I mean, she's been peeing at the bottom of our garden and we haven't said owt. Have we?

**Ted**    Well no . . .

**May**    And it's killed all his rhubarb, hasn't it . . . ?

**Ted**    Well it's not done it any good!

**Sylvia**    Well I don't know about that . . .

**May**    I'm not having you come round here and say our lad's sly, not when your bloody house stinks of chip fat.

**Ted**    Now, May.

**May**   And Frank's in the club every verse end . . .

**Sylvia**   Well now I know where he's getting it from!

**May** *becomes extremely upset and irrational.*

**May**   I mean she never washes, and when she does there's clothes on the line for a fortnight.

**Ted**   Hey now listen . . .

**May** (*builds to tears*)   I'm not having it, Sylvia . . . I'm not having it! It's not fair . . . Ted's sent him to bed and you come around here playing little hell! Good God, what do you want, a pound of flesh?

**May** *exits. She is very upset.*

*Silence.*

**Sylvia**   Well I'm only saying . . .

**Ted**   Aye well!

*A beat.*

**Sylvia**   I mean . . . I didn't know about our Angela but . . .

*A beat.*

**Ted**   It's not about him writing on the wall, Sylvia love . . .

**Sylvia**   Well I mean . . .

**Ted**   Her mam's not so well, so she's a bit highly strung at the moment. Don't put much by what she says, she says owt sometimes . . .

**Sylvia**   Aye well, I'm not having her call our Angela . . . I mean, I'm having problems with her as it is . . .

*A beat.*

**Ted**   I'll get a bucket and come and wash your wall down.

**Sylvia**   Oh don't bother with that, I'll do that . . . I was only making a point!

**Ted**   No . . . I'll do it.

**Sylvia**   I mean, I didn't know about her mam like . . . I hope she gets better anyway!

*A beat.*

**Ted**   There's not much chance of that, Sylvia love.

**Sylvia** *exits.* **Ted** *stands, picks up the bike, attempts to straighten out the front wheel and slowly exits.*


### Scene Seven

*The present.*

**Steve** *enters with a number of small dining chairs. As he does,* **Jack Willis** *enters. He is a tall thick-set-looking man in his mid-forties.* **Jack** *has a lugubrious manner but the air of someone successful about him. He swings car keys into his pocket as he enters his mother's house.*

**Jack** (*as he enters*)   Are you there, Mam?

**Steve**   Is that Mr Willis?

**Jack**   That's right.

**Steve**   I bet you don't remember me?

**Jack** *considers* **Steve**.

**Jack**   I know the face.

**Steve** (*easily mocking*)   I know the face? Tha doesn't remember, does tha?

**Jack**   Hang on . . .

**Steve**   Steve Hardy.

**Jack**   Oh right.

**Steve**   I was in Mr Dean's tutor group.

**Jack**   Oh right.

**Steve**    I knew tha wouldn't remember me. Can't you remember when you dragged me out of technical drawing for farting?

**Jack**    Well?

**Steve**    You were on cover for Mr Dawson!

**Jack**    Was I?

**Steve**    I did an essay about them worms that my grandfather kept, can you remember that?

**Jack**    I don't . . .

**Steve**    Tha must remember smacking Steve Woodhead.

**Jack**    Oh aye I remember that!

**Steve**    For feeling Jackie Grahame up . . .

**Jack**    I remember that . . .

**Steve**    I married her tha knows.

**Jack**    Really . . . ?

**Steve**    Divorced now like but . . .

**Jack**    Well anyway . . . nice to see you again . . .

**Steve**    It was dog eat dog down at that school, wasn't it? I used to say to my mam, 'I don't know how the teachers stand it!' I mean, it was bad enough for the kids!

**Jack**    It wasn't that bad, was it?

*A beat.*

**Steve**    Sorry to hear about thee dad.

*A beat.*

**Jack**    Can I give you a lift with anything?

**Steve**    No I'm right.

**Jack**    Are you sure?

**Steve**    Do you know, it's funny because I was talking about you the other day to Col Mawhinney! Can tha remember Col? You had that gym in block two toilets, didn't you? 'Mr Willis' Office' it said on the door. Can tha remember? Thought tha was the Fonz or sommat.

**Jack**    It was the only place I could go to train.

**Steve**    Do you still do it?

**Jack**    I'm forty now, you know?

**Steve**    Hey . . . I'm twenty-five. Three kids . . .

**Jack**    I joined a gym a couple of months ago and I could still bench as much as these lads, but they didn't go dizzy when they stood up . . .

**Steve**    All that writing keeps you fit eh?

**Jack**    Some of them pens are heavy . . .

**Steve**    I was telling thee mam, good to see tha's got on.

**Jack**    Cheers.

**Steve**    I've seen thee on t' telly a couple of times.

**Jack**    Well.

**Steve**    She says they're making a film?

**Jack**    She's told you everything, has she?

**Steve**    Mini series, is it?

**Jack**    She should be my agent!

**Steve**    Worth a few quid now then?

**Jack**    Well . . .

**Steve**    I'll swop you jobs . . .

**Jack**    Pays the wages . . .

**Steve**    Pays the wages, bloody hell, tell us another.

**Jack**    Anyway.

*A beat.*

**Steve**    You never forget where you were brought up, do you? Some things stick with you!

**Jack**    They do and all!

**Steve** (*starting work*)    Better get cracking . . .

**Jack**    I'll settle up with you later, will a cheque do?

**Steve**    Well if you've got cash . . .

**Jack**    Cash fine, no problem.

**Steve** *exits, and* **Jack** *follows him to the back door.*

**Jack** *stands alone, as the ball from next door comes into the garden followed by a small plastic tractor. It has been deliberately thrown into the garden.* **Sonja** *can be heard shouting.*

**Sonja** (*off stage*)    Shasa you little twat, stop it! Right, you'd better go and ask her if you can have it back . . .

**Jack** *looks at the tractor. Picks it up and throws it back over the fence into next door.*

**Sonja** (*off stage*)    Thanks. Can we have the ball and all?

*He then gets the ball and takes it with him into his mother's.*

**Jack** (*softly*)    Come and get it!

*He walks into the house and off stage.*


## Scene Eight

*1974.*

**May** *enters. She is now dressed as a forty-year-old woman would in 1974. She sits herself down in one of the sofa chairs. It is a very warm and sunny day, and once she is settled in the chair, she sits and reads a book she has with her. After a while* **Ted** *enters with a tray full of cups and buns for afternoon tea.*

**Ted**    I've made you a cup . . .

**May**    You needn't have bothered . . .

*A beat.*

**Ted**    You all right?

**May**    I'm all right.

*Silence.*

**Ted**    I mean there's nowt I can say, is there?

**May** (*holding back tears*)    No.

**Ted**    I mean he was a bugger, but . . .

*Silence.*

**May** (*wipes a tear*)    Oh dear my dad . . .

**Ted**    It's one thing after another, isn't it? Three years ago your mam! Then my dad, and now your dad . . . And to top it there's him and his bloody A levels.

**May**    I don't know where the time goes!

*A long silence.*

**Ted**    No wind out there today is there . . .

**May**    Well there isn't, but now you've come in here there's every possibility there might be . . .

**Ted**    'Hey.'

**May**    'Hey.'

*A beat.*

**Ted**    I can't get over that phone!

**May**    Just because we've got one doesn't mean you've got to use it.

**Ted**    I haven't used it, I just keep looking at it.

*Silence.*

**Ted** *stands and walks around the room. He parks himself by the downstage area.*

**Ted**   I don't know. One minute we're putting the privets in and the next thing you know, I'm cutting half a foot off 'em because you think they've grown too high.

**May** (*doesn't look up from her book*)   Funny.

**Ted**   I wonder how he's going to get on.

**May**   Well he's got his head up his behind half the time so if that's what they're looking for he should get a place.

**Ted**   He'll never get his A levels, he's always farting about.

**May**   Well he'd better, now we've bought that bloody phone.

**May** *laughs.* **Ted** *takes in the calming day.*

**Ted**   This is more like it . . .

**May**   I'm glad we've got that coal house done.

**Ted**   Aye, it took some nagging but you finally got it done!

**May**   Eighteen years.

**Ted**   I said I'd get around to it!

**May**   Once we get that kitchen finished it'll be lovely in there.

**Ted**   I might even look at having a car-port built on!

**Ted** *sits, pours a cup of tea. And begins to eat a small cake.*

**May**   Don't sit like that.

**Ted**   Like what like that.

**May**   Like that.

**Ted**   I'll sit how I like.

**May**   Sit up!

**Ted**   Shut up and get your tea.

**May**    It'll give you indigestion, sitting like that.

**Ted**    How do you know?

**May**    It'd give me indigestion.

**Ted**    Well you're not sat like this, are you?

**May**    No, but if I was it'd give me indigestion!

**Ted**    Oh shut up and read your book!

**Jack** *enters. He is eighteen. He wears clogs and a pair of tight yellow loons with no fly hole. He carries a small table with him and two cheap table-tennis bats and sets up the table tennis.*

**Jack**    Right, table tennis . . .

**May**    Well I'm not playing in here . . .

**Jack**    What's new?

**May**    I'd beat you anyway . . .

**Jack** *puts the table down and arranges a few books for a net.*

**Ted**    You can't play on that.

**Jack**    Course you can . . . Come on!

**Jack** *gives his father a bat and they go to their respective ends of the table. He and his father start to play table tennis. It is very slow and quite pointless.* **May** *has no interest in the game but comments on it from her book.*

**May**    You're both useless . . .

**Jack**    I played this kid in the sixth form who said I was a cheat because I made the ball spin.

**May**    You shouldn't spin!

**Jack** *(confused)*    You what?

**May**    That's why I'm not playing!

**Jack**    That's the whole point of the game!

*Silence.*

*The two men play table tennis. It is very plodding but strangely watchable. As they play* **May** *begins to look at* **Jack**.

**May**    What are you wearing anyway?

**Jack**    Eh?

**May**    What have you got on?

**Jack**    These are them loons my Auntie Margaret bought me!

**May**    Bloody hell!

**Jack**    What?

**May**    Well you look a bugger in them!

**Jack**    Don't start . . .

**May**    Let's have a look at you.

**Jack**    I'm doing sommat . . .

**Ted**    What's score?

**Jack**    We're just warming up!

**Ted**    I thought we'd started.

*They still play table tennis.*

**May**    What do you look like in them?

**Jack**    They're all right!

**May**    Where do you go to the toilet?

**Jack**    You don't.

**May**    Isn't there a zip?

**Jack**    Aye there's a zip.

**May**    Where?

**Jack**    I'm doing sommat!

**Ted**    What's score . . . ?

**May**    If you get caught short in them . . .

**Jack**    I'm doing sommat!

**May**    You'll end up with prostate problems with trousers like that. I mean fancy not having a zip!

**Ted**    Have we started?

**May**    You'll mess your bloody self in them if you're not careful. You don't want to be going to Ponte in them, you know, they've shut them public toilets. And you don't want to be taking them to college, if you get in. You'll end up doing yourself some damage in them sods!

**Jack** *can stand it no more. He grabs the bat from his father and carries the table towards the kitchen.*

**Jack**    Right . . .

**Ted**    What?

**Jack**    Forget it . . .

**Ted** (*disappointed*)    Is that it?

**Jack**    I can't concentrate with her going on . . .

**May**    Well they're disgusting they are, at the front, you can see all you've got . . .

**Jack**    Shut up, you silly sod!

**May**    Swearing now!

**Jack**    I can't do owt without her going on . . .

**May**    Oh don't be so touchy.

**Jack** *takes the table off stage.* **Ted** *calls after him.*

**Ted**    Are we playing or what?

**Jack** (*shouts*)    I'm not playing with that silly cow watching me!

**May**    'Hey?'

**Ted**   'Hey?'

**Jack**   Hey nothing!

*Silence.*

**May**   You can't say owt to him . . .

*A beat.*

**Ted**   Mind you, some of the stuff your Margaret buys him are bloody ridiculous.

**May**   Don't you start!

**Ted**   I mean she bought him that fisherman's smock and he's never worn it. He looks backward in it!

**May**   I don't know who he thinks he is shouting at me like that!

**Ted**   Look at that ashtray she bought him for his eighteenth, he doesn't even bloody smoke, and she bought him an ashtray on a stand!

**May**   You can't say owt to him without he's marching off!

**Ted**   I mean look at them clogs she bought him, he looks like Frankenstein's bloody monster in 'em and then she plays hell when he doesn't wear 'em! He can't bloody walk in 'em, that's why he doesn't wear 'em.

**May**   I don't know what he'll be like if he gets to college.

*A beat.*

**Ted**   Why you had to go on about them bloody trousers is beyond me!

**May**   Well he looks a bugger!

**Ted**   You're enough to wear anybody down.

**May**   How's he going to pee with a zip at the side?

**Ted**   You're off again, look . . .

**May**   He'll have to pee around corners with them on!

**Ted**    Off again!

**May** *stands. She is working herself into quite a frenzy. She picks up the buns and the tea tray.*

**May**    I can't believe you and our Jack, you know!

**Ted**    Off again!

**May**    We've just buried my dad and I can't open my mouth.

**Ted**    Off again!

**May**    I mean we're in mourning in this house and he's wearing bloody silly trousers with no fly hole.

**Ted**    Here we go.

**May**    I just can't believe him!

**Ted**    And she wonders who he takes after . . .

**May**    If I can't express an opinion about his fly hole then it's a bugger . . . And I'm not arguing about it out here!

**May** *makes her way to the kitchen. Taking the tea tray with her.*

**Ted** (*following her*)    Here we go, off again!

**Ted** *follows her forlornly.*


### Scene Nine

*The present.*

**Steve** *struggles his way on stage with a small chest of drawers.*

**Steve**    Bloody hell! (*To himself.*) This is brilliant!

**Sonja** *enters over the fence and into the living room. She is very slatternly.*

**Sonja**    Seen a ball?

**Steve**    What?

**Sonja**　A ball?

**Steve**　No.

**Steve** *puts the chest of drawers down.*

**Sonja**　She going?

**Steve**　Son's bought her a villa or sommat. Did you know him at school?

**Sonja**　I didn't go to school round here . . .

**Steve**　Loaded!

**Sonja**　It's all right for some!

**Steve**　Writes books.

**Sonja**　I said to Les, I bet it's not long before she's off!

**Steve** (*picking up the chest*)　Anyway . . .

**Sonja**　I don't know where that ball's gone!

**Steve** (*heaving*)　Awkward bloody . . .

**Sonja**　She's probably taken it. Les'll go blue if she has.

**Sonja** *suddenly shouts at her kids who are off stage.*

**Steve** *struggles with the chest of drawers.*

**Sonja**　Come off that car-port you slack getts! How many times have I told you?

**Sonja** *takes her shouting off stage.*


### Scene Ten

*1979.*

**Ted** *comes into the living room and begins to polish a sideboard. He has a duster and a spray. He stops as* **Jack** *enters.* **Jack** *is wielding a cricket bat. He is now a graduate and looks quite summery.*

**Ted**　Oh thee mother!

**Jack**   What's up with her?

**Ted**   It's non-stop. She wants a bloody fridge now!

**Jack**   Tell her she can't have one.

**Ted**   You tell her!

**Jack**   This back lawn needs cutting!

**Ted**   She's got me on this. I'm gunna do that later.

*He begins to dust. Then stops.*

She's getting worse!

**Jack**   I wouldn't mind a word if you've got a minute.

**Ted**   Don't thee set me going, for God's sake. Or I'll end up cutting every bloody garden on the estate. Because I either take it out on the lawn or I take it out on your mother, which do you think is best?

**Jack**   Well I know which would be the most effective!

**Ted**   Exactly!

*He commences the dusting once more. Then he stops.*

What do you want me for?

**Jack**   Well . . .

**Ted**   What?

**Jack**   I've got a bit of a problem.

**Ted**   What sort of problem?

**Jack**   A downstairs problem.

**Ted**   What in that flat?

**Jack**   No.

**Ted**   Where then?

**Jack**   Downstairs . . .

**Ted**   Talk bloody English.

**Jack**   In my pants.

*A beat.*

**Ted**   Oh right!

**Jack**   I've got a sort of discharge thing.

**Ted**   Oh right.

**Jack**   So er . . .

**Ted**   Bloody hell.

**Jack**   I thought it might go away but . . .

**Ted** (*resigned*)   Bloody hell!

**Jack**   I've had it for a month now.

**Ted**   Who is she? Don't tell me! The less I know about it the better. Hey don't tell thee mother . . .

**Jack**   I'm not thick.

**Ted**   You make me wonder.

**Jack**   Aye I know.

*A beat.*

**Ted**   You'll need to go to Wakefield then with that!

**Jack**   That's where they send 'em, is it?

**Ted**   Department thirteen!

**Jack** *laughs. He swings lightly.*

**Jack**   Unlucky for some.

**Ted**   I'm serious.

**Jack**   Like sending somebody to Coventry, is it? If they get clap they send them to Wakefield?

**Ted**   You'll not be laughing when the doctor gets hold of you!

**Jack**   Oh right!

**Ted**  Oph!

**Jack**  Oh right.

**Ted**  When they put a red hot spatula down your pipe . . .

**Jack**  Bloody hell . . .

**Ted**  What's up . . . ?

**Jack**  That's too much information.

**Ted**  I haven't got to the best bit yet.

**Jack**  I've got the picture, thanks . . .

**Jack** *stands for a while.*

**Ted**  And I thought tha was a queer.

**Jack**  Eh?

**Ted**  Well we've never heard owt about women, have we?

**Jack**  What did you want, a written report?

**May** *enters. She seems fine and completely happy with herself.*

**May**  I thought you were going to cut the lawn?

**Ted**  I was, but you wanted this dusting and then we got talking about the good old days . . .

**May**  What, when he didn't leave hair in the sink?

**Jack**  That's my dad . . .

**May**  When he wasn't running around looking for a job?

**Ted**  He's had three interviews, he's bound to get one of 'em.

**Jack**  Law of averages.

**May**  He'll probably get that one down the road and end up living at home and us looking after him.

**Jack**  Well you wouldn't be bothered, would you?

**Ted**  You could stop here for ever for your mam.

**May** *sits.* **Jack** *re-acquaints himself with the cricket bat.*

**May**   I say, Angela, remember Angela from next door, she's having her second now, you know?

**Ted**   He's not interested in owt like that, are you?

**Jack**   Not me . . .

**Ted**   Plenty of time for all that.

**May**   And their Kenny's in Armley. Two years he got for robbing that bookie's.

**Jack**   He didn't get in to Oxford then?

**Ted**   He left school at fourteen, didn't he?

**May**   Aye, got himself a bloody job. Not like some people.

**Ted** (*warmly*)   She's a sarcastic sod . . . How do we put up with her?

**Jack** (*easily*)   I've no idea.

*The phone is heard ringing in the kitchen.*

**May**   Phone's ringing.

**Ted**   Well, go and answer it.

**May**   I'm not answering it.

**Ted**   She never answers it.

**May**   It's not for me.

**Ted**   She never touches it. She hasn't rung a number yet.

**May**   I don't like using it.

**Ted**   How do you know, you never used it?

**May**   It's never for me!

**Ted**   How do you know until you answer it?

**May**   I bet it's not for me, now then!

**Ted**   Well I bet it's not for me.

**May**    How do you know?

**Ted**    It's never for me, is it? Every time I answer it, it's your Margaret for you!

**Jack**    I don't why you got one.

**May**    We got one for you . . .

**Ted**    That's why we got one . . .

**May**    For when you went to college.

**Jack**    Aye I know that.

**May**    So you go and bloody answer it then.

**Jack**    Because every time it rings it's for me, isn't it?

**May**    Well it's never for me!

**Jack** *exits.*

**Ted**    Look at you . . .

**May**    Come on let's go outside and you can push me on t' swing . . .

**Ted**    You'll break that . . .

**May**    Come on, you can push me high and I'll see what Sylvia's having for her tea.

*He grabs her around the throat jokingly.*

**Ted**    I'll tell you what I should do! You?

**May**    What?

**Ted**    Arghh!

**Sylvia** *is heard shouting off stage.*

**Sylvia** *(off stage)*    May. May . . . Oh hell. Are you there May?

**Ted**    Another bloody fire . . .

**May** *(calls off)*    Jack, fill a bucket up!

**Sylvia** *arrives on stage and into* **May***'s living room. She is not as sprightly as previously and she is very worried.*

**Sylvia**    It's Frank . . . can you come . . . I'm sorry, love, but can you come and look at him?

**May**    Well I'll come, Sylvia, but . . .

**Sylvia**    I think he's gone this time!

**May**    Are you sure . . . ?

**Sylvia**    Come and have a look, will you . . . I mean his face's gone blue . . .

**Ted**    Well it makes a change, Sylvia, because he usually goes red . . .

**May**    I'll come and look but . . .

**May** *and* **Sylvia** *exit.* **Ted** *stands around in his living room.* **Jack** *enters.*

**Ted**    Thee mam's popped next door to Sylvia's. Frank's had another drinking do by the sounds of it.

*A beat.*

**Jack**    They've offered me that job down at school!

**Ted**    Well isn't that what you wanted?

**Jack**    I don't know if I want to teach though.

**Ted**    Well it's a bit late to start thinking like that, isn't it? I mean you've just spent the last four years studying to be an English teacher!

**Jack**    I know but . . .

**Ted**    Well what have you been doing at college? Don't answer that, I think I've got a pretty good idea!

**Jack**    I asked them to call me back anyway, when I'd had a think about it!

**Ted**    Well you've got some bloody cheek, I'll say that much . . .

**May** *enters through the back door.*

**May**    Right, Ted?

**Ted** (*referring to* **Jack**)    Have you heard this here . . .

**May**    Frank's gone!

*A beat.*

**Ted**    Oh bloody hell . . .

**May**    He's gone!

**Ted**    Oh hell . . .

**May**    So we'd better go and . . .

*A beat.*

**Ted**    And what?

**May**    Well he wants laying out, doesn't he? Sylvia can't do it on her own, can she?

**Jack**    Hey mam . . . ?

**May**    Not now, kid, let's get Frank sorted. It's bloody awful in there, Ted, you're going to have to help me . . . Sylvia's gone to pieces!

**May** *exits.*

*Silence.*

**Ted**    You know what the next thing'll be, don't you?

**Jack**    What?

**Ted**    How long will Sylvia stay in that house for?

**Jack**    She'll live for ever, won't she?

**Ted**    Will she?

**Jack**   Well she smokes sixty a day, drinks like a mad woman and has lived on nowt but chips for the last twenty years! They always live for ever . . .

**Ted**   I'd better go and give her a hand . . .

**Jack**   Before she starts sorting out their funeral arrangements!

**Ted** (*considering*)   Bloody hell. Poor old Frank!

**Jack**   Ar!

**Ted**   Well, it wasn't work that killed him, was it, so the NCB can relax.

*The phone rings off stage.*

**Jack**   Phone . . .

**Ted**   Who's that then?

**Jack**   It'll be school for me.

**Ted** *makes his way off stage.*

**Ted**   How's tha know that?

**Jack** *makes his way off stage.*

**Jack**   I'm a teacher, aren't I? They know everything!

**Jack** *exits towards the house.*


### Scene Eleven

*The present.*

**Steve** *struggles across the stage with a single wardrobe. He puts it down and leans on it for a moment. He wipes his face, then attempts to pick it up once more.* **May** *comes to him from the kitchen with a cuppa.*

**May**   This cup of tea's going cold . . .

**Steve**   Oh you needn't have bothered.

**May**    Well I was making one for our Jack.

**May** *hands him the tea. He sips and she looks around the house.*

**Steve**    So when do you fly out then?

**May**    I'm going to stay with him for a couple of days. And if the kids don't finish me off, I'm going on Thursday.

**Steve** *sips his tea.*

**Steve**    Are you from round here then?

**May**    Born and bred mining stock.

**Steve**    Different world now!

**May**    Aye it is . . . generations just lost!

**Steve** *sips his tea and looks off stage.*

**Steve**    I was just thinking, that car-port looks good!

**May** (*looks*)    Aye well!

**Steve**    Adds value to the house!

**May**    We must have spent thousands on it over the years but . . .

**Steve**    Looks well . . .

**May**    It's not worth owt now. Thirty-five thousand we've let it go for.

**Steve**    Somebody's getting a bargain!

**May**    Thirty-five thousand. It's what second-class footballers get a week! It's all wrong, you know?

*A beat.*

**Steve** (*looking*)    Yes, it's good to have a car-port!

**May**    We bought this when they were selling 'em cheap! Six thousand! It was worth twelve, but we got it half price. Depending how long you'd lived in it. Mrs Thatcher's idea . . .

**Steve** (*sips his tea*)   Oh aye.

**May**   I mean Ted was Labour through and through but he wanted his own house . . . He said they'd all buy 'em on this corner.

**Steve**   It's changed has this estate, my auntie used to live on Rose Close.

**May**   Well it all changed after the strike, didn't it?

**Steve**   Not much, I used to work at Frickley and now look at me!

**Steve** *hands his cup back to* **May**.

**Steve**   Smashing that!

**May**   Do you miss the pit then?

**Steve** (*struggling to lift the wardrobe*)   Oh aye like a hole in the head!

**Steve** *exits*.

**May** *looks around her*.

*As . . .*

## Scene Twelve

*1984.*

**Jack** *enters with a large sack full of coal. He is now a teacher and is living at home.* **May** *remains still and watches her son.*

**May**   What you got there, you silly sod?

**Jack**   A sack of coal, got it from Mrs Bird!

**May**   Doesn't she want it?

**Jack**   She says she can do without a sackful in weather like this. I told her we'd got none.

**May**   How did you know she'd got some?

**Jack**   Her grandson's in my tutor group, he's a right big mouth. So I nipped around after school. She knew my grandad she said.

**May**   You'll get where water won't.

**Jack**   I can take it back!

**May**   Stick it out in the bunker before anybody sees it. I've made a sandwich, do you want one?

**May** *exits.* **Jack** *stands with the sack.*

*Silence.*

**Ted** *enters through the kitchen.*

**Ted**   Some more trouble at Orgreave. It's them bastards from the Met tha knows! Chief Constable of West Yorkshire was on; he said most of the police and miners are getting on. Ralph Butcher works in Method Study, he's to get through t' picket at Cortonwood. He says the lads there are right as rain wi' him because he's making the pit good. Keeping the fans working. He says it's these bastards that they're bringing in from the Met.

**Jack**   Can't prove owt though!

**Ted**   I'm telling thee, it's these bloody Southerners. Met bastards. They think we're all flat caps and whippets up here. They think they can come up here and kick the shit out of us. I mean, I've never had a flat cap tha knows. Never! . . . I've had a flat bloody head a time or two like but . . . It's bloody end of the pits is this! She's had it in for the miners, right from day one has Thatcher.

**Jack**   Stock piling coal, wasn't she?

**Ted**   Everything Scargill's on about is right!

*A beat.*

What's tha got there?

**Jack**   Sack of coal from Mrs Bird.

**Ted**   Well put it down or that'll rupture thee sen! Tha's sweating!

**Jack** *puts the sack of coal on the carpet.*

**Jack**   What will you do then?

**Ted**   I might retrain as a brain surgeon.

**Jack**   Daft question eh?

**Ted**   A bloody teacher? I don't know!

**Ted** *moves towards the sack of coal.*

**Jack**   Can you manage that?

**Ted**   What's tha think I am?

**Jack**   I know what you are, I just wondered if you could manage.

**Ted** *goes to pick up the sack. It is a struggle for him.*

**Ted**   I used to throw these at birds.

**May** *enters with a cup of tea and a sandwich.*

**May**   There's a fry-up for you on t' oven top! And get that taken round the back before any bugger sees it.

**Ted** *exits with the sack.* **Jack** *and* **May** *stay silent and eat their tea.*

**Jack**   They reckon it could go on all year.

**May**   They've not lost yet!

**Jack**   It's a bloody war, isn't it? And no bastards bothered really.

**May**   Hey . . .

**Jack**   Hey . . .

**May**   There's money coming in from Poland, you know? I mean they're even collecting in London.

**Jack**    A few half-soaked liberals, and thespians putting money in a bucket in Hampstead's not going to get my dad back to work.

**May**    Oh shut up, you don't know what you're talking about!

**Jack**    She's been after the unions for years, and when she beats the miners she'll have beaten every working man in this country.

**May**    Where did you learn to think like that?

**Jack**    Well if you can't see it . . .

**May**    That's what they teach you, is it?

**Jack** (*exasperated*)    I'm on your side . . .

**May**    You can walk out of here tomorrow! Get another job. I've seen the application forms in your bedroom. You've always been the same, you take the path of least resistance! You've never stood up for yourself, even as a kid; you let Angela and Kenny Bostock next door shit all over you.

**Jack**    Well hello, Kenny Bostock's a bloody madman. He's been in prison half his life!

**May**    The number of arguments I've had over you . . .

**Jack**    Here we go!

**May**    I can't understand you, I don't know where that comes from. You're not like me and your dad, we've allus stood up for ourselves. We've had to do . . .

**Jack** *could argue back but concedes.*

**Jack**    Hey!

**May**    You bloody 'hey'!

**Jack**    You should be leading the miners . . .

**May**    And I'll tell you sommat else while I'm on, we're not benefiting from it like some of them are.

**Jack**    How do you mean?

**May**    Them soup-kitchen hand-outs down at the Welfare. We're not getting any of that.

**Jack**    Well you would do if you went down, everybody's entitled to it, that's what it's all about.

**May**    I wouldn't demean myself, I've got more pride.

**Jack** (*to himself*)    You can't win, can you?

*A beat.*

**May**    Why don't you nip down to the pub with your dad?

**Jack**    Because I've got some work to mark . . .

**May**    Just nip down to the Arms with him? Take his mind off it. If he watches the news once more I'll end up in bloody Stanley Royd. It's not doing him any good.

**May** *holds him and looks at him. He is still a boy of seven to her.*

Bloody hell, look at you. Six feet tall!

**Jack**    Six feet of nonsense.

**May**    Time eh . . . ?

**Jack**    Time is a clock with no hands . . .

**May**    Which smart arse said that then?

**Jack**    Me . . .

**May**    Where are you going now?

**Jack**    Get a bath, and then I'll take my dad for a drink.

**May** *remains on stage. She looks around the room. She is back to being seventy-one and coughs badly, as if she is quite ill. She remains stage centre.*

**Scene Thirteen**

*The present.*

**Steve** *enters down the staircase. He is covered in sweat. He is struggling with the mattress of a single bed, which he tries to slide down the stairs.*

**Steve**    I'm going to go for me dinner after this, love.

**May**    Right oh.

**Steve** *struggles throughout the scene.*

**Steve**    I'm gunna get some chips, do you want any?

**May**    I wish I could, doctor would have a fit. I've heart problems . . .

**Steve**    Oh dear.

**May**    He says I'm not supposed to fly but once I'm there . . .

**Steve**    Well they've got all the best stuff, haven't they? I mean, schools, trains run on time! No waiting lists, and to top it all they've got all the bloody weather! If we have two days' sunshine here we all go mental!

**May**    Once I'm there, I should be all right!

**Steve**    I've brought the rest of the stuff downstairs. So that shouldn't take me above two hours.

**May**    Aye, once I'm there, all being well.

**Steve**    When are they moving in?

**May**    This afternoon . . .

**Steve**    Bloody hell, I'd better get a move on! Or I'm going to be meeting 'em coming the other way.

**Steve** *begins to struggle with the bed once more.*

**May**    I can get our Jack to give you a hand if you want . . . He's sorting the loft out.

**Steve** (*struggling*)    No love, I'm fine . . . (*To himself.*) We wouldn't want him to twist his hand and not be able to write, would we?

**May**    I said it'd be a struggle for you . . .

**Steve** (*struggling*)    No . . . I'm actually making it look much more difficult than it actually is . . .

**Steve** *disappears off stage.* **May** *remains.*


## Scene Fourteen

*1986.*

**Ted** *enters from the kitchen. He is wearing pyjamas. He is much older-looking now and this is the first time that we really feel that he is turning into an old man. He is crying.* **May** *is part in dream and part in the reality.*

**May**    Ted . . . Ted! Go back to bed, love . . . It's half-past four. There's nowt to get up for . . .

**Ted**    I keep seeing all the lads in the cage as it's going down . . .

**May**    Come back to bed.

**Ted**    I can smell the baths, I can smell all the men down there . . .

**May**    Ted, come on! Come on, let it go, love!

**Ted**    There's no pits . . . bloody hell . . . there's no pits left. She's beaten us.

**May**    Go back to bed, love.

**Ted**    She's beaten us!

**May**    Go and relax, love!

**May** *exits towards the stairs.* **Ted** *goes back into the kitchen.*

**Ted**   They've beaten us, May. The bastards have beaten us!

*He exits slowly in tears. We can hear wailing from the kitchen . . .*

They've beaten us . . . oh my God, the bastards have beaten us!


## Scene Fifteen

*The present.*

**Jack** *enters from the staircase. He has his coat off and has clearly been in his mother's loft. He carries a carpet over his shoulder. As he does,* **Les**, *a dangerous and wild-looking man, comes over the garden fence and enters the garden. He is smoking heavily and looks like trouble.* **Jack** *arrives at the front door with the carpet over his shoulder.*

**Les**   Seen a ball, mate?

**Jack**   I'm not your mate!

**Les**   Eh?

**Jack** (*looking daggers at* **Les**)   Sorry?

**Les**   Ball's come over . . .

**Jack** (*abstracted*)   Not seen it . . .

**Les**   Sonja reckons she's taken it!

**Jack**   Who?

**Les**   Old lass!

*A beat.*

**Jack**   Do you mean my mam?

*A beat.*

**Les**   Not seen it then?

**Jack**   No.

*A beat.*

**Les**    Tha used to teach down at school, didn't you?

**Jack**    Close the gate when you go!

**Les**    Useless school that!

**Jack**    Oh I dunno.

*A beat.*

**Les**    I want that ball back. It's kid's!

**Jack**    It's not here.

**Les**    She said it'd come over . . .

**Jack**    Well I've not seen it.

**Les**    Right then.

**Les** *exits, taking his time as he does so.* **Jack** *watches him. As he does, his mobile phone rings. He answers it quickly.*

**Jack**    Hello! Candace . . . How are you? No . . . I'm at my mother's . . . So what's the story?

**May** *has entered and gives him a cup of tea.*

**May**    I thought you were still in the loft . . .

**Jack** (*to the phone*)    Have you heard anything?

**May**    I was stood there shouting up!

**Jack**    Have you spoken to Steven?

**May**    I thought you were ignoring me, I bet there's still a load of stuff up there, isn't there?

**Jack**    Well we did ask for a quick turn around! I mean they've had it three months.

*He drifts off stage speaking into the phone.*

Well can't we get hold of someone and find out what's going on?

**Jack** *has gone with the carpet over his shoulder and the mobile phone in his other hand.*

**May** *stands alone.*


## Scene Sixteen

*1989.*

**Ted** *enters from the kitchen. He is clearly older but much more sprightly than we saw him previously. He is wearing a large sombrero and is singing to the tune of 'Viva Espania'.*

**Ted**   'Oh last week we went to sunny Spain, Oh *viva Espania!* We got on the East Midlands Airport plane, hey *viva Espania.* We brought some cigs back for next door, and a bull, some sandals, gin and port, *Espania por favor*!'

**May** *(still watching)*   You silly sod!

**Ted**   Do I look like Julio Anglais?

**May**   Do you hell!

**Ted**   Well you bad pig, and I thought I was the spit.

**May**   Have you been at that brandy?

**Ted**   I've only had a tot!

**May**   Turn around, let's have a proper look at you!

**Ted** *does a spin.*

**May**   No, it's no better. Go and put a bag on your head, you might look more like him then.

**Ted**   'Hey.'

**May**   'Hey.'

**Ted**   Right, where's them cigs for Sylvia . . . ?

**May**   Still in the case, aren't they?

**Ted**    I think we've dropped a clanger there, you know? I think she smokes Embassy.

**May**    Well I've no idea!

**Ted**    And we've gone and got her six hundred Marlboro.

**May**    Well you look a bugger in that hat.

**Ted**    'Hey'. I'm wearing this everywhere I go. I might even go down to the Arms in it!

**May**    Where did you get it from?

**Ted**    I got it from Spain.

**May**    Well I never saw you buy it!

**Ted**    I don't tell you everything!

**May**    'Hey.'

**Ted**    'Hey.'

**Jack** enters. *He is dressed quite smartly with a shirt and tie. His wife* **Sharon** *is with him. She is a shy but pleasant girl in her late twenties. They have been married a year.*

**Jack**    Now, then . . .

**Ted**    *Buenos dias . . .*

**Sharon**    Oh that's very good!

**Jack**    It's *Buenos tardes*, isn't it?

**Ted**    Aye that's right. It's afternoon, isn't it?

**Jack**    *Donde servicios por favor.*

**May**    Oh he's off.

**Ted**    What's that then?

**Jack**    Where's the bogs?

**Sharon**    Typical of him!

**Jack**    Very handy phrase that in Spain!

**Ted**   Aye you bloody need 'em, Sharon.

**May**   Your dad caught a bug.

**Jack**   Well if anybody was going to catch anything, it'd be my dad!

**Sharon**   Did you have a good time?

**May**   Fantastic! Wasn't it?

**Ted**   Taking off was a shock . . .

**Jack**   I told you it was fast.

**Ted**   I didn't know it was that bloody fast.

**May**   When it banked to one side your dad nearly embarrassed himself!

**Jack**   Now I don't believe that for one minute!

**May**   You should have seen his face!

**Sharon**   So you'd go again?

**Ted**   Fantastic, and the drinks, the bloody drinks. I'm not kidding, I asked for a brandy and he must have given me half a pint!

**May**   Your dad wanted to stop for a fortnight . . .

**Sharon**   Better than working?

**May**   He says he could go live there.

**Ted**   I could live there, I could honest!

**May**   Get an apartment he says . . .

**Ted**   I could get an apartment over there, no problem!

**May**   He says we should have had some of that years ago!

**Ted**   We should have had some of that years ago, Sharon. I mean your mam and dad went out with Laker's, didn't they?

**Sharon**   Well there you go then! Get yourself off!

**Ted**   Except that we haven't got the money.

**May**   Aye that's the only problem.

**Ted**   Everything we got from the redundancy's gone on the house.

**May**   He'll never go and live there, Sharon, take no notice of him!

**Ted**   It's either all gone on the house or been spent in Marks and Spencer's! She's a Marxist is Jack's mam, Sharon, did you know . . . ?

**Jack**   You've told her that one.

**Ted**   Have I?

*A beat.*

**Sharon**   The car-port looks good!

**Ted**   I've had to fight tooth and nail for that!

**Sharon**   You didn't build it yourself, did you?

**May**   Did he bloody hell . . .

**Ted**   I was going to tell her I had.

**May**   Sylvia's Kenny next door did it.

**Jack**   Oh he's back out of prison then?

**Ted**   Well he was . . .

**May**   Gone back in for theft . . .

**Sharon**   Oh dear!

**May**   A post office this time.

**Ted**   It's a shame about him, he's a nice kid really.

**Jack**   He is except that he's tried to kill his girlfriend twice.

**Ted**   I think first time was an accident!

*A beat.*

**Sharon**    Did you try any of the tapas bars?

**Jack**    Did they hell!

**Ted**    Well it was full board anyway so . . .

**May**    It's the first time we've been abroad; don't expect us to eat their food and all, you know?

**Jack**    You probably didn't go out of the hotel, did you?

**Ted**    Hey we're not that bad!

**May**    They had a group on every night, didn't they?

**Ted**    Maurice and Carmen!

**May**    She'd been a flamenco dancer, hadn't she?

**Ted**    She'd been a flamenco dancer, Sharon!

**May**    She could move, couldn't she?

**Ted**    She'd been a flamenco dancer!

**May**    Go and get their presents.

**Ted**    What do you think to my hat, Sharon?

**Sharon**    Do you know I didn't even notice it . . .

**Ted**    Hey Sharon, be careful, you haven't been in the family long enough to make jokes yet!

**Jack**    No, it's just polite conversation at the moment, jokes come after the first ten years.

**May**    Aye, if you're lucky! Go and get their presents. What do you think they've come for?

*A beat.*

**Jack**    Well actually, we've come to tell you something!

**Ted**    You're not packing in teaching, are you?

**Jack**    Not yet!

**Ted**   Because you're bloody silly if you do, I know he fancies this writing lark, Sharon, but.

**May**   Oh shut up you . . . !

**Ted**   I'm only saying . . .

**May**   What is it then?

*A beat.*

**Jack**   Well . . .

**May** (*to* **Ted**)   Take that bloody silly hat off.

**Ted**   I'm leaving it on . . .

**May**   He's drunk is your dad.

**Ted**   I'm not drunk.

**May**   He's bought this cheap brandy and he can't keep off it! Take that bloody silly hat off!

**Ted**   I shan't!

**May**   Take it off!

**Ted**   It's only cheap brandy but I love it, Sharon!

**May**   Aye, we've bought you a bottle, you'll be all right with that!

**Ted**   It's only cheap but . . .

**May**   They'll not know any different anyway!

**Ted**   It's only cheap but I love it!

**May**   Aye he loves it coz it's cheap!

*A beat.*

**Jack**   Well it's Sharon really . . .

**May**   What's up then?

*A beat.*

**Sharon**   Well . . . I'm having a baby . . .

*Silence.*

**May** (*delighted*)    Well about bloody time and all . . .

**Ted** *begins to become rather over-active.*

**Ted**    Well bloody hell, well done the pair of you! A bloody granddad! I think I'll open some more of that brandy. I'll open their bottle! They'll not drink it anyway, it'll not be good enough for 'em! They don't drink cheap bloody brandy do they?

*He dances about.*

**May**    Take that silly hat off.

**Ted**    Granddads wear hats like this, you silly old sod! Your mother knows nothing, does she . . . Come here.

**Ted** *hugs* **Jack** *tightly.*

**Jack**    Don't break my back!

**Ted**    That's my bloody lad!

**Ted** *is euphoric.*

**May**    So when is it due then?

**Sharon**    August! We weren't sure but . . .

**May**    Come here the pair of you . . .

**May** *hugs* **Sharon** *and* **Jack**.

**Sharon**    I didn't want to tell you until it'd all been . . .

**Jack**    You're the first to know, we're on our way to Sharon's mum's.

**Sharon**    Jack didn't want to tell you until it was born.

**May**    Silly sod.

**Jack**    I didn't want anybody to know, that we'd actually done it . . .

**May**    What's he bloody like?

**Ted** *has gone silent and still. He takes his sombrero off.*

**Jack**    Are you all right, Dad?

**Ted**    Aye . . .

**Jack**    Are you sure?

*Silence.*

**Ted**    Oh ar!

**Ted** *sits in the armchair.*

**May**    He always has to overdo it!

**Ted**    I feel sick that's all.

**May**    He's had all that brandy!

**Ted**    Oh shut up.

*A beat.*

**Jack**    Are you sure you're all right?

**Ted**    Is it warm or is it me?

**Jack**    It is quite close.

**Ted** *is experiencing his first angina attack.*

**Ted**    I feel bloody . . .

**Jack**    Dad?

**Ted**    Oh hell!

**Ted** *swoons and feels pains in his chest.*

**Sharon**    I think we need to get a doctor!

**Ted**    Oh hell!

**May**    Ted?

**Ted**    Oh hell!

**Jack**    Dad?

**May**    Ted . . . !

**Jack**   Bloody hell what are you playing at?

**Ted** *swoons on the chair as* **Sharon** *and* **Jack** *hold him.*

**Sharon**   I've got him . . .

**Ted**   It's too warm . . .

**Jack**   We've got you . . . Phone nine, nine, nine . . . Mam, phone the ambulance!

**May**   I don't like using it . . .

**Jack**   Phone the bloody ambulance . . .

**Mam**   I can't . . . I've never used it . . .

**Jack** *and* **Sharon** *comfort* **Ted**.

**Sharon**   Let's get him some fresh air!

**Jack**   Come on, let's get him out in the back garden! Have you got the heating on, it's barmy in here with the heat!

**Jack** *and* **Sharon** *help* **Ted** *out towards the kitchen. They have gone.*

*Silence.*

**May** *is in present time and is remembering the whole event as though it was yesterday.*

*May*   Sharon phone, phone the ambulance! Phone the ambulance will you . . . somebody do something!


**Scene Seventeen**

*The present.*

**May** *is standing alone on the stage. She begins to become emotional. As she stands,* **Steve** *enters through the front door with a bag of chips, and stands looking at her, eating chips.*

**Steve**   Want a chip?

**May**   No thanks, love . . .

**Steve**   Go on, one'll not kill you!

**May** *takes a chip.*

**Steve**   Finish them off if you want . . .

**May**   No, I'm not eating in my front room. I've never done that, don't want to do it now!

**Steve**   Right, we'll have a look at the kitchen now, shall we?

**Steve** *exits.* **May** *stands alone.*

*Loud disco music pulsates. As a plastic tractor and a kid's spade are thrown over the garden fence.*

**May**   Here we go! Bloody noise . . . Jack? Jack?

**Jack** *enters from the staircase. He is more hassled than previously.*

**Jack**   What's up?

**May**   Have you heard this!

**Jack**   Oh just forget it.

**Sonja** (*voice only*)   Turn it up, Les, I love this, it's brilliant!

**May**   Go and tell 'em to turn it down!

**Jack**   Just leave it!

**May**   Can't you do sommat to help me just for once?

**May** *exits into the kitchen. The volume of the music increases.*

**Jack** *walks through the house to the front door. He sees the tractor and the spade and takes then back into the house and then he walks slowly off stage.*

# Act Two

**Scene One**

*1996.*

*As the house lights go down we see* **May** *enter the living room. She looks around the room and picks up an old photo. As she holds the photo* **Ted** *enters. He is much older now and wears slippers and a cardigan, though he is not ill.*

**Ted**   Put their hands up who wants a cuppa!

**May** *is still looking at the photo.*

**May** (*to herself*)   Bloody hell, Ted!

**Ted**   Put their hands up who wants a cuppa tea!

**May** (*to herself*)   Bloody wedding anniversary and all!

**May** *puts her hand up.*

**Ted**   Right that's one cuppa tea for in here then.

**May** (*to* **Ted**)   I'll make it!

**Ted**   I'll make it, you sit down, and get yourself right. You've just come out of hospital.

**May**   You're not well yourself.

**Ted**   'Hey.'

**May**   'Hey.'

**Ted**   Come on here, you know what the doctor said, take it steady. Get yourself sat down, you can't be running about with heart problems.

**May**   Who'd've thought it? Me and you with heart problems!

**Ted**   You've only got 'em because I've got them. You're only jealous!

**May** *notices someone through the window in the fourth wall. She walks towards the window and looks out.*

**May**    Our Jack's here by the looks of it.

**Ted**    I thought he'd gone to London to talk to this agent thing?

**May**    Well he's obviously back, isn't he?

**Ted**    I'd better put that kettle on . . .

**May**    Sharon'll do it . . .

**Ted** *sits. As he does* **Jack** *and* **Sharon** *come through the front door upstage.* **Sharon** *enters first.*

**Sharon**    Hello . . .

**May**    Hello!

**Sharon** *enters the living room, and offers* **May** *a card.*

**Sharon**    Happy anniversary!

**Ted**    I thought he was going to London?

**Sharon**    Got back last night!

**Ted**    How did he get on?

**Sharon**    You know your Jack, you can't get two words out of him.

**May**    He should stay in teaching. It's security now; he's got two kids!

**Sharon**    I know that!

**May**    Where are they?

**Sharon**    They're at my mam's . . .

**May**    I thought you'd've brought them.

**Sharon**    Well, we were but . . .

**Jack** *enters. He is more casual than before. He carries a small present with him.*

**Jack**   Now then. Happy anniversary. And the winner is!

*He kisses his mother and hands her the present.*

**May**   Oh you needn't have bothered.

**Jack**   Aye, you say that, and the year I don't buy you owt you have a dickie fit!

**May**   A card would've been enough.

**Sharon**   How are you feeling?

**May**   Well, I've felt better, Sharon, let's just say that.

**Jack**   What did the doctor say then?

**May**   It's my valves or sommat, isn't it? I'm not working properly anyway, let's just say that.

*She begins to unwrap the present. It is a piece of Lladro pottery.*

Oh isn't that lovely. Ted, isn't that nice?

**Jack**   I thought it'd go on the mantelpiece.

**May**   I thought you'd've brought the kids.

**Jack**   Well we were but . . .

**May**   Are they all right?

**Jack**   Oh aye . . .

**May**   So what's up then?

**Jack**   How do you mean?

**May**   Well I know that there's sommat up because of the look on your bloody faces!

**Jack** (*to* **Sharon**)   There's nowt up is there?

**Sharon**   No!

**May**   Well something's not right, I can tell! I knew when Sharon came in!

**Sharon**   Well I never said . . . !

**May**    You didn't have to!

**Jack**    It's nothing anyway . . .

**Sharon**    We've dropped the kids at my mum's because we've had a bit of a do in the car, that's all . . .

*A beat.*

**May**    I knew there was something.

**Jack**    It's nothing, leave it, don't spoil your day!

**Sharon**    He was going off on one in the car, so we dropped them off . . .

**May**    Well, don't bring your problems here, we've got enough!

**Sharon**    We're not doing . . .

**Jack**    Well, what did you have to mention it for . . . ?

**Sharon**    I didn't, it was your mum.

**May**    She didn't have to!

**Sharon**    There's no point pretending everything's all right!

**May**    I've known something's been going on for the last six months so you needn't worry about that, Sharon!

**Jack**    Oh here we go . . .

**May**    Hey!

**Ted**    Now hey . . . Don't start having a barney here. It's our wedding anniversary, now have more sense!

**Jack**    She's always got to open her mouth!

**Sharon**    I didn't say anything!

**May**    You shouldn't have come if you're going to do this on us.

**Jack** (*to* **May**)    It's nothing, don't worry about it!

**Sharon**    No, just let him keep on hitting me, like he's always done!

**Ted**    Hey now, hey . . .

**Jack**    Here we go . . . !

**Sharon**    He thinks it's normal behaviour!

**May**    Ted, now tell him!

**Ted**    What can I say?

**Sharon**    All he's doing is writing a book; you'd think he was the first person in the world to write one! And when things aren't going well . . .

**Jack**    Why don't you just shut up?

**Sharon**    This is what I get every night.

**May**    Now, hey, both of you, leave it!

**Sharon**    You don't know what he's like . . .

**Jack**    I tell you what, I'll go shall I . . . ?

**May**    Hey, hey!

**Sharon**    We're onto that now! Empty threats!

**Jack**    They're not empty as it happens!

**Sharon**    I have this every night!

**Jack**    Well I'll go shall I, is that what you want . . . ?

**Ted**    Well, aren't we blessed?

**Jack**    I'll go, and then you'll have the kids all to yourself!

**May**    Now listen to me, you!

**Jack**    Listen to you? I've had about enough of listening to all the bloody lot of you!

**Ted**    I don't know if it's right about you hitting her but . . .

**Sharon** (*to* **Ted**)    What are you saying, that I'm a liar!

**Ted**   . . . You want to give that a bloody miss.

**Jack**   I'm not stopping here listening to this!

**Sharon**   Well go then . . .

**Jack**   I will do.

**Sharon**   Go on then.

**Jack**   And if I go I'll not come back!

**Sharon**   More threats!

**Jack**   I mean it!

**May**   Well go then because we don't want all this upset. Just go, you've been the same all your bloody life, whenever things aren't going your way! Bloody go, go and write your little book, life goes on, you've got two kids and you want to write, you're bloody pathetic! I don't know why you can't be happy with what you've got, you've got a nice little life at that school! You're bloody pathetic at times!

**Jack**   Am I?

**May**   Pathetic. (*To* **Ted**.)   Ted, say something to him.

**Ted**   Well, now hey!

**May**   We're not having this, not from you, not from anybody!

**Jack**   Well, don't worry because I'm going!

**May**   Well, go then and let's have done with it! If you can't live together bloody go, and good riddance to you!

**Jack** *leaves the house.* **Ted** *walks after him.*

**Ted**   Jack, hey now, hey . . .

**Jack**   Oh leave it, Dad eh?

**Jack** *exits through the front door.* **Sharon** *and* **May** *remain in the room and* **Sharon** *becomes very upset. She cannot get her breath.* **Ted** *is by the front door.*

**Sharon**   He's like this with me . . . all the . . . bloody time. Oh I'm sorry . . . I can't get my breath . . .

**May**   Are you all right?

**Sharon**   Have you got a bag. I'm having a panic do!

**May**   Ted, a paper bag!

**Ted** (*entering*)   A paper bag, what for?

**May** *looks as* **Ted** *rummages through the dustbin and produces a crisp packet.* **Ted** *gives* **Sharon** *the paper bag that the present came in, and* **Sharon** *begins to breathe deeply into it.* **Ted** *exits after* **Jack**.

**May**   Aren't we all right?

**Sharon** (*breathing into the bag*)   I'm sorry . . .

**May**   Just get your breath back.

**Sharon** (*into the bag*)   I'm sorry.

**May**   Calm down!

**Sharon**   He's been like it for the last year. He takes it out on the kids . . .

**May**   Just settle down.

**Sharon**   He keeps saying he's going to leave . . . says he can't stand teaching, says he can't write. I don't know what he wants!

**Ted** *enters through the front door.*

**Ted**   He's gone.

**Sharon**   This is what he does, he shoots off in the car, we don't know where he goes . . . And then he comes back two hours later right as rain, as if nothing's happened.

**May**   Our bloody Jack!

**Sharon**   I mean he grabs me sometimes, I think he's going to kill me!

*A beat.*

**Ted**    There isn't another woman, is there?

**May**    Ted?

**Ted**    Well, I mean look at him at college.

**May**    Don't be so bloody tactless . . .

**Sharon**    I'm sorry . . .

*A beat.*

**May**    Well, this is one anniversary that we'll not forget in a hurry.

**Sharon**    He says he hates me that often he must bloody mean it!

**Ted**    He doesn't know when he's bloody well off our Jack!

*A beat.*

**May**    Is that kettle on?

**Ted**    It can go on. Hands up who wants a cuppa tea?

**May**    Ted?

**Ted**    I'm only trying to make light of it . . . Hands up.

**Sharon** *and* **May** *put their hands in the air.*

**Ted**    That's two teas in here then.

**Sharon**    I'm sorry to bring an argument into your house.

**May**    An argument?

**Ted**    That wasn't an argument, was it, May?

**May**    Was it bloody hell, that's the trouble with these young 'uns, they don't know how to argue!

**Ted** *takes* **Sharon** *off stage . . .*

**Ted**    Come on, I'll show you my privets . . . They're me pride and joy at the moment, now I know that's sad, but that's how you get when you get older, Sharon!

**Ted** and **Sharon** *have gone.* **May** *is standing alone on the stage. She picks up the small piece of pottery* **Jack** *has brought her and holds it in her hands.*

## Scene Two

*The present.*

**Steve** *enters through the front door.* **May** *stands holding the piece of pottery which she now puts back among the packed furniture.*

**Steve**    I'm back, Mrs Willis!

**May**    No sign of your mate then?

**Steve**    I've phoned him! He went to Sheffield last night and he broke down apparently.

**May**    Oh dear.

**Steve**    Well, that's what he says, it's more likely he found a woman and ended up back at her house.

**May**    How do you work that out?

**Steve**    Well, he always seems to break down when he goes to Sheffield! Now either that's a huge coincidence or they've got to do sommat about the state of that road through Rotherham!

**May**    Why's that?

**Steve**    Because he's had four punctures, two blow-outs, his water pipe's burst, his exhaust's come off, and he says that last night, his big end went. I know where it's gone and all if you ask me!

*A beat.*

I'll get started on this . . . Has your Jack gone?

**May**   He's on the phone.

**Steve**   Have these chairs to go?

**May**   No, no, we're leaving them.

**Steve**   Bloody hell they're getting a bargain with you.

*He picks up a tea-chest.*

He must have money to burn, your young 'un . . .

**Steve** *exits upstage and out through the front door.*


**Scene Three**

*1997.*

**May** *remains on stage.* **Ted** *enters. He has just been doing the garden and is fatigued.*

**Ted**   Oh, I'm buggered!

**May**   You're doing too much in that garden.

**Ted**   Oh shut up!

**May** *raises her hand.*

**May**   Are we going to have some music on?

**Ted**   Who?

**May**   Bing.

**Ted**   I'm buggered.

*Bing Crosby music starts to play.* **Ted** *sits in one of the easy chairs and* **May** *eventually sits in the other.* **Ted** *sings along to the music.*

**May**   Don't sing, Ted, you're killing it.

*A beat.*

**Ted**   I'll do some ironing.

**May**   Can't you sit still?

**Ted**   I can't just sit, you know that!

*A beat.*

**May**   Well, I never thought he'd actually leave her . . .

**Ted**   No . . . !

**May**   I never thought he'd leave her and not come bloody back!

**Ted** *exits to the kitchen and comes back with an ironing board and a load of washing in a washing basket.*

**Ted**   I don't know how we get so much washing!

**May**   He doesn't see a lot of the kids!

**Ted**   Shall I do the shirts or the sheets?

**May**   I say, he doesn't see . . .

**Ted**   I heard what you said.

**May**   He's living in a flat Sharon said! She's had to go back to work.

**Ted**   I'm not getting into it!

**May**   I mean we never brought him up like that . . .

**Ted**   He's my lad and that's that!

**May**   That's the trouble with you, you turn off.

**Ted**   I turn off because you never do.

**May**   You turn off!

**Ted**   I've got to do!

**May**   He can bloody rot for me!

**Ted**   Now you don't mean that!

**May**   After all we've done for him!

*A beat.*

**Ted**   He'll be back teaching before too long!

**May**    And Sharon looks shocking!

**Ted** *irons. A moment's silence.*

**Ted**    Well, things can only get better according to Mr Blair!

**May**    I didn't vote!

**Ted**    Well, at least we've got rid of Mrs Thatcher. Eighteen bloody years. Things can only get better. That's what they're saying!

**May**    If it hadn't been for Mrs Thatcher we wouldn't have been able to buy this house.

**Ted**    If it hadn't been for Mrs Thatcher, I'd've still had a job, and we could have saved up, gone and lived somewhere else, and maybe I wouldn't be doing the bloody ironing!

**Ted** *continues to iron. As he does, we can see* **Jack** *enter through the front door upstage.* **Candace**, *a strikingly attractive and flamboyant young American woman, enters with him. As he enters the music fades.* **Jack** *is now every inch the aspiring author.*

*Silence.*

**Jack**    Now then?

*A beat.*

**Ted**    Now then?

*A beat.*

**May**    Who's this then?

**Ted**    Don't be like that with him!

**May**    Runs off and then just turns up!

*A beat.*

**Jack**    I didn't know if I'd be welcome but . . . !

*A beat.*

**May**    Why didn't you ring?

**Jack**    I knew you wouldn't answer the phone!

*A beat.*

**May**    He thinks he's funny.

*A beat.*

**Jack**    This is Candace, Mam, a mate of mine . . .
She's my agent's assistant!

**Candace**    Hi!

**Ted**    Hi!

**Jack**    We were just passing through, thought I'd drop
in . . .

**May**    You been to see the kids . . .

**Jack**    We just popped.

**May**    How's Sharon, is she all right? Coz she looked awful
when I saw her!

*A beat.*

**Candace**    We were just passing, weren't we . . .

**Jack**    We're driving down from Edinburgh!

**Candace**    Have you ever done the Festival? It's great!

**May**    She says the kids are all over the shop!

**Jack**    They're only young, Mam . . . they'll not even . . .

**May**    I know how old they are!

*A beat.*

Give us a hand up, Ted, will you.

**Jack**    I'll . . .

**Jack** *steps forward to attempt to help his mother.*

**May**    Your dad'll do it!

**Ted** *comes and helps* **May** *to her feet.*

**Ted**   I'll put the kettle on, shall I?

**May**   You do what you want, I'm going out.

*A beat.*

**Jack**   Well I thought if you wanted we could have a run to the Rogerthorpe and have a bit of sommat to eat!

**May**   Well I'm not going!

*A beat.*

**Jack**   Well, it looks like they're going publish my book. So I thought I could treat you!

*A beat.*

**May**   It was foggy here this morning, wasn't it, Ted?

**Ted**   Oh aye, it was foggy this morning!

*A beat.*

**Candace**   It's the same people who did *The English Patient.* Everyone in the office is delighted for Jack. It's quite an achievement!

*A beat.*

**May**   Well I'm going over to Jean Burton's. Can you remember her?

**Jack**   Oh aye!

**May**   She's got breast cancer now, you know?

**Jack**   No I didn't!

**May**   I go and sit with her for an hour or two, keeps her company.

**May** *exits.*

*Silence.*

**Ted**   She's pleased to see you!

**Jack**   That's right.

**Ted**   I was just ironing. She can't do so much now because of her arthritis. She's got arthritis you know.

**Canda**   Has she tried massage oils at all?

*During this sequence **Ted** tidies away the ironing board.*

**Ted**   Always washing, that's why she's got arthritis. I'll get shut of this stuff and put the kettle on. We've got decaffeinated you know, if you fancy that. May has it because normal gives her palpitations. Normal doesn't give me palpitations, it gives me stomach ache so I drink lemonade, I'm a secret lemonade drinker!

**Ted** *clears away the ironing board into the kitchen.*

**Jack** *and* **Candace** *are left alone.*

*Silence.*

**Jack**   Sorry!

**Candace**   So I'm your mate? That's new!

**Jack**   I couldn't think of anything to say!

**Candace**   Pretty good for a writer, Jack!

**Jack**   Sorry, I didn't mean it like that!

**Candace**   Wishful thinking?

**Jack**   Absolutely!

*A beat.*

**Candace**   Your mother could be a heritage centre. D.H. Lawrence in the flesh!

**Jack**   Don't mention Lawrence in here.

**Candace**   Why's that?

**Jack**   He was from Nottingham.

**Candace**   Eastwood.

**Jack**    Near enough! Any mention of anything to do with Nottingham and my dad has a stroke.

**Candace**    Oh yeh?

**Jack**    They didn't support the miners. You can't talk about Nottingham Goose Fair, Nottingham lace, Brian Clough or Robin Hood in this house any more! It's a big loss to conversation, but a sad fact!

**Candace**    It sounds it!

*A beat.*

**Jack**    Gor, the same old chairs! I had my first sexual encounter in this room!

**Candace**    Well, you're not having one today, so I'd forget that!

**Jack**    Pity!

**Candace**    You don't give in, do you?

**Jack**    I thought it was all part of the service.

**Candace**    We get you published, Jack, we don't get you laid!

**Jack**    I have to take care of that myself, do I?

**Candace**    What did you think?

**Jack**    Well, I did think that you and me going to Edinburgh was a signal.

**Candace**    For what?

**Jack**    Well . . . ?

*A beat.*

**Candace**    Sorry!

**Jack**    My fault. I've always been keen to get to the end of a story!

**Candace**    Sorry.

*A beat.*

**Jack**   Another mistake!

**Ted** *enters.*

**Ted**   We have got proper coffee if you'd prefer . . .

**Jack**   I think we're going to get off, Dad . . .

**Ted**   It's no bother.

**Jack**   I think we'll get off. I've got to drop Candace at her flat anyway!

*A beat.*

**Ted**   Getting off?

**Jack**   Yes!

**Ted**   It's a long run!

**Candace**   But it's downhill all the way!

*A beat.*

**Ted**   A full-time writer now then?

**Jack**   I do some part-time teaching!

**Candace**   Jack's got a good eye for comedy.

**Ted**   It's all about timing, isn't it?

**Jack**   Oh I don't know about that!

*A beat.*

**Ted**   No, you're right there!

*A beat.*

**Candace**   Can I use the little girls' room?

**Ted**   Bottom of the stairs, love . . . don't use them towels that's hung up though, they're just for show, she'll go barmy if you use them. There's usually an old towel in the bottom drawer.

**Candace**    I'll be one minute!

**Candace** *makes her way through the door and off stage.*

**Ted**    Nice lass!

**Jack**    Yes but . . .

**Ted**    Go steady, you know!

**Jack**    No danger there, Dad, I've been reading it all wrong!

**Ted**    Story of my bloody life! Fantasy and reality that's what that's all about!

*A beat.*

**Jack**    Listen, this was a mistake I know that but er . . .

**Ted**    I'll tell thee what's been a mistake: leaving Sharon . . . that's been thee biggest mistake and them kids. That's been a bloody mistake and all.

*A beat.*

**Jack**    My mam's true to form!

**Ted**    Thee mam's all over t' shop.

**Jack**    Is she?

**Ted**    She's in and out of Ponte hospital.

**Jack**    I have been meaning to get back and catch up a lot more but what with this book lark . . .

*A beat.*

**Ted**    Sylvia's gone, you know? Got herself a little bungalow on the close.

**Jack**    So what's happening next door?

**Ted**    Don't know!

**Candace** *arrives.*

**Candace**    I hope I've used the right towel . . .

*A beat.*

**Jack**    Anyway! We'd better get off!

**Candace**    Pleasure to meet you, Mr Willis, and I hope we can get you down to the office some time!

**Jack**    See you, Dad! Say 'hey' to my mam for me!

**Ted**    Aye, I will. I will that!

**Candace** *and* **Jack** *exit.* **Ted** *walks them to the back door. Then he slowly re-enters, picks up the washing basket and walks with it into the kitchen. He is very upset.*

**Ted**    My bloody lad! My bloody lad!

*As he moves about, an older-looking* **Sylvia** *enters. She knocks on the front door and comes immediately into the house. She is clearly an older woman, but still smokes with a gay abandonment.*

**Sylvia**    Are you there, May?

**Ted** (*calling*)    Come in, Sylvia.

**Sylvia**    Is she in?

**Ted**    She's over at Jean's.

**Sylvia**    I was just passing, do you want owt bringing from t' Asda because I'm going down that way?

**Ted**    Now you're all right asking me, Sylvia, you know that. I'd live on tinned bloody ham if it was left to me.

**Sylvia**    Because I can get some stuff if you want . . .

**Ted**    She's over at Jean's . . .

**Sylvia**    Have you heard about Len Picton? Died last night.

**Ted**    Dear me.

**Sylvia**    In Ponte.

**Ted**    Dear me!

**Sylvia**    Kidneys!

**Ted**   Dear me!

**Sylvia**   Digging the garden one minute and . . .

**Ted**   Dear me . . .

**Sylvia**   That's five on this estate in as many months. I'm glad I'm down in t' bungalow, I mean I said to her next door, they're dropping like flies up here.

**Ted**   Dear me!

**Sylvia** *makes to move.*

**Sylvia**   Right, she's over at Jean's, is she? I'll go and have ten minutes, mind you I always say I'm going to have ten minutes and, you know me, I stay a bloody hour. I always outstay my welcome, I always have done, see you later . . .

**Sylvia** *is almost at the door. She stops.*

Was that your Jack, driving off?

**Ted**   That's right!

**Sylvia**   I haven't seen him for bloody years. What's he doing up here then?

**Ted**   Practising his timing.

**Sylvia**   Oh right then . . .

*A beat.*

**Ted**   I tell you what, I'll come over to Jean's with you . . .

**Ted** *starts to move off towards the front door.*

**Sylvia**   That's it, you come and have a bloody natter with us! Mind you, I don't know why you're coming, you'll not get a bloody word in!

**Ted** *and* **Sylvia** *exit.*

**Scene Four**

*The present.*

**May** *enters from the kitchen into the living room. She is carrying a small box which is suffering from having been sprayed with a hosepipe.*

**May** (*calling*)    They're going bloody mad with a hosepipe them kids next door. Jack? I say, have you seen 'em with that hosepipe? I'm wet through. It's all coming over onto our side! They've been a bloody nuisance since they moved in. Two years, I've had this . . .

**May** *moves through the house.*

Jack? Jack? I bet he's on the bloody phone!

**May** *exits.*

*As . . .*

**Scene Five**

*1997.*

*At the space behind* **May**'s *home* **Les** *enters. Lights pick out that area. He is carrying a few boxes, which he dumps on the floor.* **Sonja**, *dressed more vulgarly than we have seen previously, also brings some boxes into the room.*

**Les**    Drop this off and I'll make a start on t' shed.

**Sonja**    Where's the kids?

**Les**    In t' garden wi' dogs!

**Sonja**    Do you want a fag?

**Les**    I wouldn't mind a fuck . . .

**Sonja**    Let's get this done first.

**Les**    Urgh!

**Sonja**    I'm away tonight you know!

**Les**   Where at?

**Sonja**   Wath.

**Les**   What is it?

**Sonja**   Social club.

**Les**   Who's taking you?

**Sonja**   Mark.

**Les**   He's gay, isn't he?

**Sonja**   Is he?

**Les**   He'd better be . . .

**Sonja**   Why had he?

**Les**   Nowt to worry about then, have I?

**Sonja**   Jealous or what?

*A beat.*

**Les**   I'm gunna get a C.B. rig and all . . . Put an aerial up in the garden.

**Sonja**   One nine for a copy . . .

**Les** (*American*)   We got ourselves a convoy!

**Sonja** *investigates the carpet in the room and through the door.*

**Sonja**   This carpet's all right, isn't it?

**Les**   We can sell some of them pups on the market.

*A beat.*

**Sonja**   I'm gunna need some more stuff and all you know . . .

**Les**   What sort of stuff.

**Sonja**   For t' club . . .

**Les**   What's up with what you've got?

**Sonja**    I've had it ages!

**Les**    Are you sure you want some?

**Sonja**    Yeh!

*They have completed this room.* **Les** *has one thing on his mind.*

**Les**    Right, let's go upstairs then!

**Sonja**    What for?

**Les**    I want to show you sommat.

**Sonja**    Oh I haven't got time for that.

*A beat.*

**Les**    Upstairs.

**Sonja**    Oh!

**Les**    Sonja!

**Sonja**    I've got to sing tonight, you know . . .

**Les**    I'll make you sing!

**Sonja**    Les?

**Les**    No, come on upstairs!

**Sonja**    Oh!

**Les** *grabs her around the waist and forces her out of the room.* **Les** *and* **Sonja** *exit through the door. They are giggling as they depart.*


### Scene Six

*The present.*

**Jack** *enters. He is in his shirtsleeves and is on the phone. He has been sweating and shows signs of perspiration. He walks from the front door past the bottom of the stairs to the living room.*

**Jack** (*to the phone*)   What do you mean, it's not funny? Of course it's funny. Listen there's only two types of funny, it's either funny or it's not!

**May** *enters.*

**May**   Has he taken that microwave?

**Jack**   Did they want it ha ha funny or ho ho funny?

**May**   I'm leaving that . . .

**Jack**   Because nobody said!

**May**   You've come to help you know!

**Jack**   Or did they want it: 'I've shit my pants' funny?

**May**   And stop swearing on the phone!

**Jack**   Tell them to read it again with some flippers on . . . see if it's funnier then.

**May**   Hey . . . ?

**Jack** (*to* **May**)   Hey off!

**Jack** *starts to move off stage . . .*

**May**   Is he taking the right boxes . . . ?

**Jack** *disappears upstage.*

**Jack**   And try a big red nose and all! And if that doesn't work tell him to try a flower up his arse . . .

**Jack** *has gone.*

**May**   I said we should have got Mason's . . .

**May** *sits and listens to the whole of the next scene.*

**Scene Seven**

*1998.*

**Sonja** *enters. She is dressed in a club singer's off-the-shoulders dress. She would look good but there is something extremely cheap about her. As she enters she calls to the kids off stage.*

**Sonja**    Sasha? What are you doing? Don't hit him like that, you twat! . . . I'm trying to get ready, aren't I? Gooor. Do you think I've got nothing better to do?

**Sonja** *begins to sing the 'Preacher Man'. As she sings she gets ready. She is a good singer but there is nothing showy about what she is doing. As she sings,* **Les** *enters. He has clearly just got up and appears to be either drunk or on drugs.*

**Les**    What are you shouting for?

**Sonja**    Sasha's always hitting him!

**Les**    Stop shouting!

**Sonja**    I'm trying to get ready!

**Les**    Stop shouting!

**Sonja**    They're my kids!

*A beat.*

**Les**    What do you look like . . . ?

**Sonja**    This is that new dress . . .

*A beat.*

**Les**    You look like muck!

**Sonja**    What?

**Les**    Muck!

**Sonja**    You didn't say that last night . . .

*A beat.*

**Les**    Who are you trying to impress?

**Sonja**   It's just a dress!

**Les**   That Mark?

**Sonja**   No!

*A beat.*

**Les**   I'll stitch that bastard if he touches you!

**Sonja**   He hasn't touched me!

**Les**   Why, what's up with him, is he a bummer or sommat?

**Sonja**   How do I know?

*A beat.*

**Les**   You look like you've had more prick than a second-hand dartboard!

**Sonja**   I thought it looked okay . . .

*A beat.*

**Les**   Anyway they can go back and live with their dad them kids if you keep shouting at 'em!

**Sonja**   Why?

**Les**   Coz they can!

**Sonja**   No, they can't!

**Les**   Yes, they can!

**Sonja**   You know what he's like with 'em . . . He's all over 'em, and I'm not having that again!

**Les**   Well shut up then!

**Les** *pulls on a coat.*

**Sonja**   Where are you going anyway?

**Les**   I'm going out . . .

**Les** *starts to leave.*

**Sonja**    But I was going out!

**Les**    You're out every night!

**Sonja**    It's my job!

**Les**    Job?

**Sonja**    Yeh!

**Les**    Job?

**Sonja**    It's what I do!

**Les**    You should get down the social and flog your hole instead of doing that shite! Nobody listens to you anyway!

*A beat.*

**Sonja**    Who's going to look after the kids if you go out?

**Les**    It's all right! They're old enough to put themselves to bed.

**Sonja**    Les?

**Les**    I'm only going down to the social anyway, they know where I am!

**Sonja**    Les please, please . . . it's the only bit of pleasure I get.

**Les**    What sort of pleasure do I get? You slobbering all over me with your big white arse? I can get that anywhere!

**Sonja**    Les . . .

**Les**    You're muck . . .

**Sonja**    Les?

**Les**    Muck!

**Les** *has gone.* **Sonja** *is in a real state.*

**Sonja**    Les, please, please . . . Les, please don't go, I'm begging you! Please let me go out, please!

**Sonja** *pathetically makes her way out of the room and off stage.*
*As* . . .

## Scene Eight

*The present.*

**May** *is on stage. She remains exactly where she was in the previous scene set in the present.* **Jack** *enters from the kitchen. He is still on the phone, attempting in a desultory manner to remove things.*

**Jack**    That's good is that, Candace, but I thought you said it was the funniest script you'd read? No! It was you who said I was a comic genius! I thought you said they were bound to like it?

**Jack** *walks around the room and out into the kitchen.* **May** *watches him go off stage* . . .

**Jack**    No, it's your bullshit, Candace! That's what you said! No it's not my bullshit! My bullshit is very messy! Your bullshit is crumbling down around you, girl. Well, can't you talk to somebody who can make a frigging decision? Look I'm not saying it's your fault, I'm just saying it's your bullshit!

**Jack** *has gone.* **May** *is motionless as she watches him depart.*
*As* . . .

## Scene Nine

*1999.*

**Ted** *enters. He is markedly older and more run-down than we have seen previously. He is working himself into a real lather. We can also hear the annoying bass beat of music as it emanates from* **Sonja** *and* **Les***'s house.* **May** *is looking out of the window in the fourth wall.*

**Ted**    I've put some wire across the privets where the dogs come through!

**May**   Did you say owt to 'em?

**Ted**   You only get an earful if you do!

**May**   Is it their kids?

**Ted**   Course it bloody is! Forty years we've had them privets! The youngest has been stood on their shed peeing into my rockery. Little sods. And he's just up at the window laughing at me!

**May**   They're not his kids, are they!

**Ted**   Our Jack rang, by the way. They're not coming this weekend, he's going to America or sommat!

**May** *is still looking out of the window.*

**May**   I'm just looking at these out here with that ball. They're in and out of Mrs Bird's garden.

**May** *and* **Ted** *stand in silence. It is only now that we get a sense of the noise coming from next door.*

**Ted**   Can you hear that? Thump, thump, thump, every bloody Sunday!

**May**   Stop swearing.

**Ted**   I'll start bloody swearing if they keep on!

**Ted** *moves towards the kitchen.*

**May**   Where are you going?

**Ted**   For an angina tablet.

**May**   I told you, you were getting worked up!

**Ted**   I'm not getting worked up, I'm going for my four o'clock tablet!

**May**   You're getting worked up!

**Ted**   I'm not getting bloody worked up!

**Ted** *exits to the kitchen.* **May** *looks out towards the fourth wall.*

**May**   They're going out. I say, they're going out! He looks backward if you ask me. And she's a bloody mess she is. They reckon she's a singer. I don't know what she sings . . . all I've ever heard her do is shout. Mind you, it's more shouting than singing these days.

**Ted** *re-enters. He is more angry than before. He takes his tablet.*

**Ted**   Well, you wouldn't bloody believe it. They've knocked all the bloody privets over, I've just been out there and all! They've been standing on top of the car-port and jumping off by the looks of it!

**May**   We should have never had that car-port put on.

**Ted**   Well, Sylvia never jumped off it!

**May**   It's been nowt but trouble that car-port!

**Ted**   Don't talk such bloody rubbish.

**May**   All the money we've spent on this house, all the money we've thrown away, and now they're jumping off the car-port!

**Ted** *sits. He is beginning to feel unwell as the stress of the situation takes its toll.*

**Ted**   You're not doing me any good, you know?

**May**   They'd all buy their own houses you said! All this estate will buy their own houses. All the miners will want to own their houses!

**Ted** (*shouting*)   I've heard you!

*Silence.*

**May**   I could bloody weep when I think about it!

*A beat.*

**Ted**   I'll go and tie them privets up.

**May**   You're doing too much you are . . . You're up and down like a sodding yo-yo! You'll end up back in t' hospital you! You're doing too much!

**Ted** *is almost off stage through the kitchen.*

**Ted**   Oh shut up . . .

**May** *remains on stage, remembering.*

*As . . .*


**Scene Ten**

*The present.*

**Steve** *enters from the front door. He is sweating heavily. He walks into the living room.* **May** *stands looking at her furniture.*

**Steve**   There's no need to go abroad you know! It's like Spain out there!

**May**   It is next door with them with that bloody hosepipe!

**Steve** *bends to pick up a small box of seventy-eight records.*

**Steve**   Are these all seventy-eights?

**May**   They want binning!

**Steve**   They're worth a few quid are these, you know?

**May**   I can't see any fun in keeping 'em.

**Steve**   I'll have these if you want, I can car-boot such as this . . .

**May**   Do what you want!

**Steve**   I mean it's a shame to throw 'em away, isn't it?

**May**   You can throw all the bloody lot away for me, they don't mean anything to me any more.

**Steve** *grabs a few boxes and makes his way out of the room and out through the front door.*

**Steve**    Goor, it's a bloody scorcher today . . . I could do with standing under that hose myself!

**Steve** *has gone.* **May** *stands alone.*

*As . . .*

### Scene Eleven

*1999.*

*Late afternoon.* **Sharon** *enters from the kitchen. She has a plateful of butterfly buns with her. She is dressed smartly but a little more nervous than we have seen her before. It appears the separation has certainly taken its toll on her.*

**Sharon**    Do you want a butterfly bun? I've brought a cartload. I didn't bake 'em, I haven't had time. I got 'em from Cooplands in Donny!

**May**    No, I'm all right, Sharon love . . . I'm supposed to keep off sweet stuff!

**Sharon**    I've tried to keep my weight down since Jack came back.

**May**    Oh go on then, I shouldn't but . . .

*She treats herself to a butterfly bun.*

Where are the kids?

**Sharon**    Kitty's around by the garages playing, and Tom's helping Jack and his dad patch up the privets.

**May**    That's a full-time job.

**Sharon**    Is it getting any better?

**May**    I take my hearing-aid out so . . .

**Sharon**    Kitty'll be all right playing around by the garages, won't she?

**May**    Well our Jack played there all his life!

**Sharon**   It's different now though, isn't it?

**May**   I don't know what it's coming to!

**Ted** *enters through the kitchen. He is extremely tired.*

**Ted**   Bloody hell!

**Sharon**   Butterfly bun?

**Ted**   I'm not supposed to but . . .

**Ted** *treats himself to a bun.*

**Sharon**   It'll not kill you.

**Ted**   Actually Sharon, it might do.

**Sharon**   How are you feeling?

**Ted**   Two heart attacks and I'm still here.

**Sharon**   Well you look well.

**Ted**   I'm getting to know 'em quite well in Ponte A and E now! You know you've arrived when the porters wink at you.

**May**   I said he was doing too much!

*A beat.*

**Ted**   How are you, love?

**Sharon**   We're all right.

**Ted**   No more bloody tantrums?

**Sharon**   He's on his final warning!

**Ted**   Good for you!

**May**   It didn't happen in our day!

**Ted**   There's no excuse for it. He can't go about lashing out just because he can't get his own bloody way!

**May**   I was disgusted with him I was.

**Ted**   Well it's all over now, that, so . . . !

**May**    He stills sees this bloody Candace though, doesn't he? When he brought her here I thought he was shacking up with her!

**Sharon**    So did he!

**May**    Silly sod him!

**Sharon**    She's all right actually. She's got this American film company to buy the rights to one of his first books. She says they think it's very funny . . . She says, if it comes off we'll be talking serious money!

**Ted**    All money's serious, Sharon, especially when you've bloody well got none!

**Jack** *enters from the kitchen.*

**May**    All done?

**Jack**    Well aye but . . .

**May**    What's up?

**Jack**    Kitty's crying.

**Sharon**    Why, what's happened?

**Jack**    She's been over by the garages and some big kids have hit her.

**Sharon**    Where is she?

**Jack**    She's in the back having a drink of orange. She's all right.

**Sharon**    What have you let 'em hit her for?

**Jack**    I didn't . . .

**Sharon** *exits through the kitchen.*

**Sharon**    Kitty . . . are you okay, darling?

**May**    Who's hit her did you say?

**Jack**    She says some tall lass.

**May**    Has she got blonde hair?

**Jack**    I've no idea, I didn't see. I've been patching the privets up!

**May**    I bet it's her next door, the eldest. They're a pigging nuisance . . . if she's hit our Kitty, I'll sodding rag her!

**Jack** *stands in the living room as the voice of reason.*

**Jack**    Wow, hang on! You can't go around smacking people just because our Kitty's been hit.

**May**    They're a bloody nuisance!

**Jack**    Well aye but . . .

**May**    A bloody nuisance . . .

*Music begins to pulsate from next door.* **Jack** *is silent and hears it for the first time. It is 'Let me down' sung by Bettye Lavette, a soul classic.*

**Jack**    What's that?

**May**    Oh it's like that regular.

**Ted**    That's what it's like every night. That's nowt that. Sometimes we lay in bed and the bloody bedside lamp is rocking. I've been around to talk to him but all you get is abuse!

**Jack**    He probably hasn't got a lot to think with!

**Ted**    It gets on your mother's nerves . . .

**May**    I can't bloody stand it!

**Jack**    Well you know . . .

**May**    Let me go in the kitchen and have a look at her.

*She begins to exit into the kitchen.*

I mean she doesn't want hitting does she?

**Jack**    I know she doesn't but . . .

**May**   Our Jack's always been like that . . . he'll let people walk all over him.

**May** *has gone.*

**Ted**   We could go around if tha wants!

**Jack**   Eh?

**Ted**   We could go around . . .

**Jack**   And what?

**Ted**   Well, have a word with 'em!

**Jack**   Dad, you've got a bloody heart condition!

*A beat.*

**Ted**   Thee granddad would have been round and given them a pasting tha knows!

**Jack**   Just ignore 'em.

**Ted**   You don't live here. It's killing your mam is this, you know?

**Jack**   Have you called the police?

**Ted**   They're not bothered. There's only one bobby for these three villages. I'll go and see what's happening in t' kitchen, I mean fancy hitting our Kitty.

**Jack**   They've got to grow up.

*A beat.*

**Ted**   They want to be doing karate!

**Jack**   Dad?

**Ted**   Never mind bloody ballet and playing the sodding piano, a good bout of karate won't hurt her . . . You're bringing up a set of bloody nancy girls.

**Jack**   She's only six.

**Ted**   I'm telling thee!

**Jack**    Right!

**Ted**    Because, this with thee mother? She's down at Dr Diggle's three times a week tha knows, with her nerves! I've told her to save on petrol and go and bloody live there!

**Ted** *exits.* **Jack** *is left alone on stage.*

*As . . .*


## Scene Twelve

*1999.*

**Sonja** *bursts onto the stage through the door. She has a can of beer with her and is laughing loudly. She is half dressed, après coitus.*

**Sonja**    That's it now! I'm not doing it again today, no way! (*To herself.*) Not with you anyway!

*She dances to the music, drinks and then walks to the door and shouts through it.*

Les! If you're going to the shops get some more cigs, will you! And some more nappies . . . There's twenty quid in the top drawer. And turn it up a bit, I like this . . .

**Sonja** *stands by the door. The music volume doesn't increase.*

I'll turn it up myself then!

**Sonja** *exits. The bass beat increases.*

*As . . .*


## Scene Thirteen

*1999.*

**Jack** *remains on stage. The bass beat from next door can be heard pulsating and getting slightly louder.* **Sharon** *enters from the kitchen.*

**Jack**    She's all right, isn't she?

**Sharon**    Well she's burst her lip! And it's shook her up!

**Jack**    It happens!

**Sharon**    I thought you were watching her?

**Jack**    It'll toughen her up!

**Sharon**    I don't want her toughening up. She's a little girl and she's six. I don't want her turning out like Johnny Rambo!

**Jack**    She can't turn the other cheek all through her life!

**Sharon**    I mean she's only a tot!

**Jack**    It gets to me and all, you know?

**Sharon**    I could bloody well go round there myself.

**Jack**    What good would that do?

**Sharon**    Well your mum's having a fit about it . . .

*A beat.*

What's that noise?

**Jack**    That's them next door!

*A beat.*

**Sharon**    It's a bit loud, isn't it?

**Jack**    It's all right, isn't it?

**Sharon**    Good grief!

**Jack**    Just leave it!

**Sharon**    That's not reasonable, is it?

**Jack**    Just leave it, don't set my mam off!

**Sharon**    Can't you go and say something?

**Jack**    Like what?

**Sharon**    Well . . .

**Jack**   What?

**Sharon**   Oh sometimes.

**Jack**   What?

*A beat.*

**Sharon**   I'll go and say something then!

*A beat.*

**Jack**   All right. I've got the message.

**Sharon** *exits back into the kitchen.*

**Jack**   I've got the message!

**Jack** *remains on stage. He bangs on the wall lightly. As he does the music from next door increases in volume. As he stands* **May** *enters with a small box from the kitchen.* **Jack** *exits through the front door as* **May** *stands on stage and looks at her furniture. She walks off stage through the kitchen door. Music swells.*

*As . . .*


**Scene Fourteen**

*1999.*

**Sonja** *is lit upstage, singing at the top off her voice. She dances and smokes. She is quite celebratory. As she sings* **Jack** *enters. He is shy and nervous. He stands watching her dance for a while. The music fades under.*

**Jack**   Sorry . . .

**Sonja**   Eh?

**Jack** *comes closer to* **Sonja**.

**Jack**   I did knock.

**Sonja**   What?

**Jack**   I did knock!

**Sonja**    What do you want?

**Jack**    I wondered if you could keep the music down?

**Sonja**    Eh?

**Jack**    Can you turn it down a bit?

**Sonja**    Can I hell!

**Jack**    It's just that my mum and dad are both getting on a bit . . .

**Sonja**    So what?

**Jack**    What?

**Sonja**    So what?

*A beat.*

**Jack**    Actually I think one of your kids has just hit my little girl . . .

**Sonja**    So . . .

**Jack**    Eh listen . . .

**Sonja**    Can't she stick up for herself?

**Jack**    She's only six!

**Sonja**    So what?

**Jack**    Well she's at her gran's, and she's not from round here!

**Sonja**    What's that got to do with it?

**Jack**    Unlike me!

**Sonja**    It's nowt to do with you what my kids do!

**Jack** *moves close to* **Sonja** *and in a moment he has grabbed her by the throat.*

**Jack**    Listen, you slack bastard, turn the music down or I'll eat you!

**Sonja** *plays this all very sexually charged.*

**Sonja**    Yes, that'd be nice!

**Jack** *lets her go and then comes away from her.*

**Jack**    Just watch it!

**Sonja**    You wait while Les comes back . . .

**Jack**    Let him come back . . .

**Sonja**    Now piss off!

**Jack** *moves towards the exit.*

**Jack**    You don't know what you're fucking dealing with!

**Jack** *moves to exit.* **Sonja** *follows him.*

**Sonja** (*screams*)    We're not scared of you! Who do you
think you are coming round here? Think you're somebody
do you? Wait till I tell Les, he'll kill you! We live here now,
we live here, you smarmy bastard! So we'll make as much
noise as we like! And don't think we won't . . .

**Sonja** *exits. The music gets louder as* **May** *enters and looks towards*
**Sonja** *and* **Les***'s house. The music eventually fades.*

*As . . .*


**Scene Fifteen**

*The present.*

**May** *enters from the kitchen. As she does,* **Sharon** *enters from the
front door. She is dressed rather smartly. She has a bag with her and
dangles her car keys.*

**Sharon**    Sorry I'm late, the traffic in Leeds! By the time
I'd dropped the kids off! Is everything all right?

**May** (*fighting the tears*)    Well, I feel a bit . . .

*A beat.*

**Sharon**    Where's Jack ?

**May**    He's giving the removal lad a hand to move some stuff from the garage. He's spent half the day on the bloody phone. And these kids next door?

**May** *exits through the kitchen at the same time as* **Steve** *enters through the front door.*

**Steve**    Not long now!

**Sharon**    Do you want a hand?

**Steve**    You should have been here this morning . . . I've nearly done it all! Sweating like somebody not right but . . . !

**Steve** *struggles with one of the large tea-chests from the living room. As he does,* **Jack** *enters from the front door.*

**Jack**    Hiya!

**Steve**    He's still strong, you know, this one . . . (*Struggling.*) Bloody hell! I think I've twinged my back. I'll need your mam to sign for all this stuff and then we can settle up.

**Steve** *exits.* **Jack** *wipes sweat from his brow and pecks* **Sharon**.

**Sharon**    How's it been going?

**Jack**    Balls and nappies all over the back garden, and then they set the hosepipe on her. And I've had bloody Candace on for the last half hour!

**Sharon**    I thought you'd come to help?

**Jack**    Hey!

**Sharon**    Hey!

**Jack**    There might be a problem with this American lark. She's spoken to the development bloke who's told her they think it's not funny!

**Sharon**    What?

**Jack**    Enough! It's not funny enough! That's it, I'm changing agents!

**Sharon**    I thought you needed that cash for your mam's apartment?

**Jack**    She's ringing back when she's spoken to somebody who can actually tell her how funny it's supposed to be! They've probably got an expert who can do that!

**Sharon**    Don't give up the day job . . .

**Jack**    It is my bloody day job.

**May** *enters from the kitchen.*

**May**    Nearly done?

**Jack**    Just about.

**May** *looks at the walls of her living room. She moves to them and starts to rub the walls down.*

**May**    Look at the muck on them walls. You think you're clean, don't you, until you start moving stuff.

**Jack**    It's a bit late for that now, Mam!

**May**    I'll just give 'em a wipe down . . . It'll not hurt, I expect people would do it for me! Look at the muck on these walls. Mind you there must be thirty coats of emulsion on 'em! They'll never get this paper off!

**Jack**    I'll go settle up with laddo!

**May**    There's some cloths in the passage, Sharon love, go and get some and we'll give these walls a rub down!

**Sharon**    Oh right!

**May**    Not tek us two minutes!

**Sharon** *(hesitating)*    I'll go and get a cloth then!

**Jack** *exits through the front door.* **Sharon** *exits to kitchen.* **May** *walks and inspects the walls.*

**May**    I told you to wipe 'em down, Ted. Never did what you were told did you?

*She stands still.*

*As . . .*

## Scene Sixteen

*2000.*

**Ted** *enters. He is wearing pyjamas. He has a tray of tea with a slice of bread and jam on it. A glass of water and some tablets.*

**Ted**    I've brought your tablets. I was going to have 'em all myself and end it, but I thought it would only spoil the fun for you. There you go. One for your heart, one for your blood pressure, one for your stomach, one for your kidneys, one for your mood swings!

**May** *takes the tablets.*

**May**    Ha ha!

**Ted**    I'm on more than you.

**May**    Show-off!

**Ted**    'Hey.'

**May**    'Hey.'

**Ted**    When they cut me open I wouldn't be surprised if I didn't look like a tube of Smarties.

*They both sit and get comfortable on the chairs.*

Well I'm buggered and I've done nowt.

**May**    Are my feet swelling up?

**Ted**    No.

**May**    They are.

**Ted**    They're bloody not.

**May**    I don't know where I ache the most.

**Ted**    Time is it?

**May**   Nine o'clock.

**Ted**   Watch the news.

**May**   I'm going to bed in a minute.

**Ted**   If you go to bed any earlier you'll meet yourself getting up.

**May**   I can't sleep when I'm in bed anyway.

**Ted**   So why go to bed so early?

**May**   Well at least I'm laid down.

**Ted**   Oh you make me bloody laugh!

**May**   Why aren't you laughing then?

*Music begins to pulsate from next door. We see* **Sonja** *dance through the wall.*

**Ted**   Bloody hell! If it isn't her wailing it's this racket!

**May**   I can't hear it, if I take my hearing-aid out.

**Ted**   Can't hear it, you must be bloody deaf.

**May**   I am deaf, aren't I!

*A beat.*

**Ted**   I can hear it when it's not playing!

**Ted** *gets up and begins to patrol the room slowly.*

*The pulsating music increases slightly.*

**May**   Just leave it.

**Ted**   This is . . .

**May**   Put the telly on.

**Ted**   This is just.

**May**   Go to bed, because if you set off on another bout tonight, I'll put my head in the sodding oven!

**Ted**   Hellfire!

**May**    Look at you!

**Ted**    Every sodding night.

**May**    You'll make yourself bad you will!

*A beat.*

**Ted**    They are bloody things that pair next door! He's put that bloody C.B. thing at the bottom of the garden and that looks a sodding eyesore.

**May**    I thought you said you couldn't see it?

**Ted**    I wish we'd never bought this house!

**May**    You wanted to buy it.

**Ted**    Bloody things!

**May**    This is the Labour party this is! They're bringing 'em all up here from Park Avenue. Sylvia told me. They've got drug problems down there and they're bringing 'em all up here. That's the bloody Labour party for you!

**Ted**    Bump, bump, bump!

**May**    And them who's making the decisions live somewhere bloody else!

**Ted**    Bump, bump, bump . . .

**May**    They're not bothered . . .

**Ted**    Bump, bump, bump!

**May** *suddenly explodes, and screams.*

**May**    Shut up . . . pack the bloody noise up!

*She gets up and begins to bang on the wall.*

For God's sake give it a rest . . . We've not had one night without this for the past year!

**May** *is banging on the wall, crying and making herself poorly.* **Ted** *follows* **May***'s lead and begins to bang on the wall with her. There is a foreboding sense of madness in the air.*

**Ted**   Turn it down!

**May**   Look at us . . . Just look at us!

*She comes away and sits in the chair. She is exhausted.*

Oh I feel bloody dizzy . . .

**Ted** (*bangs the wall*)   Pack it in, you filthy sods!

*As* **Ted** *bangs,* **Les** *enters the room next door. The music volume increases slightly.* **Les** *is wearing nothing but a pair of dirty underpants. He smokes heavily and looks as though he is the worse for drink or drugs or both. He starts to shout to the wall.*

**Les**   Are you banging?

**Ted**   Are they banging?

**Les**   Can't we have a bit of fun?

**May**   Are they banging?

**Les**   Are you banging?

**Ted**   Are they banging?

**Les**   Are you banging?

**May**   Are they banging?

**Les**   Don't bang me . . .

**Ted**   I'll bang the sods!

**Les**   It's only nine o'clock, you banging bastards!

**Sonja** (*laughing*)   Are they banging?

**May**   Are they banging back?

**Les** (*to the wall*)   I'll set the dogs on you in a minute!

**May**   Are they shouting?

**Sonja** (*shouts to the wall*)   He shouldn't have grabbed me!

**Les** *grabs* **Sonja** *sexually as they are shouting. He kisses her on the mouth.*

**Ted**   Bloody banging back!

**Les** (*shouting, and suddenly manic*)   If he comes round here again I'll kill him!

**May**   Are they banging back?

**Les** (*madness*)   And I'll kill you!

**Sonja** (*laughing*)   Ha ha . . . !

**May**   Are they're shouting?

**Les**   And then I'll kill your grandkids!

**Ted**   Bloody banging me back! You bastards!

**Ted** *is becoming completely wild. He is patrolling around the room.*

**May**   Hey, hey, now sit down, you've made your point!

**Ted**   Who's he to bang me back?

**May**   You've made your point, now leave it!

**Ted**   Bastards!

**May**   Call the police!

**May** *is up on her feet attempting to stop* **Ted** *from going too far.*

**Ted**   I'll go round there in a minute!

**May** (*screaming*)   No you won't, you've done enough now! Now you've said enough now. Look at you!

**Les**   Not banging now, are you? You silly old bastard!

**Ted**   I'm not having this . . . I'm not having this.

**May**   Oh leave it, for God's sake, Ted, leave it! I'm begging you, I'm begging you on my hands and knees. Look at me. Look at me, I'm begging you!

**May** *gets on her knees and begs him . . . It is an unedifying sight, a woman of seventy begging on her knees.*

**Ted** (*shouting*)   Look what she's doing! Look at what you're making her do! You bastards!

**May**    Ted, look at you . . . Look at you!

**Ted**    I'm not having this!

**Sonja** (*to* **Les**)    Turn it up . . .

**Les** *goes out of the room.* **Sonja** *dances to the music. The volume of the music increases.* **Les** *returns and starts to dance with* **Sonja**. **Ted** *screams and leaves the room.* **May** *stands and starts screaming . . .*

**Ted**    I've worked all my sodding life for a bit of peace and bloody quiet . . . I'm not having this!

**May**    Ted! Ted! Ted!

**Sonja** *and* **Les** *dance out of their room. They are all over each other. As they exit their room, the music swells and then cuts out to silence dramatically.*


## Scene Seventeen

*The present.*

**May** *is standing alone. She is very upset. She stands in silence for quite some time.* **Jack** *enters. He is uncomfortable. He looks around the house. Almost everything has been removed from the living room by this time.*

**May**    He never came back, Jack. He never came back.

*A beat.*

I still can't believe he's gone.

**Jack**    I know.

**May**    Heart attack in their garden! Of all the bloody places! Covered in dog mess he was in the ambulance! Dog mess, nappies and God knows what!

**Jack**    Mam!

**May**    I told him to leave it!

*A beat.*

He used to drive me mad but . . . Hey . . . we used to say! Hey! When any one of us was getting upperty. Hey! It meant a million bloody things . . .

**Jack**    I know.

**May**    And he always voted Labour. Allus voted Labour and look what we had to deal with! It's getting worse!

**Jack**    I don't know that it is!

*A beat.*

**May**    What would I do if I didn't have you? What would they do to me, where would they put me? I couldn't stay here, could I? Nobody could!

**Sharon** *enters from the front door.*

**Sharon**    We've got a bit of problem out here.

**May**    Another bloody problem . . .

**Sharon**    It looks like Mr Shifter's slipped a disc.

**May**    I said he wouldn't be able to manage. I mean he's like a streak of tap water that lad.

**Sharon**    He's laid down by the side of his van waiting for you to sign before he tries to get up. And the other removal van's here, but he can't get past because of that skip, his van and our cars so . . . !

**May**    I told you we should've had Mason's! I'll go and sign up then.

**May** *exits through front door.* **Jack** *and* **Sharon** *are silent.*

**Sharon**    It's chaos out there! Battle of the removal vans! And the kids are running all over!

*A beat.*

**Jack**    It looks like the film's off, by the way!

**Sharon**    Why?

**Jack**    Candace's just called me. They've decided it's definitely not funny enough! Not enough fart jokes, I bet!

**Sharon**    Well, can't you put some in?

**Jack**    Do you think I should?

**Sharon**    People love fart jokes!

**Jack**    What sort of people . . . ?

**Sharon**    Well, you do!

*A beat.*

**Jack**    I feel a bit emotional!

**Sharon**    Well, you're bound to.

**Jack**    I thought it wouldn't bother me but . . . (*Crying despite himself.*) It'll always be my home!

**Sharon**    I'll go and move my car!

**Sharon** *leaves through the front door as* **May** *enters.*

**Sharon**    Move my car!

**May** (*calls*)    That's it then, Sharon, I've signed all my stuff away!

**Sharon** *exits as* **May** *enters the living room.*

**May**    Have you paid him?

**Jack**    Cash. I've no change left now!

*A beat.*

**May** (*very sad*)    Oh well!

*A beat.*

**Jack**    When we get in the car don't look back!

**May** (*tears*)    School holidays and all next week; all them privets will be down!

**Jack**   Are you listening to me?

**May**   Be like little hell in that back garden!

**Jack**   Don't look back, promise me . . .

**May** (*tears*)   I'll try!

*As they stand, **Lance**, a huge and quite bizarrely dangerous-looking man in his late fifties enters. He has the air of something not right about him and carries with him a large ghetto-blaster covered in paint, and a holdall. He wears a gypsy bandana, heavy earrings and biker's leathers; he is clearly a Hell's Angel of some standing.*

**Lance**   Are you there?

**Jack**   Through here, mate!

**Lance** *enters the living room and surveys his new home.*

**Lance**   Now then!

**Jack**   How are you?

**Lance**   Not bad!

**Jack**   This is my mam!

**Lance**   Sorry to go, are you?

**May** (*tears*)   I am!

**Lance**   Aye my mam was the same when she moved; after my dad had hung hissen. She was lost without him!

**May** (*tears*)   Oh dear!

**Lance**   Mind you, she couldn't handle being on her own! That's why she finished up in t' nut house!

*A beat.*

**Jack**   Anyway!

**May**   Well, I hope you're as happy as we've been!

**Lance**   I'll go start unpacking!

**Lance** *exits.*

*Silence.*

**May**    It'll be interesting to see if he gets on wi' them next door!

**Jack**    I would have thought so!

**May**    Bloody hell!

*A beat.*

**Jack**    Oh aye, they reckon he's a right nutter! Eleven brothers he's got, and they're all like him apparently.

*A beat.*

**May**    What does he do then?

**Jack**    He works for a security firm as far as I know, but he breeds animals!

**May**    Well, he should get on with them then.

**Jack**    Oh aye that's about it.

*A beat.*

**May**    What does he breed then?

**Jack**    Snakes! Reptiles really! Iguanas and all, I think! He took some bloody finding! There was him and a newly-wed couple after it! He offered the same as them but I thought that he was such a nice bloke so I let him have it cheap! Shall we get off?

**May** *is utterly delighted and moved to tears by this amazing checkmate her son has pulled off. She touches* **Jack**'s *face with an affectionate sense of pride.*

**May**    Eleven brothers and he breeds snakes . . .

**Jack**    I think he's got about eight . . . Twenty-foot-long one of 'em!

**May**    What about them kids next door though?

**Jack**    Wait at the gate, I'll back the car up! And don't look back.

**Jack** *has gone.* **May** *stands by the door for a moment. She breaks down in tears.*

**May**    My bloody house!

**May** *leaves her home for the last time. As she does she is sprinkled with water from next door.*

**Les** *(off stage)*    Go on, you sad old cow!

**May** *exits in tears.*

*Lights upstage as* **Sonja** *enters and music plays.*

**Les** *enters a moment later. He has a can of beer and he finds something extremely amusing.*

**Les**    I got her, she was wet through! Sasha threw some nappies over and I got her with t' hosepipe. I was trying to get the son!

**Sonja**    I wonder what happened to that ball?

**Les**    She took it!

**Sonja**    You can go around and get it then . . .

**Les**    I will do . . .

**Les** *grabs* **Sonja**.

**Sonja**    Oh no . . .

**Les**    Yes! Come on . . . Hey turn the music up!

**Les** *and* **Sonja** *exit. The music volume increases.*

*In the other space* **Lance** *enters with two large snake boxes. He carefully places the boxes on the floor and has a look around his new home, in the kitchen and the bottom of the stairs.* **Lance** *listens to the pulsating music, then he bangs on the wall.*

**Lance**    You can pack that in for a start!

*He plugs in his own ghetto-blaster and plays a piece of music. The music drowns out the music from* **Les** *and* **Sonja**. **Lance** *sits with a large basket. As the lights fade,* **Lance** *takes a huge snake from a basket and puts it around his neck. Lights fade to blackout as the music swells.*

**Christmas Crackers**

## Characters

**Keith**, *fifty, a security guard*
**Alan** *forty-six, an ambulance man*
**Kath**, *forty, an A and E nurse*
**Holly**, *twenty-four, an A and E nurse*
**Len**, *sixty-five, a smoker*
**Billy**, *thirty-two, a balloon clown*
**Anna**, *forty, a lady*
**Lilly**, *twenty-three, a street girl*
**Stevo**, *thirty-three, a druggie*
**Man**, *forty-six, Prague man*
**Mike**, *forty-six, Kath's dead husband*
**Franz**, *thirty-two, a mime*
**Hans**, *forty-six, a puppet master*
**Mik**, *thirty-two, a male puppet*
**Kit**, *twenty-four, a female puppet*

*Directed by* John Godber
*Designed by* Pip Leckenby

*Christmas Crackers* was first performed by Hull Truck Theatre Company in December 2006 at Spring Street Theatre, Hull, with the following cast:

| | |
|---|---|
| **Keith** | Rob Angell |
| **Alan** | Rob Hudson |
| **Kath** | Una McNulty |
| **Holly** | Amy Thompson |
| **Len** | Rob Hudson |
| **Billy** | Matt Booth |
| **Anna** | Una McNulty |
| **Lilly** | Amy Thompson |
| **Stevo** | Matt Booth |
| **Man** | Rob Hudson |
| **Mike** | Rob Hudson |
| **Franz** | Matt Booth |
| **Hans** | Rob Hudson |
| **Mik** | Matt Booth |
| **Kit** | Amy Thompson |

# Act One

## Scene One

*4.30 a.m.*

*The set is the entrance to a large Accident and Emergency department of an East Yorkshire hospital. There is one central entrance and a forecourt area where an ambulance may park. Everything about the set is real. There are even flurries of snow in the corners of the downstage wall. We may even hear the chaos of A and E from time to time, from within the doors. Downstage of this forecourt is a small wall, and we may imagine that we have cut away this wall in order to see the action. It is near to Christmas, very late at night or very early in the morning depending how you look at it. The lights from within A and E will glow, since most of this shift is spent in complete darkness. It is extremely cold.*

**Keith** *enters. He is a fifty-year-old security guard. He is gaunt and nasty-looking, dressed against the late night. He looks out towards the night, breathes the fresh air and wanders around the forecourt aimlessly. After a while* **Kath** *enters. She is a forty-year-old nurse, tired, emotionally upset but still with a sparkle of attractiveness about her. She attempts to hide her tears.*

**Keith**   All right?

**Kath** (*upset*)   Yes, yes!

*A beat.*

**Keith**   Fresher out here!

**Kath** (*gaining composure*)   That's right!

*A beat.*

**Keith**   Quieter now!

**Kath**   That's it!

**Keith**   Crackers tonight!

**Kath**   Well it's Christmas, isn't it?

*A beat.*

**Keith**   You all right now then?

**Kath**   Yes!

**Keith**   That's good then!

**Kath**   Just . . . you know . . . it gets to you!

**Keith**   Oh aye!

**Kath**   Christmas eh?

*A beat.*

**Keith**   It never stops, does it?

**Kath**   What's that?

**Keith**   Time!

**Kath**   You're not wrong.

**Keith**   It never stops.

*A beat.*

**Kath**   No, you're not wrong there.

**Keith**   Bloody Christmas!

**Kath** (*pulling herself together*)   Oh well!

*A beat.*

**Keith**   Bloody crackers at Christmas! Parties, hen dos, bloody madness!

*A beat.*

Fancy fuckin' dress, they all end up down here.

*A beat.*

Cold one tonight, Kath.

**Kath**   Boiling in there.

*A beat.*

**Keith**    I mean I know I shouldn't be out here, but I can't take that heat.

**Kath** *is becoming more settled.*

**Keith**    It's not healthy.

**Kath**    I don't have much choice.

**Keith**    It's false air isn't it? You're breathing somebody else's air.

*A beat.*

Quieter now though.

**Kath**    Don't speak too soon.

*A beat.*

**Keith**    Nearly done.

**Kath**    Three more hours.

**Keith**    Over the worst though.

**Kath**    You never know though, do you?

**Keith**    Well aye, I suppose that's right.

*A beat.*

**Kath**    Keeps you on your toes.

**Keith**    I'm always on my toes.

**Kath**    Are you?

**Keith**    Oh aye.

*A beat.*

I mean my mind wanders off but I'm always there.

**Kath**    Where?

**Keith**    Here.

*A beat.*

**Kath** (*dryly*)   You should be in there though!

**Keith**   It's too stuffy for me in there. I can't breathe. I mean I'm here for you, but sometimes my mind wanders off.

**Kath**   So you've said.

*A beat.*

**Keith**   I suppose you can't do that, can you?

**Kath**   No, not really.

*A beat.*

**Keith**   Oh aye, sometimes I just stand here and wander off and an hour's gone.

**Kath**   Really?

*A beat.*

**Keith**   You can't afford to do that, can you?

**Kath**   No, and you shouldn't be wandering off into the never-never either. You're here to do a job.

**Keith**   I'm still here.

**Kath** (*dead*)   Are you really?

**Keith**   Oh aye, I'm still here . . .

**Kath**   Well that's a good trick then because you've just told me you wander off.

*A beat.*

**Keith**   You can't though, can you, you're stuck with it.

**Kath**   You're not wrong.

**Keith**   Christmas and all.

*A beat.*

**Kath**   So what's he bringing you then?

**Keith**  Me?

**Kath**  What's he bringing you?

*A beat.*

**Keith**  Nowt.

**Kath**  No, I know what you mean!

*A beat.*

**Keith**  Why, what's he bringing you?

**Kath**  I don't know; what do you give the girl who's got everything?

*A beat.*

**Keith**  Nothing.

*A beat.*

**Kath**  Aye that'll be about it.

*A beat.*

Hey you might get lucky though, he might bring you a sense of humour.

*A beat.*

**Keith**  I don't want one.

*A beat.*

**Kath**  You need one though, doing this job.

**Keith**  Once you're laughing on this job, you are as good as dead.

**Kath** (*sad*)  Oh dear.

*A beat.*

**Keith**  I hate Christmas anyway.

**Kath**  Do you?

**Keith**    I hate Christmas, I hate to see people enjoying themselves. It's all a fake to me. They spend most of the year stopping in, and then come Christmas they go bloody crackers.

**Kath**    Part-timers eh?

*A beat.*

**Keith**    Mind you, I hate New Year and all.

**Kath**    Oh right!

*A beat.*

**Keith**    And summer, I hate summer, long nights summer.

**Kath**    Is there anything you do like?

**Keith**    Going home.

**Kath**    Oh yes, there's that.

**Keith**    I like being on my own.

**Kath**    Do you?

**Keith**    Well, I've no choice, have I, since I lost my mam . . .

*A beat.*

**Kath**    Yes well . . .

**Keith**    I like to go home . . .

**Kath**    And wander off?

*A beat.*

**Keith**    There's a lot of scum down here!

**Kath**    Eh?

**Keith**    A lot of scum!

**Kath**    Well, I wouldn't say that . . .

**Keith**    Oh aye, everybody tries to be liberal, but I see it different.

**Kath**   Do you?

**Keith**   If you want to find out about the country and how well it's doing, spend a day in A and E; scum a lot of them and that's the truth.

**Kath**   Oh right.

*A beat.*

**Keith**   I don't think you should treat half of them, it's their own fault. I mean, I'm not saying don't treat old women and that, but half of them in here tonight are here because it's their own silly fucking fault.

**Kath**   Well there you go . . .

*A beat.*

**Keith**   Druggies . . . bloody foreigners . . . lasses off the street. Piss artists.

*A beat.*

**Kath**   And that's just the staff.

**Kath** *is becoming emotional.*

**Keith**   Well you've got to deal with them, but they're a load of scum to me.

**Kath**   Oh aye, we have to deal with them, no matter what they're like, no matter what they say to you, no matter what colour they are, we have to deal with them. And sometimes no matter how hard you try, it gets to you if you lose one, it gets to you if they don't make it. And that's the bloody truth and all.

**Kath** *exits into the hospital.*

*A beat.*

**Keith**   Bloody Christmas!

*Lights fade slowly to blackout.*

## Scene Two

*4.55 a.m.*

**Keith** *remains outside the hospital. Time has moved on. He has been joined by* **Holly**, *an attractive and tired junior nurse. She is lively but not too intellectually blessed, though very likeable. As the lights fade up* **Keith** *is already in full flow.*

**Keith**   Oh aye, I've always been able to wander off.

**Holly**   Have you?

**Keith**   I'm just talking and before you know it, I've gone.

**Holly**   Just wandered off?

**Keith**   The power of the imagination that is, you know.

**Holly**   I know, you've told me.

**Keith**   Coz we're just a bag of chemicals really!

**Holly**   Yes, you've said.

*A beat.*

**Keith**   And my dreams are really real, are yours?

**Holly**   No, no, they're not, not really!

*A beat.*

**Keith**   I think I'm in the wrong job to be honest.

**Holly**   Do you think so?

**Keith**   Don't you?

**Holly**   I don't know.

*A beat.*

**Keith**   Yeh, sometimes I stand here and I could be anywhere.

*A beat.*

**Holly**   Christmas.

**Keith**    I hate Christmas.

**Holly**    I hate this Christmas.

**Keith**    You should love Christmas, Christmas is for the young, like you and Darren.

*A beat.*

**Holly**    Oh don't! Men, Keith!

**Keith**    Oh aye!

**Holly**    Men.

**Keith**    Bastards.

*A beat.*

**Holly**    All they want is sex.

**Keith**    I know that!

**Holly**    That's all they're after.

*A beat.*

**Keith**    That's what Darren wants, is it?

**Holly**    I want him to respect me as a person, but all he wants is sex.

*A beat.*

**Keith**    Can't he do both?

**Holly**    It doesn't look like it, he wants it all the time! And that's not respecting me, is it?

**Keith**    Well no, I don't suppose it is!

*A beat.*

**Holly**    Anyway so I've I dumped him.

**Keith**    Oh dear.

**Holly**    And do you know what he said to that?

**Keith**    Go on!

**Holly**   He said he could go paint-balling at Christmas now instead of coming to my mother's.

**Keith**   Oh right then!

**Holly**   I wanted him to change and want me for who I am, and us to get back together but he just said that he'd go paint-balling instead.

**Keith**   Oh dear!

**Holly**   And he's bloody loaded, lives up in West Ella. I mean I've got no money, I've spent up on presents. I've gone mad this year trying to impress him. Men, Keith? That's all they're after.

*A beat.*

**Keith**   Kath's a bit . . .

**Holly**   Is there any wonder?

*A beat.*

**Keith**   It's a year, isn't it?

**Holly**   Last Christmas.

*A beat.*

**Keith**   You don't know what to say, do you?

**Holly**   No, and then we've got this lot in here, and then that old man's just died. I doesn't help that he lived next door to her and Mike, does it? He'd been sat in his house for six days with the fuel off, did you hear?

*A beat.*

He froze to death. Couldn't pay his fuel bill. I mean what's happening to this country, Keith?

*A beat.*

**Keith**   Politicians!

**Holly**   I don't understand it!

*A beat.*

**Keith**  I didn't vote, I've never voted; would they vote for me do you think?

**Holly**  Probably not.

**Keith**  Exactly, fuck 'em.

*A beat.*

**Holly**  At least we're on with Rojinsky.

*A beat.*

**Keith**  Oh aye, they're all coming over here that lot.

**Holly**  He's ever so nice though.

**Keith**  They're coming over here taking our jobs.

*A beat.*

**Holly**  They're not taking your job though, are they?

**Keith**  They can bloody have it for me!

**Holly**  You don't mean that.

**Keith**  I do.

**Holly**  You'll still be here when you're fifty.

*A beat.*

**Keith**  I am fifty.

*A beat.*

**Holly**  What would you be doing, Keith, if you weren't doing this though?

**Keith**  I'd be at home doing my studying.

**Holly**  What is it you're doing?

**Keith**  Open University.

**Holly**  Oh right that's it, you've told me!

*A beat.*

**Keith**   I'm only on level one like but . . .

**Holly**   Sounds good though, Keith.

*A beat.*

**Keith**   Modern literature and art.

**Holly**   I don't read me at all. I don't read, well, apart from *OK* magazine. I mean after a night like this, I just want to stop in and eat a box of chocolates. And curse Darren!

*A beat.*

**Keith**   Only three more hours now, Holly.

*A beat.*

**Holly**   Three more hours then you can wander off as much as you like.

**Keith**   I do that anyway!

**Kath** *re-enters. She is short-tempered and harassed.*

**Kath**   Rojinsky's back from cardiology, can you get somebody to take some X-rays down, and find Mr Patel, he's on a ward. I've got an issue with Mrs Preston, and we're waiting for Mr McDonald to come back in.

**Keith**   I'll come and find him if you want.

**Kath**   No, I don't think we want you on the wards, that'd be enough to give anybody a fright.

**Kath** *exits.* **Holly** *looks at* **Keith**.

**Holly**   Oh she loves you really.

**Keith**   No, she doesn't, she doesn't even know my name!

**Holly**   Oh Keith, she does!

**Keith**   She thinks I'm boring!

*A beat.*

**Holly**  Well, you are really aren't you?

**Keith**  Well, thanks a bunch for that!

**Holly**  I'm only joking!

**Holly** *exits.*

**Keith**  No, you bloody weren't!

**Keith** *is alone against the night.*

*Lights fade to blackout.*


**Scene Three**

*5.30 a.m.*

*The lights fade up slightly later.* **Keith** *shuffles against the night. An ambulance siren can be heard. He reacts to it and looks in the direction from which the noise is coming. When the noise has disappeared into the distance he stands once more and warms himself. As he gets comfortable* **Len** *enters: a man in his late sixties, he has a comb-over haircut and wears clothes that have seen better days. He appears to be slightly drunk. He takes out a cigarette and begins to smoke. As he smokes he coughs heavily. He appears to be quite ill and speaks with real aggression.* **Keith** *watches him with real interest.*

**Len**  Ophh . . . eh . . . (*Coughs.*) A right do . . . ( *Coughs.*)

**Len** *coughs heavily and has another draw on his cigarette.*

Been here bloody ages. Doctor's foreign. (*Coughs.*) What is he, Polish? Bloody NHS, run by Pakis, isn't it? (*Coughs.*) If it's not Pakis it's Poles now. (*Coughs.*) Bloody ambulance took ages. Heart attack they've said. (*Coughs.*) Crackers in there earlier. Friday neet. (*Coughs.*) I told her, 'You're all right being badly on a Friday, there'll be nobody on who knows owt, especially at Christmas all good 'uns will have buggered off!' (*Coughs.*) Friday night, full of druggies and what have you . . . They've no time for you. (*Coughs.*) You pay your national insurance, and when you need 'em you get Poles, Greeks, Czechs, owt but bloody English. (*Coughs.*)

Been here hours, she's just laid in a corridor now, they say she's to have some tests. I heard a nurse say it didn't look so good! I know that! They can't find anywhere to put her with it being so busy. (*Coughs.*) There's no beds, so I don't know what they're going to do with her. (*Coughs.*) Eh dear!

*A beat.*

(*Coughs.*) I've said to her before don't be ill here, if you're going to be ill, be ill in Leeds at your Sally's, they've got all the stars, haven't they?

**Keith**   No idea, mate.

**Len**   It's only a one-star, isn't it?

**Keith**   I don't know.

**Len**   Bloody one-star. Typical, if it was a hotel, I wouldn't stop there. Bloody one-star.

*A beat.*

**Keith**   They did all right by my mother.

**Len**   Aye but did she get better?

**Keith**   Well no but . . .

*A beat.*

**Len** (*coughs*)   Aren't we all right? Staff look at you like you're backward, my nerves are shot sat in there, they took her away and you're just sat there aren't you, don't know what's going off. Nobody's got a clue what's happening.

*A beat.*

Nobody's a bloody clue! Nobody knows who the boss is, do they? (*Cough.*) Didn't they take somebody t' wrong leg off last week?

**Keith**   I don't know, mate.

**Len**  It was in the *Daily Mail*. Bloody one-star, mind you it's better than nowt I suppose. Nobody's a bloody clue what's what, it's too big, isn't it?

**Keith**  I don't know, mate.

**Len** *draws once more on his cigarette.*

**Len**  I mean she's all I've got. (*Coughs.*) We're just stuck in it, aren't we. We're just stuck in a system. It's like when I was at work, we're stuck in a system and nobody really knows what's what. We're just numbers, aren't we? I've told her we're just numbers really.

**Keith**  Well aye!

**Len**  It's at times like this you wished you believed in sommat, isn't it?

*A beat.*

I'll go and see what's what.

**Keith**  Good luck.

**Len**  Luck? I've never had any luck in my life. Christmas, fuck Christmas and fuck New Year and all. I mean we're supposed to be going to Reighton Gap in March, looks like that's fucking well had it! Last fag and all, look at this.

**Len** *crumbles up his fag packet.*

Set of bastards in here you know, they're not bothered, it's just a job to them, isn't it? I hope I get hit by a bus I do, I don't want to end up in here. And tha's got a right job an't tha, just standing there doing sod all. What's it coming to when we need security in bloody hospitals, fucking hell it's the staff tha' wants to watch. (*Coughs.*) What's it coming to?

**Len** *wanders into the hospital, as another ambulance siren is heard.*

**Keith** *looks to where the siren is coming from as the lights fade to blackout.*

## Scene Four

*5.45 a.m.*

*Slightly later.* **Billy Bubbles**, *a children's entertainer, is now standing outside the hospital. He is still wearing his children's entertainer's costume and a full face of clown make-up. He has one arm in a sling and is on the phone, holding the phone with his other hand. He moves animatedly around the forecourt.* **Keith** *watches him like a hawk.*

**Billy**   Eh? No, I'm still here. I'm not a priority. It's nearly six o'clock. You tell me, I've been here since one, well I didn't realise it was killing me because I'm on these pain killers for my back. My back? No, I did that last week. I know it's Christmas. Eh? No, I've had an X-ray. I'm waiting for the results. God knows where they've taken it to. Nobody's got a clue. Chaos earlier, I think the doctors went home. Eh? No, nobody, a couple of nurses. Been an accident at Melton. No, I didn't have time to get changed. Eh?

**Billy** *wanders around under* **Keith***'s watchful eye.*

**Billy**   No I'm still in my stuff, or yes, really amusing that. Billy Bubbles! I know, I tried to call Colin to get him to bring me sommat down but he was still at Fuel at half three. Eh? Well it could have been worse, I could have my Father Christmas on. Eh? Keep smiling, you try it! Eh? I know and I've got all them bookings for the New Year. Just pushed me down a flight of stairs. How am I gunna bend a balloon with one hand? Eh? I'm a balloon bender not a friggin' ventriloquist. Eh? No, she's gone home. I think she's seeing somebody to be honest. I don't trust her. Well she said she was working with Sammy Smiles. Eh? I can't hear you. Eh? You what? No, I'm not playing Swanland again. Eh? You're breaking up . . . no sod 'em! Listen my arm's killing me, no that arm's killing me, but this arm's killing me now, my arm I'm holding the phone with. Eh? I'll call you back if I hear owt. Eh? Can you hear me? Eh? Can you hear me?

**Billy** *puts the phone away and shakes his phone arm. He looks at* **Keith**.

**Billy**   Couldn't hear me.

*Silence, awkwardness.*

All right?

**Keith**   Yes!

**Billy**   Good!

**Keith**   Yes.

**Billy**   That's good then.

**Keith**   Yes.

*A beat.*

**Billy**   Shouldn't you be in there?

**Keith**   Been in all night.

**Billy**   Quieter now.

*A beat.*

Car accident!

*A beat.*

That woman fighting with her boyfriend? Sorted that out, didn't you?

*A beat.*

Did you have to kick her or what?

**Keith**   She kicked me first. Bloody scum, mate!

*A beat.*

**Billy**   See some sights eh? That bloke with an axe in his head, I thought it was a joke at first but . . . blood all over, what was that all about?

**Keith**   Domestic that!

*A beat.*

**Billy**   It's been like a bloody circus in there.

*A beat.*

**Keith**   You'd feel at home then.

**Billy**   Eh?

**Anna** *enters, a smart woman in her forties. She wears an expensive evening gown, and wraps a small coat around her cleavage. She looks wonderfully out of place except for the fact that she has a large bandage around her head and has a patch over one eye. She stands with* **Billy** *and* **Keith** *in silence.* **Keith** *looks at* **Anna** *but doesn't say a word. He looks at* **Billy** *and* **Billy** *looks at* **Anna**. *Nothing is said.*

**Anna**   Brrr.

*A beat.*

**Keith**   Fresh this morning!

*A beat.*

**Billy**   Been here long?

**Anna**   Since half two.

*A beat.*

**Billy**   I've been here nearly half a day now! I'm thinking of staying here. X-ray department's got my arm.

**Anna**   Oh dear.

**Billy**   I don't think it's here, I think they've taken it to Newcastle.

*A beat.*

**Anna**   Well, they say if you're going to be ill don't go into hospital.

*A beat.*

**Billy**   Is it your eye?

**Anna**    Is what my eye?

**Billy**    Your eye! Is it your eye?

**Anna**    Oh yes, it's my eye.

**Billy**    Somebody crack you?

**Anna**    I got poked!

**Billy**    I got pushed. Flight of stairs. Swanland. Fell over a doll's house.

*A beat.*

**Anna**    I was dancing at Willerby Manor . . . Charity Ball . . .

**Billy**    Bang over a doll's house, thirteen steps!

**Anna**    A consultant, I think.

**Billy**    Little girl and all!

**Anna**    He hit my husband. He's still in there. I don't usually dance but what with it being Christmas . . . You've got to join in, haven't you!

**Billy**    How am I going to bend a balloon with one hand?

**Anna**    I've no idea!

**Len** *enters and lights up a cigarette.* **Len**, **Anna**, **Billy** *and* **Keith** *stand in silence outside A and E.* **Len** *lights his cigarette, takes a few draws and coughs heavily.*

**Len**    Aren't we all fucking right? (*Coughs.*)

*Silence. No one is quite sure what to say.* **Billy** *breaks the silence.*

**Billy**    I'll just go see where my arm is.

**Billy** *exits.*

*Silence between* **Anna**, **Len** *and* **Keith**.

**Len**    Aren't we all right? (*Coughs.*)

**Anna**    That doesn't sound so good!

**Len**   It doesn't look so good!

**Anna**   Oh dear.

**Len**   No, it looks a bit rough at the minute . . .

**Anna**   Oh dear!

**Len**   They're waiting for a Czech to come and see her, I don't know, there's some problem, nobody knows what to do with her. Been the same all her life, bloody awkward.

**Anna**   Oh dear!

**Len**   Bloody hospitals. (*Coughs.*)

**Keith**   It was worse last night.

*A siren is heard drawing near to the hospital.*

**Len**   Here you are, look, another lucky winner.

*The siren gets louder as* **Keith** *makes his way into the A and E.* **Len** *and* **Anna** *stand outside the hospital.* **Len** *smokes and smokes, and coughs and coughs.*

**Len**   Is it the eye?

**Anna**   Yes, it's the eye!

**Len**   She's critical, they say. (*Coughs.*) In the next hour owt could happen, and there's nowt but a bloody Czech to see her. Aren't we all fucking right?

*Lights fade to blackout.*


**Scene Five**

*6 30 a.m.*

**Lilly** *enters. She is dressed in a Duffer sweat top, a short mini skirt. She wears her hood up and has long matted hair. She has sunken eyes and looks rough. She stands against the cold and wipes her nose. We notice she is wearing far too much fake gold.* **Keith** *comes out into the* *forecourt. He is slightly offended at being unable to help but he resumes his position watching the day break.*

**Lilly**    Hiya.

**Keith**    Not bad.

*A beat.*

**Lilly**    All right then?

**Keith**    Not bad.

*A beat.*

**Lilly**    You all right then?

**Keith**    Yes not bad!

*Silence.*

**Lilly**    You want business?

**Keith**    Eh?

**Lilly**    You want business!

**Keith**    Business?

**Lilly**    Yes.

**Keith**    What sort of business?

**Lilly**    Eh?

**Keith**    What sort of business?

**Lilly**    Business.

**Keith**    No, I don't want any business.

*A beat.*

**Lilly**    Come on, what's up wi' you?

**Keith**    What?

**Lilly**    Don't you want a quickie?

**Keith**    A what?

**Lilly**   A quickie?

**Keith**   Do I heck!

**Lilly**   It's Christmas.

**Keith**   I know it's Christmas.

**Lilly**   Well then . . .

**Keith**   I thought you were in there?

**Lilly**   I am.

**Keith**   Well, get back in there with your mate then.

*A beat.*

**Lilly**   Twenty quid, no messing!

**Keith**   No!

**Lilly**   A tenner!

**Keith**   No.

*A beat.*

**Lilly**   Well, what're you looking for?

**Keith**   You, to go back in there.

**Lilly**   Well, what are you willing to pay?

**Keith**   Nothing!

*A beat.*

**Lilly**   Come on, you twat, it's Christmas!

**Keith**   Eh?

**Lilly**   A tenner over by the dentist's.

**Keith**   Eh?

**Lilly**   What's up with you?

**Keith**   You.

**Lilly**   It's Christmas.

**Keith**    Go away.

*A beat.*

**Lilly**    You a puff?

**Keith**    Yes.

**Lilly**    Are you?

**Keith**    No!

**Lilly**    Come on, a tenner over there . . .

**Keith**    Go away, you don't know what you're dealing with.

*A beat.*

**Lilly**    You got a match then?

**Keith**    Yes, your face my arse.

**Lilly**    I could report you for that.

**Keith**    Eh?

**Lilly**    I could report you for that!

**Keith**    Go on then.

**Lilly**    Think you're funny?

**Keith**    No . . .

**Lilly**    Tosser.

**Keith**    Eh?

**Lilly**    Tosser.

**Keith**    Oh dear!

**Lilly**    Tosser . . .

**Keith**    Get off . . .

*Silence.*

**Lilly**    You're pathetic!

**Lilly** *re-enters the hospital.* **Keith** *watches where she goes.*

**Keith**    You're the tosser! Wanker!

*He looks towards where she stood and mimes making a slow-motion punch towards her head as the lights fade to blackout.*

## Scene Six

*7.15 a.m.*

**Keith** *warms his cold hands against the cold morning, though it still looks like night. As he stands* **Stevo** *enters, a dangerous youth in a filthy hoody, with dirty and ripped jeans. He wears baseball boots and looks nervous but agitated. He stands against the cold but he is a live wire and speaks with a peculiar drawl and at speed.*

**Stevo**    Am I friggin' invisible or wha'?

**Keith**    Eh?

**Stevo**    Do I look invisible to you?

**Keith**    No!

**Stevo**    Well I must be because nobody seems bothered about me nobody seems bothered about what I want I mean that Polish doctor's shite!

*A beat.*

**Keith**    Czech!

**Stevo**    Eh?

**Keith**    He's Czech.

*A beat.*

**Stevo**    I'm not bothered what he is he's shit all t' staff are shit that old nurse's got a face like a friggin' wet week what's her problem then?

**Keith**    Her husband died last Christmas.

**Stevo**    What and it's my fault it is her job!

**Keith**    He jumped off the bridge.

*A beat.*

**Stevo**    And that young 'un wants a good length up her waken her up a bit it's shit in here it's shit Hull's a shit tip isn't it?

*A beat.*

**Keith**    Don't you like it?

**Stevo**    It's shit mate!

**Keith**    Go and live somewhere else then.

*A beat.*

**Stevo**    Hey you ever seen two blokes snoggin'?

**Keith**    Who?

**Stevo**    You ever seen two tramps tonguing each other?

**Keith**    Well it's not usually sommat I look out for!

*A beat.*

**Stevo**    Are you a puff?

**Keith**    Me?

**Stevo**    I saw two blokes snogging on Hessle Road toneet. You ever fired a gun?

**Keith**    Me?

**Stevo**    Hear about that kid with that goat? He got caught wi' a goat! Everybody on the train was watching him with a goat. You hear about that, that kid shagging a goat, it wa'on t' news!

*A beat.*

**Keith**    It wasn't you was it?

**Stevo**    Eh?

**Keith**    Just wondered!

*A beat.*

**Stevo**   Does it make you feel hard that uniform?

**Keith**   No!

**Stevo**   What you wearing it for then?

**Keith**   To not feel hard!

*A beat.*

**Steve**   Is your head the same shape as that hat?

**Keith**   Is yours?

*A beat.*

**Stevo**   Think you're hard?

**Keith**   No!

**Stevo**   My brother does martial arts.

**Keith**   My brother does!

**Stevo** *is becoming more agitated, and animated.*

**Stevo**   Nobody's fucking bothered about me in there . . . all they're bothered about is a load of old women they should leave 'em they're nearly dead anyway full of foreigners, isn't it? I'm English I want to be seen to by an English doctor I don't want some Pole sorting me out I don't want no Pole getting me sorted send the fuckers back I'm English. You English mate . . . ?

**Keith**   Me?

**Stevo**   Who am I talking to my fucking self you English?

**Keith**   No I'm Yorkshire!

**Steve**   I'm English pal I want to see some English doctors not somebody I can't understand, you know what I'm saying, you go to Hull Fair?

**Alan** *enters. He is dressed in his green ambulance suit. He has a shaved head and looks useful. He is jolly but direct and carries a* *solitary Christmas cracker, which he uses as a baton.* **Alan** *and* **Keith** *are almost a double-act.*

**Alan**    Right, Steven Chiko, my old mucker, Mr Patel's back, he's looking all over for you.

**Stevo**    About friggin' time and all I've been here ages. What is it with these in here tonight; I just want to get sorted!

*He strops off stage into A and E.*

That's all I'm after getting sorted . . .

**Alan** *and* **Keith** *look at each other for a moment.* **Alan** *offers* **Keith** *a cracker to pull.*

**Alan**    Here you go, pull this!

**Keith**    Get off!

**Alan**    Go on, pull it with me and I'll kiss you! But I want the party hat!

**Keith**    Get off!

**Alan**    That clown's left it in there. Come on, what's up with you?

*A beat.*

**Keith**    Do you know him then?

**Alan**    Stevo? He's come for his fix. Pharmacy's closed.

**Alan** *plays the next scene with the cracker in his hand.*

**Keith**    I was just going to give him a fix.

**Alan**    Were you?

**Keith**    Right up his arse!

**Alan**    Yes, that'd fix him.

*A beat.*

**Alan**   Cold enough for snow! I think there's been some already! Roads are lethal!

*A beat.*

Four dead tonight! A domestic, two cardiac and some poor sod who looked like he'd drank himself to death.

*A beat.*

An accident at Melton! Joy-riders!

*A beat.*

And there's some teenage kid from Brough who's got a hoover stuck up his arse!

*A beat.*

**Keith**   Why?

**Alan**   No idea!

*A beat.*

**Keith**   What bit is it, is it the engine bit?

**Alan**   No, it's not the engine bit, it's the pipe bit, he's gone and got the pipe stuck up his arse.

*A beat.*

**Keith**   Well, how's he done that then?

**Alan** (*shaking his head*)   Don't ask me!

*A beat.*

**Keith**   Bloody teenagers!

**Alan**   It's a funny old world, Keith.

**Keith**   They're sticking hoovers up their arses now!

*A beat.*

**Alan**   His mother was going mad when we got there. She's got all t' cleaning to do for Christmas and hoover's ruined!

**Keith**    I bet his arse is in a mess!

**Alan**    I don't know, I didn't really have chance to look!

*A beat.*

**Keith**    My mam got one of them Dysons!

**Alan**    Well, you're safe with them, Keith; you couldn't really get one of them up your arse, could you?

**Keith**    It's bagless!

*A beat.*

**Alan**    Did you hear about that woman yesterday?

**Keith**    Which woman?

**Alan**    There was a woman yesterday whose husband's died on her.

**Keith**    When?

**Alan**    Yesterday!

**Keith**    What shift was it?

**Alan**    He's died on her, a big lad, Kenny knows him, he used prop for East Hull.

**Keith**    How's he died on her then?

**Alan**    She's only got him to tie her to the bed and he's died on her.

**Keith**    How's he died on her then?

**Alan**    Well, he's died on her, hasn't he?

*A beat.*

**Keith**    Well, how's she got him off then?

**Alan**    Baby-sitter's got him off by all accounts.

**Keith**    Baby-sitter?

**Alan**   She's tied to the bed, he's died on her and the baby-sitter has had to come and get him off and untie her. They've been getting ready for a Christmas party and wanted to start early. They're having a shot at it and he's just, bang, heart's gone and he's died on her and she's had to call the baby-sitter who's just arrived to pull him off. Died on her, nearly twenty stone and all; just his arse there looking at us!

**Keith**   How could his arse look at you?

**Alan**   Aye, the baby-sitter's pulled him off and he nearly went through the ceiling. They live just off Sutton Park and you know what them houses are like. She was more concerned with the crack in the plaster than him dying on her if you ask me.

*A beat.*

**Keith**   They were thrown up, them houses!

**Alan**   In fact somebody said she'd planned it.

**Keith**   Planned it?

**Alan**   How the bloody hell you plan that is beyond me, but if she could plan that she's in the wrong job!

**Keith**   What job is she in then?

**Alan**   She works at that garden centre on the way to Hornsea. They reckon she's got a fella there; and she wanted to get rid of the husband.

*A beat.*

**Keith**   They've got some good stuff in there!

**Alan**   Aye they have, I looked at a fish pond from there once!

**Keith** (*after much thought*)   Bloody Christmas.

*Silence.*

**Alan**   I see Kath's in a foul mood.

**Keith**    Aye well.

**Alan**    I thought I might have stood a chance there once but . . .

*A beat.*

**Keith**    A sad story that . . . redundancy, you know.

**Alan**    Didn't he hit the bottle?

**Keith**    Big time, there was sommat not right!

**Alan**    Aye, I thought I might have stood a chance there but . . . Last May, Vicky's birthday at that do at t' Station Hotel. Craig Leach was on. We had one dance, and I thought it was going to develop but . . . she's not ready for it yet, is she?

*A beat.*

**Keith**    I think there's a consultant.

**Alan**    I wouldn't be surprised.

**Keith**    Rojinsky!

**Alan**    I did wonder.

**Keith**    He's a Czech.

**Alan**    He's a Czech with a cheque book, Keith, he can give her what we can't. Mind you, they have to put up with some shite.

**Keith**    I wouldn't have it.

**Alan**    Mind you, we had a load of kids throwing bottles at the ambulance last month.

**Keith**    Where's this?

**Alan**    Orchard Park. Bonfire night. Ten o'clock, fire brigade had taken ages getting in, we turn up, somebody's had a stroke and we couldn't get in! Ten-year-olds throwing stuff at the ambulance, what's that about?

**Keith**    That's about a kick up the fucking arse, that's what that's about.

**Alan**    Life's a shit sandwich, Keith.

*A beat.*

**Keith**    And then you die.

**Holly** *enters. She is terribly warm. She stands and cools off. She is tired out.*

**Alan**    She's here, look, the apple of my eye; nearly all done!

**Holly**    Hiya Alan!

**Alan**    And that's all I get, Hiya Alan. Go on pull this!

**Alan** *offers* **Holly** *the cracker.*

**Holly**    No, I'm not in the mood.

**Alan**    I've got sommat else you can pull if you want!

**Keith**    She's been dumped.

**Holly**    I dumped him.

**Alan**    Is there nobody good enough?

**Holly**    I'm looking for somebody special!

**Keith**    All men want is sex, she says.

**Alan**    Bastards.

**Keith**    That's what I said.

**Alan**    We're not like that, are we?

**Keith**    Well I'm not.

*A beat.*

**Holly**    I'm tired out!

**Alan**    Boiling in there.

**Keith**    These have finished now!

**Holly**   Been a long one tonight. I was going to work another hour but I've got four days off so . . .

**Alan**   Four days off? Lucky sod, I wish I'd got four days off. I've got the kids, our lass and the bloody in-laws. I need a rest from that to be honest. Christmas in our house and my blood pressure is through the roof, I've got to have a drink to get through it, my father-in-law. He's the most boring bloke on the planet.

**Holly**   What, more boring than Keith?

**Kath** *enters. She is rather anxious.*

**Alan**   Oh here she is, look. Here you go, Kath, you'll pull it with me, won't you?

**Alan** *offers* **Kath** *the cracker but she blanks him, she is not in the mood.*

**Kath**   Have you been in my lockaway?

**Holly**   Who?

**Kath**   You!

**Holly**   No, why?

**Kath**   Well somebody has, I've been just getting my stuff sorted.

**Alan**   Why, has something gone missing? You should give it to Jenny, she puts it behind the desk!

**Kath**   No, nothing's gone missing but somebody's been in my bag.

**Holly**   Why, what have they taken?

**Kath**   They haven't taken anything but they've left something!

**Alan**   Aye, aye look out! Father Christmas!

**Holly**   Eh?

**Kath**   Somebody's left a reference number on my coat.

**Alan**   Well it's not me coz I don't do vouchers!

**Holly**   A what?

**Kath**   A reference number.

**Holly**   For what?

**Kath**   For Easy Jet.

**Holly**   It's a what . . . ?

**Alan**   It's a wind-up, it'll be Kenny, pissing about!

**Kath**   It's not a wind-up because Jen's just rung up to check the reference.

**Holly**   So what is it, a present or . . .

**Kath**   Well I think so, I mean somebody's been in my stuff tonight and must have put it there.

**Alan**   I might check my bag, see if I've got owt!

**Holly**   So what is it?

**Kath**   It's two tickets for a city break.

**Holly**   Is it you, Alan?

**Alan**   It's not me, I don't throw my money away. I bet it's Keith.

**Keith**   Oh aye that's right!

**Holly**   So what happened?

**Kath**   I checked my bag to sort out my phone and check my messages and there was an envelope with a reference number on.

**Alan**   It'll be Rojinsky.

**Holly** (*certain*)   I bet it is . . . !

**Kath**   Eh?

**Alan**   Of course it is. It's a bloody consultant. It'll be Rojinsky.

**Keith**  It might be Father Christmas.

**Kath**  I don't know who it is, or what to do with the tickets.

**Alan**  Well you'll have to go, bloody hell!

**Holly**  Where's the flight to?

**Kath**  Prague!

**Alan**  Oh lovely, stag nights, and hen dos, it'll be like a night in Hull.

**Holly**  Have you been?

**Alan**  Course I have!

**Kath**  Well I'm not bothered what it's like . . .

**Holly**  Why, aren't you going?

**Kath**  Course I'm bloody going.

**Holly**  Are you?

**Kath**  I bloody am, our Emma can stop at mi mam's!

**Holly**  I wonder who's done it though?

**Kath**  Well it's obviously somebody in the hospital because they know I've got time off.

**Alan**  It's a consultant, I bet you, I bet you it's a consultant! I tell you what: I'll come with you, sod our lass.

**Kath**  No, Holly's coming with me!

**Holly**  Me?

**Kath**  Well what do you want me to do, take Darren?

**Alan**  I've said you can take me if you want!

**Holly**  Can I come then?

**Kath**  Why not?

**Alan**  You jammy bastards, eh Keith?

**Kath** (*overjoyed*)   Things like this don't happen to me! I've got to get home, pack, sort out a hotel, our Emma, mi mam! Mi life!

**Holly**   Am I coming then?

**Kath**   Why, don't you want to?

**Holly**   Hello!

**Kath**   I've got to see if Rojinsky's about for the new shift's notes!

**Alan** (*groans*)   What to thank him?

**Kath** (*jokingly*)   Oh you're only jealous!

**Kath** *exits.*

**Alan** (*calls after her*)   I bloody am and all!

**Holly**   I can't believe that we're going just like that! I mean Kath deserves it really, doesn't she?

**Alan**   She does, but you bloody don't, you jammy gett!

**Holly**   Hey shut up you, you cheeky sod!

**Alan**   Hadn't you better get in there and save somebody's life? Or would that be another first.

**Holly**   I mean I don't know where we're staying, where we're flying from and I've got sod all to wear, to be honest! I can't believe it.

**Holly** *exits excitedly.*

**Alan**   Bloody consultants. Flashing their money about! Playing God!

**Keith**   Oh aye!

**Alan**   Lucky bastards.

**Keith**   Oh aye!

**Alan**   They'll be fannying about in Prague and I'll be stuck with our lass stuffing sommat from Iceland and playing Cluedo with her father!

**Keith**   Would you do it?

**Alan**   What?

**Keith**   Buy somebody some tickets?

**Alan**   No, not unless there was something in it for me!

**Keith**   Like what?

**Alan**   Get real, Keith, there's no such thing as a free lunch. She's all over him like a rash, there's been sommat going on there for ages. That's why Mike went off the rails. I mean such as us don't stand a chance. It's just a bit of flirting isn't it, make Rojinsky feel good, the Czech bastard!

**Keith**   Well . . .

**Alan**   I don't know, bloody Prague! Mind you, they're probably cheap tickets. Typical of consultants: smart cars, fancy ties and two cheap tickets! I bet it's not set him back fifty quid and he's set up when they come back!

**Keith**   It might not be him!

**Alan**   Kath Wood in Prague, God help 'em, she's crackers when she's had a drink. And Holly, I don't think she's ever been out of Hull. What I wouldn't give to be a fly on the wall. Nurses, Keith, never go to bed with one, they know too much!

**Keith**   How do you know?

**Alan**   I'm telling you.

**Keith**   I'll try to remember that!

*Gentle flakes fall from the rig.*

**Alan**   I can't see some bastard buying me tickets to go to Prague with our lass. I wouldn't want to go with her anyway in all honesty she's such a moody sod! Oh starting to snow now! I'm in for a coffee, do you want one?

**Keith**    No, I'm staying out here.

**Alan**    I'll see if I can get Jenny to pull my cracker! It's no use asking thee because tha's such a miserable gett! Anyway Keith, before I forget: Merry Christmas.

**Keith** *is away.*

**Keith**    Eh?

**Alan**    I said Merry Christmas!

**Alan** *exits.*

**Keith**    Oh aye! Ho! Ho! Ho!

*Snow falls onto* **Keith** *as he stands centre stage.*

*A huge Slavic soundtrack can be felt rumbling. The lights slowly start to fade on* **Keith** *as the snow continues. We get a sense that* **Keith** *is just about to 'wander off'. The music swells and increases in volume as we fade to blackout.*

# Act Two

*Music. Snow.*

*The city of Prague, night time. Smog drifts. The A and E setting of Act One is struck by **Keith** and **Alan** and backstage staff, revealing a large open space. Upstage of the false pros is hard flatage. **Kath** and **Holly** are caught in a central spotlight. They are dressed in very fetching outfits, fit for part fantasy and part reality, but probably unsuitable for the weather in Prague. **Holly** wears boots and an extremely short skirt, **Kath** has also dressed much too young. They stand centre stage in the spotlight, carrying what limited hand-luggage they have brought with them. They are extremely nervous about their new adventure.*

**Kath**  I can't believe we're in Prague, it's like being in a fairy tale.

**Holly**  Except we can't read the words.

**Kath**  Eh?

**Holly**  The words, we can't even read where the toilet is.

**Kath**  Oh shurrup you, you're boring.

**Holly**  I mean, where are we staying, where's the taxi rank?

**Kath**  We'll get the subway.

**Holly**  The subway? We'll probably get murdered. It's five o'clock in the afternoon, it's pitch black and I need the loo.

**Kath**  I told you not to drink too much.

**Holly**  I've got to have a drink or I can't get on the plane.

**Kath**  Well why didn't you go when we were on the plane?

**Holly**  I don't like standing up!

**Kath**  You don't have to stand up!

**Holly**  You do to get to the loo.

**Kath**    Well cross your legs!

**Holly**    Oh we can't stand here like this, we look like tourists.

**Kath**    We are tourists.

**Holly**    I know, but you know what I mean.

**Kath**    Only half the time.

*As they stand the* **Man** *appears. He bears an uncanny resemblance to* **Len** *from Act One. He has the same type of haircut, and he coughs heavily as he smokes. He is dressed in very simple clothes with muted colours. His face seems to be slightly powdered, as if he were perhaps not a real person, or someone from an arty Czech play.*

**Man**    Taxi!

*The girls are startled.*

**Holly**    What's he say?

**Man**    Taxi! (*Coughs.*)

**Kath**    Taxi?

**Man**    My name is Jaroslav we go!

**Holly**    Is he a taxi driver?

**Man**    You like go? (*Coughs.*)

**Kath**    Ask him if he knows the Hotel Unitas.

**Holly**    You ask him.

**Kath**    Do you know the Hotel Unitas?

**Man**    Was prison, use by secret police. (*Coughs.*)

**Holly**    The secret police?

**Man**    Come we go! (*Coughs.*)

**Holly**    Kath, let's leg it!

**Man**    We go very nice English. I take you Hotel Unitas. Goodbye! (*Coughs.*)

*The **Man** takes the cases from **Holly** and **Kath**, who remain anxiously in the spotlight.*

**Holly**   He's got our cases!

**Kath**   Yes, I can see that.

**Holly**   He's just took our cases.

**Kath**   Yes, I'm aware of that.

**Holly**   He's just walked off with our cases.

**Kath**   Yes, I know, I saw him!

**Holly**   Oh we're in a nightmare.

**Kath**   No, we're not!

**Holly**   Oh shit!

**Kath**   We just need to agree a price!

**Holly**   Of what, our bail?

**Kath**   The taxi!

**Holly**   Won't there be a meter?

**Kath**   It says to agree a price first!

**Holly**   Kath, I'm scared, I need a loo and I'm freezing!

**Kath**   Well what have you come as?

**Holly** (*to her dress*)   It's all I've got.

**Kath**   Yes, but where's the rest of it?

**Holly**   This is the rest of it.

**Kath**   Come on, let's follow him and get to the hotel.

**Kath** *and* **Holly** *are about to move when the* **Man** *reappears without the cases, but carrying a large hotel ledger.*

**Man**   Welcome, welcome, nice English girl ladies. Welcome to Hotel Unitas. But I have no you! (*Coughs.*)

**Holly**   What's he say?

**Kath**   I've no idea!

**Man**   No you! No you!

**Holly**   He says he knows you!

**Kath**   Me?

**Man**   No in book!

**Holly**   He says there's no hymn books!

**Kath**   We might need one!

**Man**   I have no you, but have room! My name is Vaclav, hello to you!

**Kath**   How much?

**Man**   No too much.

**Holly**   He says we know too much!

**Kath**   That's what the taxi man said!

**Man**   My brother Jaroslav very good. (*Coughs.*)

**Kath**   I gave him fifty!

**Holly**   Fifty what?

**Man**   You in Praha nice Christmas, good room, you too cold, sleep in clothes.

**Kath**   She's not wearing any!

**Man**   You sleep together very good. I get key my brother take you. Have good time I too busy goodbye (*Coughs.*)

*The* **Man** *disappears as quickly as he came.* **Kath** *and* **Holly** *panic once more.*

**Holly**   Too busy? Doing what do you think?

**Kath**   Boiling heads!

**Holly**   Oh I don't like it.

**Kath**   We've only been here an hour.

**Holly**    Oh I don't like it!

**Kath**    I know, I've heard you!

**Holly**    Oh I really don't like it!

**Kath**    Yes, all right!

**Holly**    I mean, we've only been here an hour and we've nearly spent up!

**Kath**    I thought you could handle anything?

**Holly**    I can handle bedpans but I've never liked horror films, and I still need the loo.

**Kath**    Well, ask!

**Holly**    You ask, it was your idea.

**Kath**    It wasn't!

**Holly**    I mean, where are we staying?

**Kath**    Nowhere, yet!

**Holly**    He said we'd to sleep in our clothes.

**Kath**    Well you're not wearing any.

**Holly**    We're staying in a prison.

**Kath**    You're over-reacting!

**Holly**    We're in a prison.

**Kath**    It's not that bad!

**Holly**    I mean, what will the food be like?

**Kath**    Hopefully there'll be none! We'll have a bowl of milk and have to make do!

**Holly**    Don't joke!

**Kath**    I'm not doing!

*The **Man** reappears with the girls' luggage. He coughs his way on stage, and positions himself between the two girls.*

**Man**   So I come now, we go now! (*Coughs.*)

**Holly**   What did he say?

**Kath** (*bewildered*)   Is it the same bloke or is it me?

**Man**   Take you to room!

**Holly**   Ask him if there's a loo!

**Kath**   You ask him!

**Man**   You follow, steps not good, roof low. We go now! My name is Gustav. (*Loudly.*) Come now please yes!

**Kath** (*anxious*)   My nerves are shattered!

**Holly**   I'm exploding!

**Man**   Walk this way!

*Lights.*

*A musical drone takes us to their room. The* **Man** *begins to carry the luggage, as* **Kath** *and* **Holly** *move downstage left and right respectively, and are caught in separate lights. They all move in sync.*

**Kath** (*to audience*)   So down we go!

**Holly** (*to audience*)   Into the bowels!

**Man**   First time in Praha?

**Holly**   And the last, the way it's going!

**Man**   Many bad things!

**Holly**   Like no toilets!

**Kath**   It's freezing down here.

**Man**   Secret police live here many years.

**Holly**   He's on about the secret police now.

**Kath**   Just watch your head!

**Holly**   Watch my head? I can't walk, I've got my legs crossed.

**Man**    Many bad things happen.

**Holly**    Did you hear that?

**Kath**    Just keep walking!

**Holly**    If he keeps on I will wet myself!

**Kath**    Well, they won't notice down here!

**Man**    Many bad things!

**Kath**    Well, I hope they're not going to happen this weekend!

**Man**    St Nikolaus time, anything can happen!

**Holly**    Yes, we're going to get eaten and boiled up for goulash!

**Man**    Here is your room! (*Coughs.*)

*The* **Man** *drops the cases.* **Holly***,* **Kath** *and the* **Man** *stop moving.* **Holly** *and* **Kath** *turn to look at their 'room/cell'.*

*Music fades away. Silence.*

**Holly**    Kath!

**Kath**    I know!

**Holly**    It is a prison cell!

**Man**    Was! (*Coughs.*)

*A beat.*

**Kath** (*audience*)    . . . with bare brick walls and in one corner a single bed.

**Holly** (*audience*)    . . . and above it a crucifix.

**Kath**    We might need that!

**Man**    Is best room in hotel apartments. (*Coughs.*)

**Kath** (*audience*)    . . . above the sink, a small window with bars at street level.

**Holly** (*alerted*)   I can hear screaming!

**Kath**   It's singing!

**Holly**   Sounds like screaming to me.

**Man**   All same! (*Coughs.*)

**Kath**   It's somebody singing Christmas carols.

**Holly**   Kath, if you believe that you'll believe anything.

**Man**   You like I show you city? (*Coughs.*)

**Kath** (*loudly to a foreigner*)   Where should we go first, so many things. Which things are good?

**Holly** *looks at* **Kath** *agog.*

**Holly**   Why are you speaking like that?

**Kath**   I'm just trying to . . .

**Holly**   Ask him where the toilet is!

**Man**   Go first Karlov Most, you say Charles Bridge? All of Praha is there. Many artists, blind singers, many stories. Many are killed there, their head on spike. (*Coughs.*) Many are thrown into Vltava and die horrible, at night hear rotting dead sing. It is very beautiful. (*Coughs.*) Toilet in corner! Goodbye!

*The* **Man** *turns and coughs his way back off stage.*

*Silence.*

**Kath** *and* **Holly** *look at each other. This is serious.*

**Kath**   What are you looking at?

**Holly**   You!

**Kath**   Why?

**Holly**   Because I'm scared.

**Kath**   Of what?

**Holly**   Of this hotel, Prague, going out on that bridge.
Kath I'm bricking it and I still need a wee!

*A beat.*

**Kath**   Oh come on, we work in A and E in Hull; nothing
can be that bad . . . can it?

*Blackout.*

*Music. Operatic Slavic music.*

*Mist.*

**Holly** *and* **Kath** *exit, taking their luggage with them. The solid flats
are struck, revealing a cross-section of the Charles Bridge, featuring a
number of large statues and a number of tall street lamps. Beyond the
bridge is a view of Prague Castle dressed in winter beauty, with pockets
and caps of snow lying in nooks and crannies. The bridge also has a
flurry of snowflakes which tie in with the snowflakes that were on the
hospital forecourt. We are now truly in a breathtaking fantasy.* **Holly**
*and* **Kath** *enter. They are bewildered but cold.* **Franz**, *a mime
artist, who is completely covered in blue paint and wields an umbrella,
is secreted upstage of the Charles Bridge statues.*

**Kath**   Oh now, this is more . . . What a bridge!

**Holly**   It is so cold though!

**Kath** (*without looking at her*)   Well, put some tights on!

**Holly**   I haven't brought any.

**Kath**   Well, at least you've had a wee.

**Holly**   I'm ready for another one, to be honest. Did you
see the toilet?

**Kath**   No, I'm going to wait.

**Holly**   Till when?

**Kath**   We get back home!

**Franz** *appears from behind a statue.*

**Franz**   English?

**Kath**   Oh look out.

**Franz**   English?

**Holly**   Yes.

**Kath**   Hey come on, come away . . .

**Franz**   I am Franz. You like?

**Franz** *suddenly freezes, he is absolutely still. He puts his umbrella above his head and starts to act as if he was walking against a severe wind.* **Holly** *is transfixed by* **Franz**.

**Kath**   Holly, come away!

**Franz** *(only moving his face)*   You like in Prague?

**Holly**   Did you see that?

**Franz** *(only moving his face)*   You like tour?

**Kath**   Holly?

**Holly**   Have you seen him?

**Franz** *(only moving his face)*   You like good tour?

**Franz** *animates and then freezes dead once again.*

**Holly**   See that!

**Kath**   Yes, very good, now come away.

**Franz** *animates once more.*

**Franz**   You like I show? English! I speak good. I do good tour. I show good tour, good English. Stag parties, yes, hen dos! Weekend breaks, Easy Jet! I speak good English! Divorcees parties, yes, very good Easy Jet!

**Kath**   Divorce parties?

**Franz**   Yes, yes, very good party! You like?

**Kath**   Well . . .

**Franz**    Yes, many sad face, and then much smile and then take for ghost tour, many past life! Oh, oh husband no good, he bad, good divorce much money yes! You like tour?

**Holly**    Shall we?

**Franz**    Yes, shall we? Shall we? Good English!

**Kath**    How much is it?

**Franz**    Very cheap, no too much! You buy pizza I do cheap tour!

**Holly**    Why don't we go with him?

**Franz**    Yes, yes go with him! Why don't you go with him?

**Holly**    Or we're likely to end up wandering about not seeing much and we'll probably get locked up.

**Kath**    We'll probably get locked up for wandering about with a mime artist.

**Franz**    I show you good. I stay since festival of mime, very good. I show you yes? Praha, very romantic. Yes, yes . . . I show you castle, Kafka's house, and shopping yes, you like shopping? Yes all ladies like shopping. Divorce party very good shopping! We shop till they are dropping.

**Kath**    I'm dying for something to eat to be honest.

**Franz**    To eat, yes! We can eat. I show you eat. We eat here, we eat on bridge. I tell restaurant we eat on bridge. In Prague we can do anything! Yes?

*A beat.*

**Kath**    Oh go on then, in for a penny!

**Franz**    Yes, yes, in for a penny. We eat!

*Music.*

*Lights.*

**Franz** *produces three chairs from beyond the bridge. He sits with* **Holly** *and* **Kath**, *and also produces three napkins like a magician. The three of them wipe their mouths. They have finished their meal.*

**Franz**   You like?

**Kath/Holly** (*together*)   Yes, very nice thanks.

**Franz**   You like more beer?

**Kath/Holly** (*together*)   No I 'erm. /No thanks.

**Franz**   Good beer yes?

**Holly**   Yes, very!

**Franz**   People come to Praha now from all world. Make things better! Before revolution (*He shakes his hand.*) ahah! Now good people come. Much tourist, many music, good beer: Pivo. We like Pivo in Praha: best drinking here in world I think! All things change now, before my father cannot go to university. He work all life for Skoda, you know Skoda?

**Kath**   Oh yes!

**Franz**   Now we can go England. I speak good England. I go university many years but run away to mime, my father, how you say, is pulling his head out. But I say, now I can be anything. I just pretend: ah he has a long head! So I go for tour. Goodbye!

**Franz** *picks up his chair, takes back the napkins and exits.*

**Holly** *is very much smitten.*

**Holly**   Oh well!

**Kath**   What?

**Holly**   Don't you think . . .

**Kath**   What?

**Holly**   Well, you know . . . what if something develops?

**Kath**   If anything develops it's every woman for herself.

**Holly**    I mean he's different.

**Kath**    Well he's different to Darren.

*A beat.*

**Holly**    Hey, if they could see us at work.

**Kath**    They'd never believe it. We've been picked up by a mime artist.

**Holly**    And we've only been here two hours.

*A beat.*

**Kath**    Hey, steady you.

**Holly**    What?

**Kath**    I've seen that look on your face before.

**Holly**    What look?

**Kath**    That look you had when Rojinsky started in A and E. That: 'Oh my God look what's just walked in' look.

**Holly**    You had it as well!

**Kath**    The whole hospital had it.

**Franz** *returns with zest.*

**Franz**    So yes I ask my friend to the ghost tour but we miss so I will take . . .

**Kath**    Are you sure, we don't want to . . . ?

**Franz**    In Praha many history, many stories. I take (*Striking the remaining chairs.*) before smog come and we not see too real.

**Franz** *takes the remaining chairs off stage.*

**Kath**    He doesn't give you time to say no, does he?

**Holly**    I don't know what he's on but he's flying.

**Kath**    I'll have a pint of whatever it is any day!

**Franz** *returns with zest.*

**Franz**   So yes, now come, we go!

*Music. Ghost theme.*

*Lights.*

**Franz** *picks up his umbrella and begins to mime walk,* **Holly** *and* **Kath** *fall in line and form a chevron. As* **Franz** *speaks, the eyes on the statues behind them slowly begin to shine, as if they are watching the action. Smog begins to roll up from the Vltava onto the bridge.* **Franz** *begins to play the role of ghost hunter.*

**Franz**   Many ghost on bridge: tonight very good. Smog make bridge very beautiful! King Wenceslas was killed here! Many affairs in Praha, many men jealous and kill, here they die . . . A rich lady, she gives, how you say, counterfeit money? to a beggar, next day she is found with head cut off.

**Kath**   That means don't forget to pay him, Holly!

**Holly**   Is that all true?

**Franz**   All is true, many bad things happen on bridge. Many are tied up and thrown over side! Here you must look . . . I show you!

*Musical sting.*

**Franz** *stops and turns quickly to look upstage towards the statues which have grown more sinister. He jumps on the wall. As he does,* **Mike**, **Kath**'s *dead husband appears from behind a statue. He is decaying, his suit is ripped, dusty and hanging with cobwebs.* **Holly** *screams and* **Kath** *is too shocked to respond.* **Franz** *disappears behind a statue.*

**Kath**   Oh my . . . !

**Holly**   Oh shit . . . !

**Kath**   Oh my God . . . !

**Holly**   Oh shit, this is just . . . !

*Silence.*

**Mike**   Kath!

*A beat.*

**Kath**   Mike?

*A beat.*

**Mike**   What're you doing?

*A beat.*

**Kath**   What are you doing?

*A beat.*

**Mike**   As soon as I'd gone you were off, weren't you?

**Kath**   What?

**Mike**   As soon as I'd gone.

**Kath**   That's not true!

**Mike**   Liar!

*A beat.*

**Holly**   Oh hell, Kath come away . . .

**Mike**   You killed me, Kath!

**Kath**   That's not true!

**Holly**   Kath, come away . . .

**Mike**   You're a liar . . .

**Kath**   You were drinking yourself to death.

**Mike**   I'd lost my job . . .

**Holly** (*outraged*)   This is insane . . .

**Mike**   You killed me!

**Kath**   Don't say that!

**Mike**   You were supposed to be an angel!

**Kath** (*sharp*)   Stop it!

**Mike** . . . Supposed to be an angel!

**Kath** (*louder*)   Stop it!

**Holly** (*unbelieving*)   Kath come away . . . Just come away, where's Franz gone? Kath? Oh shit, oh hell, oh bollocks!

**Mike**   I knew you were seeing somebody.

**Kath**   I wasn't!

**Mike** (*aggressive*)   Liar!

**Holly** (*scared and lost as to what to do*)   Come away, now, oh hell Kath, I think I'm going to pee myself, come away!

**Mike** and **Kath**'s *dialogue becomes argumentative.*

**Mike**   I didn't know what you got up to every night.

**Kath**   I didn't get up to anything.

**Mike**   Always working nights.

**Kath**   To try and help out . . .

**Mike**   You left me.

**Kath**   You were killing me . . .

**Mike**   You weren't there when I needed you!

**Kath**   You were drinking yourself to death!

**Mike** *stands on the wall and looks at the fall in front of him.*

**Mike**   You killed me, Kath, you killed me over and over again. And you've got to live with that!

**Kath**   Mike!

**Mike**   You've got to live with that!

**Mike** *ignores* **Kath** *and jumps from the bridge.* **Holly** *screams and* **Kath** *runs to see where he's gone.* **Franz** *appears from his position and continues his tour.*

**Kath** (*shouts*)   Mike!

**Holly**   Are you okay?

**Kath**   Eh?

**Holly**   Oh shit! I said it was freaky!

**Kath**   Did you see that?

**Holly** (*anxious*)   Of course I bloody did, I nearly pissed myself!

**Kath**   Oh hell!

**Franz** *suddenly appears.*

**Franz**   You like many ghosts yes? St John of Nepomuk was thrown from bridge here after Queen had confessed, but would not tell King confession . . . and so, ohoh! Goodbye!

**Kath**   Dear me . . .

**Franz**   Yes, yes, is good story, many stories on bridge. You like yes?

**Kath** (*lost*)   Yes, yes, very good! A good story.

*A beat.*

**Franz**   Oh you have maybe a sad face . . . Too many ghosts eh? Too many ghosts?

**Kath**   Too many something!

*A beat.*

**Franz**   Okay go shopping?

**Kath**   No, I don't think so . . .

**Franz**   Yes! Yes! Yes! You like shopping . . . ?

**Kath**   Very much!

**Franz**   So we shopping . . . You stay I bring.

**Kath**   No honestly, Franz.

**Franz**   No problem nice ladies, I bring, I show, good shopping, I know will make happy.

**Franz** *exits.* **Kath** *watches him go. She is at a loss of what to think. She sits on the downstage wall.* **Holly** *remains centre.*

**Kath**   Bloody hell, there's no stopping him, is there?

**Holly**   Are you okay?

**Kath**   I feel like I've been kicked in the chest!

**Holly**   I couldn't believe it . . . I'm still shaking!

**Kath** (*anxious*)   Shaking? I can't keep a bloody limb still. I feel sick . . . I don't know if I'm coming or going! You did see him, didn't you?

**Holly**   Yes, yes, I saw him, it was Mike.

**Kath**   I think I'm going mad!

**Holly**   I thought I was going to wet myself. I think being on this bridge doesn't help to be honest!

**Kath**   I don't want to know it honestly, can't you keep some of your bladder movements to yourself. I mean we're supposed to be on holiday and my nerves are shot to bits!

**Franz** *enters carrying several top-brand shoe designers. The carrier bags are from exclusive and expensive styles.*

**Franz**   So we like shopping here for you. Yes. Shoes, shoes, you must take many shoes. All ladies like, I know this! I think this make you happy. I go, see my friend and we make to dance. You stay I return, you try shoes, very good. See you are smiling. Goodbye!

**Franz** *exits.* **Holly** *and* **Kath** *are left with a couple of pairs of shoes each.*

**Holly**   Do you think we should try them?

**Kath**   What's the point, they won't fit us, will they?

**Holly**   No, I didn't think of that!

**Kath** *sits on the downstage wall with her bags surrounding her. She takes out a modern shoe and looks at it. It is a wonderful high-heel, multi-coloured and almost perfect.* **Kath** *is amazed.*

**Kath**  Oh wow, nice though!

**Holly**  Oh nice.

**Kath**  Well, very nice actually . . .

**Holly**  I like the back. Are they Jimmy Choo's?

**Kath**  I don't know whose they are, I can't read what it says!

**Holly**  They are nice.

**Kath**  They're a dress shoe really but he's not done bad!

**Holly**  Yes, I don't think you'd be able to work in them.

**Kath**  Turn a few heads if you did.

**Kath** *looks inside the shoe. She is in awe.* **Holly** *has a pair of her shoes.*

**Kath** (*looking in the shoe*)   Oh hell!

**Holly** (*inspecting her shoes*)   Look at these!

**Kath** (*about* **Holly***'s shoe*)   Oh yes, nice . . . definitely you.

**Holly**  These are great, I think!

**Kath**  Check inside.

**Holly**  Why?

**Kath**  Just check inside.

**Holly**  Eh?

*A beat.*

**Kath** (*amazed*)   They're even the right size!

**Holly** *checks her shoe.*

**Holly**  They're not?

**Kath** (*happy*)   I can't believe this, he's even got the right size!

**Holly**   Oh what?

**Kath**   Mike never knew my shoe size in all the time we were together. Check the other ones.

**Holly** and **Kath** *rummage through the other boxes of shoes, to check the sizes.*

**Holly** (*amazed*)   A four and a half!

**Kath** *investigates her shoes, another outrageously stylish pair.*

**Kath** (*happy*)   Oh my God, a six! A six, a six, fantastic, look at these! Oh look at these, hello Christmas!

**Holly** *investigates her shoes. Both delirious.*

**Holly**   Oh nice! I think I'm in love.

**Kath**   And me, look at these!

**Kath** *holds up the second pair of shoes.*

**Holly**   Not with the shoes, with Franz.

**Kath**   Well if he can shop like that he'll be a dream in Tesco's.

**Holly**   I think I'm falling for him.

**Kath**   I said you'd got that Rojinsky look!

**Holly**   I think I'm falling in love with him.

**Kath**   Yes, but you don't really know him though, do you?

**Holly**   No, but I didn't really know Darren either though, did I? And I didn't really know Tyrone, or Jamel.

**Kath**   And you certainly didn't know Martin.

**Holly**   No, I didn't know Martin! I mean how much do we know anybody?

**Kath**   But what does he do?

**Holly**    I know but I feel as if I've known him all my life, I mean I feel as if I've met him somewhere before.

**Kath**    It's just a holiday romance, Holly, it's even worse than that, it's a Christmas holiday romance.

**Holly**    I have never felt like this about anybody before. Oh shit, I'm that happy I could sing, Kath . . .

**Kath**    Oh don't do that for God's sake or *I'll* wet myself. You can't even hold a tune, you ruined Vicky's party with your singing and now you want to be on bloody *X Factor*!

*Music.*

**Holly** *begins to sing easily. And plays the bridge as the location for a big song. She uses the shoe carriers as she sings.*

**Holly**
It used to be that I'd be dumped
By men time after time.
Some ditched me,
so I ditched them
But now I've met a mime.
Yes, now I've met a mime.

**Kath**    Stop it, come and sit down!

**Holly**
My life won't be the same . . .
Though some say that I'm a fool . . .
But the last laugh is with me
Coz his body is his tool.
Yes, now I've met a mime.
Yes, now I've met a mime.
And these shoes will all be mine.

**Kath**    Holly, pack it in!

**Holly**
He may be blue, he may be Czech,
But our love will know no end!
And although we have no money

At least we can pretend.
Yes, at least we can pretend.

We'll mime ourselves a life style,
We'll mime ourselves a home,
We'll mime ourselves a garden,
A fish pond and a gnome.

And if people think I'm crazy
I stop and tell them all.
If the world was full of men like mine,
We would all have shoes, wall to wall!

*The song stops almost as soon as it started.*

**Kath**   You're not serious about him though, are you?

**Holly**   Anybody who can deliver like this is worth keeping.

**Kath**   Well there is that!

*A beat.*

**Holly**   I mean, I can't understand why you haven't ever met anyone?

**Kath**   Because it's that easy, isn't it?

**Holly**   Well what about Rojinsky?

**Kath**   Are you joking?

**Holly**   Don't you like him?

**Kath**   Rojinsky?

**Holly**   Yes.

**Kath**   Well, he is just about sex on a stick, but unless you haven't noticed, all the nursing staff in the hospital are after him, including you and half the male staff. So I'm well down the list.

**Holly**   That's your trouble, you diss yourself.

**Kath**   I'm not 'dissing' myself, I'm just being realistic.

**Holly**   Listen I know what happened was awful but . . .

**Kath**   And don't even go there.

**Holly**   I know but . . .

**Kath** *stands away from the wall. She is becoming agitated and moves centrally on the bridge.*

**Kath**   I mean, what are we even doing here? No, honestly, I've been thinking, why are we here? I'll tell you why, we're so desperate for a change that we took the first little farting gift that anyone left us.

**Holly**   Well, you could say that . . .

**Kath**   We don't know who, or what, or why!

**Holly**   But that's not the point!

**Kath**   And now we're pretending we're happy when we get a decent pair of shoes.

**Holly**   Well, I am happy.

**Kath**   As if that's going to make things better. Mike's dead, Holly, and there isn't a day that goes by without I think about him, and Christmas is the worst time. A year gone, like that, in a blink! The years get faster and faster, and Prague would be beautiful if it wasn't so depressing.

**Holly**   What's depressing about it?

**Kath**   Beautiful things are always depressing.

**Holly**   Why are they, it doesn't make sense!

**Kath**   Because they always have to end!

**Holly**   Oh please not here. Kath . . .

**Kath**   It's the truth, look at our Emma, fourteen now, I look at her and she makes me sad.

**Holly**   Your Emma's fantastic.

**Kath**   Yes, but one day, she won't be here. One day I won't be there for her!

**Holly**   I'm not listening to any more of this.

**Kath**   I'm only speaking the truth.

**Holly** *is becoming annoyed and animated.*

**Holly**   I don't want the truth. If I'd have wanted the truth I'd have gone to see the lights at Blackpool with my mam and dad and our Colin. If I'd've wanted the truth, Kath, I'd have stayed in A and E in Hull. I've fallen in love with a mime artist, I don't want the friggin' truth!

*Music. Slavic violin.*

**Kath** (*the music*)   What's that?

**Holly**   Listen!

**Franz** *re-enters with a violin. He begins to play. (We hear a pre-recorded version.) The music is mesmerising and haunting. The* **Man** *enters from over the bridge playing another violin.* **Franz** *and the* **Man** *are in concert.*

**Franz**   Yes you like?

**Man**   You like? (*Coughs.*)

**Franz**   Yes, yes you like?

**Holly**   Fantastic!

**Franz**   You try shoes and dance!

**Holly**   Shall I?

**Franz**   Yes, yes! I think so!

**Holly** *quickly puts on a pair of the new shoes and slowly begins to dance to the violin music, deliberate and strong.*

**Holly**   Kath, look at this!

**Franz**   You dance well.

**Kath**   I don't bloody believe this!

**Franz**    Yes we all dance . . .

*Slowly* **Franz**, *the* **Man** *and* **Holly** *start a slow Slavic-style dance routine while still playing their violins. This becomes more and more complicated and effusive as the violin-playing gets more intense. After a while the cast stop miming the violin-playing but continue to dance.* **Franz** *entices* **Kath** *to her feet during the dance.*

*Reluctantly she begins to dance and picks up the steps. The* **Man** *and* **Holly** *clap to encourage* **Kath**, *and before long she is caught up in the dance.*

**Kath**    Oh no, look at this!

**Kath** *is dancing around and around. As she does this from upstage behind one of the statues* **Keith** *appears. He seems changed, wearing a suave jacket and slacks. He looks at* **Kath** *and watches her dance. He stands on the wall to watch the dancing.* **Kath** *notices him standing on the wall. She stops dancing and the music stops, as* **Franz**, **Holly** *and the* **Man** *run away.* **Keith** *looks very attractive.*

*Silence.*

**Keith**    Is it Kath?

**Kath**    Keith? What the bloody hell are you doing here?

*Music plays wildly as the lights fade to blackout.*

# Act Three

*Music.*

*Lights.*

**Kath** *and* **Keith** *are on the bridge.* **Keith** *is easy and charming.* **Kath** *can only just believe she is having this conversation with him. She still has her bags of shoes and her mood is slightly brighter.* **Keith** *wanders around on the bridge looking over the upstage edge.* **Kath** *is sitting on the wall downstage.*

**Kath**  So what *are* you doing here, Keith?

**Keith**  Me? This and that.

**Kath**  Meaning?

**Keith**  I'm doing a bit of teaching at the moment. But I want to write: a novel, maybe a film!

**Kath**  What sort of teaching is it, then?

**Keith**  At the Open University.

*A beat.*

**Kath**  Oh right, so are you based in Prague or . . . ?

**Keith**  No, I'm based in York.

**Kath**  So how come you're here . . . ?

**Keith**  I've brought some students, we're doing a unit on Kakfa and the modern Europeans.

**Kath**  Who?

**Keith**  Franz Kafka?

**Kath**  Never heard of him.

**Keith**  Don't you know *The Trial*, or *The Castle*?

**Kath**  Ask me one about sport!

**Keith**  What about *Metamorphosis*?

**Kath**   No!

**Keith**   It's about a man who woke up to discover he'd been turned into a giant beetle.

**Kath**   It's not a comedy, is it?

**Keith**   Have you never read it?

**Kath**   Did they make it into a film?

**Keith**   His work was banned under the communist regime and erm . . .

**Kath**   Well, there's no wonder if he was writing about people turning into beetles. Did he ever work for the NHS?

**Keith**   Well he wrote about institutions.

**Kath**   Hey, I know a lot about that. I work in one. We're all just a number, Keith.

**Keith**   It's getting that way.

**Kath**   Yeh, but you try and tell that to someone who's waiting for a hospital bed.

**Keith**   Or whose X-rays are lost in the system eh?

*A beat.*

**Keith** *drifts around the bridge.* **Kath** *is fascinated by him.*

**Kath**   The last I heard about you was that you'd walked out of your job after assaulting one of the druggies.

**Keith**   Steven Chiko.

**Kath**   And that nobody knew what you were doing.

**Keith**   Well, I was studying part-time.

**Kath**   I knew that you were doing something but I never asked what.

**Keith**   And then this job in York came up!

**Kath**   It must have happened so quickly.

**Keith**   Oh yes, there was no messing about.

**Kath**   And it's so different.

**Keith**   Well, it was a bit real for me, do you know what I mean?

**Kath**   What was?

**Keith**   Working at the hospital. It was a bit too much like 'real life'!

*A beat.*

**Kath**   Oh yes, it is a bit like real life, Keith.

**Keith**   Yes, it was a bit too real for me though!

**Kath**   That's one of the drawbacks!

**Keith**   Too many people die in real life.

**Kath**   They do!

**Keith**   In literature they can come back to life . . .

**Kath**   Is that the attraction?

**Keith**   One of them!

*A beat.*

**Kath**   I suppose it's a lot different to standing in A and E letting your mind wander?

**Keith**   No, it's the same to be honest, but the hours are better.

**Kath**   I suppose that's what you were wondering about?

**Keith**   What's that?

**Kath**   How to get out of that job!

**Keith**   I don't know how you stand it.

*A beat.*

**Kath**   No, I don't sometimes!

*A lighter tone to the conversation.*

**Keith**    And now I'm here, asking whether culture cultivates.

**Kath**    And does it?

**Keith**    I hope so. I've based a term's work on it. I've got eight students looking into it, we're just here for a few days.

**Kath**    We've got one night . . . Me and Holly!

**Keith**    Have you come for the Christmas market?

**Kath**    Well we haven't got off the bridge yet, we've been here three hours, and she's just run off, so it's all a bit erm . . .

**Keith** *has another look around the bridge.*

**Keith**    Well there's some history here, Kath!

**Kath**    Oh I know that.

**Keith**    Yes?

**Kath**    Oh yes, it's been a hell of a day so far.

**Keith**    Oh right!

**Kath**    You wouldn't believe it.

**Keith**    And it's far from over.

*A beat.*

**Kath** (*almost to herself*)    Yes, that's what worries me!

*A beat.*

**Keith**    So what is it, Holly's hen do?

**Kath**    It might well be the way things are going. No, it's actually a gift.

**Keith**    From who?

**Kath**    We don't know!

*A beat.*

**Keith**   You mean you've come here and you've no idea who's paid for you?

*A beat.*

That's a bit random isn't it?

**Kath**   It is, but with one thing and another we thought we deserved a break . . .

**Keith**   But you've got a clue though?

**Kath**   We've got an idea but . . .

**Keith**   It'll be a consultant!

**Kath**   Oh don't you start.

**Keith**   Well, wasn't there some consultant at work?

**Kath**   I don't know where this has come from. Everybody in the damn hospital thinks he's gorgeous and I'm the one who's supposed to be having an affair with him! Chance would be a fine thing.

**Keith**   What was his name?

**Kath**   Do you mean Rojinsky?

**Keith**   That's the one!

**Kath**   I had some reference numbers left in my stuff so we just decided to go for it, no matter what: came by Easy Jet.

**Keith**   Cheap tickets!

**Kath**   You cheeky sod!

**Keith**   Hey, we came by Easy Jet, don't knock it!

*A beat.*

**Kath**   The truth is we don't know who paid for them, but beggars can't be choosers.

**Keith**   Well somebody's smiling on you.

**Kath**    For once.

*A beat.*

**Keith**    Father Christmas maybe?

**Kath**    I'm not bothered who it is, to be honest, I just needed to get away this Christmas.

**Keith**    So it could be Father Christmas?

**Kath**    You never know.

**Keith**    Do you still believe in him?

**Kath**    Who, Father Christmas? I don't know, do you?

**Keith**    Yes I do! I believe in him, I put a letter up the chimney and everything.

**Kath**    Christmas is for the kids, Keith, it's not the same when you grow up.

*A beat.*

**Keith**    What's so good about growing up anyway?

**Kath**    Nothing!

**Keith**    Dead right.

*A beat.*

**Kath**    I don't know what to believe in any more, to be honest!

*A beat.*

**Keith**    Well, when I was twelve everybody at our school kept telling me that there was no Father Christmas, so I went home and asked my dad. My dad usually told it how it was. He'd worked on the railways all his life, called a spade a spade. Big tough hairy-arsed bloke! He just came out with it: 'There isn't a Father Christmas, Keith!' I was gutted, but then he said: 'But I think that it's such a good idea, I still pretend that there is one!' So I thought that'll do for me. And I'm still pretending there is one.

*A beat.*

**Kath**    You know what, I think that's the best answer I've ever heard.

**Keith**    It was the best answer I'd ever heard so I've stuck with it!

*A beat.*

**Kath**    I can't believe how much you've changed.

**Keith**    Me?

**Kath**    Yes!

**Keith**    I haven't!

**Kath**    Are you joking?

**Keith**    I'm just the same.

**Kath**    Keith, you're almost unrecognisable.

*A beat.*

**Keith**    You should never judge a book by its cover.

**Kath**    Oh here we go, getting smart, don't come all intellectual with me, Keith, it'll make me feel bad.

**Keith**    Hey come on, you're not thick.

**Kath**    I sometimes wonder!

*A beat.*

**Keith**    Well, you never saw me without my uniform.

**Kath**    Is that an offer?

**Keith**    You know what I mean!

**Kath**    I did, at Vicky's party.

**Keith**    Yes, but you never spoke to me. I mean you looked at the consultants.

**Kath**    Oh here we go!

**Keith**    All you saw was a bloke in a uniform.

*A beat.*

**Kath** (*considering*)    Yes you're right, I did. I never bothered to see the person Keith.

**Kath** and **Keith** *look at each other.* **Keith** *breaks the spell by coming to the downstage wall and standing on it.*

**Keith**    What a bridge eh?

**Kath**    Don't jump!

**Keith** *is on the wall.*

**Keith**    Over five hundred metres long!

**Kath**    I feel like I've been up and down it a hundred times already.

**Keith**    Change your shoes.

**Kath**    No, I'm saving these . . .

**Kath** *has another look at her shoe bags.*

**Keith**    You've been shopping then?

**Kath**    Well, it's a long story.

**Keith** *is changing mood.*

**Keith**    Anyway I always thought that there was something going on with you and Alan . . . He was always going on about it.

**Kath**    Who?

**Keith**    Alan?

**Kath**    Which Alan?

**Keith**    You know, Alan!

**Kath**    Alan?

**Keith**    Alan!

*A beat.*

**Kath**    You mean Fat Alan?

**Keith**    Who?

**Kath**    Fat Alan?

**Keith**    Which one's Fat Alan?

**Kath**    The fat one!

**Keith**    I didn't know him as the fat Alan, I just knew him as Alan!

**Kath**    Do you mean Ambulance Alan?

**Keith**    Yes, that's him.

**Kath**    Oh that's Fat Alan!

**Keith**    Is it?

**Kath**    There's Fat Alan, that's him, Ambulance Alan, and then there's Alan in X-ray – he's just Alan, and then there's Thin Alan who works in Pharmacy! And then there's Odd Alan who's a porter, I think he's got problems to be honest, and then there's Sweaty Alan who works at the security control but we don't see a lot of him.

**Keith**    Thankfully.

**Kath**    That's right.

*A beat.*

It's a thing that me and Holly have got.

**Keith**    What, naming Alans?

**Kath**    No, naming everybody.

**Keith**    Sounds like a big job.

**Kath**    Everybody in the hospital's got a nickname.

**Keith**    That is a big job.

*A beat.*

**Kath**   Like Mr McDonald, do you remember him?

**Keith**   Wasn't he the stomach bloke?

**Kath**   Yes, well, he's called Mr Poppadam!

**Keith**   Why?

**Kath**   Well, he likes curries.

**Keith**   But there was only one Mr McDonald, wasn't there?

**Kath**   Yes and there's only one Mr Poppadam.

**Keith**   It doesn't make any sense though.

**Kath**   Fat Alan does.

**Keith**   Yes, fat Alan does.

**Kath**   You've got to have something to think about at work. Do you remember Vladimir Belkowski?

**Keith**   No!

**Kath**   The anaesthetist?

**Keith**   No, I never met him.

**Kath**   Well, we call him Mr Sleep!

**Keith**   Well, that's a bit obvious, isn't it?

**Kath**   Well, it's got nothing to do with what he does. Have you ever spoken to him?

**Keith** (*lightly*)   Well no, I never met him.

**Kath** (*friendly*)   Oh yes, sorry.

*A beat.*

**Keith**   So what about me then?

**Kath**   What?

**Keith**   Did you have a nickname for me?

**Kath**   Of course we did!

*A beat.*

**Keith**   Well what was it then?

**Kath**   Are you sure you want to know?

*A beat.*

**Keith**   Do you think I should?

*A beat.*

**Kath**   Well, there were three Keiths, weren't there, when you worked there. Fat Keith, who works in the kitchens.

**Keith**   Oh yes!

**Kath**   Tall Keith, he's a consultant.

**Keith**   Was that Mr Keith?

**Kath**   That's right, and you were erm . . .

**Keith**   What?

**Kath**   You were . . .

**Keith**   Go on!

**Kath**   . . . Scary Keith!

*A beat.*

**Keith**   Eh?

**Kath**   Yes!

**Keith**   Scary Keith?

**Kath**   Well, you were.

*A beat.*

**Keith**   Scary Keith?

**Kath**   I mean you've changed but . . . !

**Keith**   Scary Keith?

**Kath**   It was just a nickname!

**Keith**    And it was going so well . . .

**Kath**    Well, you asked me!

*A beat.*

**Keith**    Scary Keith?

**Kath**    Well, you had to have a name.

**Keith**    Yes, but did I have to have that one?

**Kath**    We couldn't think of any other.

*A beat.*

**Keith**    Scary Keith?

**Kath**    Well you had to be, doing that job! In a way it's a compliment!

**Keith**    What?

**Kath**    In a way.

**Keith**    Calling me Scary Keith was a compliment?

**Kath**    Well, it was!

*A beat.*

**Keith**    I think I would have preferred Fat Keith to be honest!

**Kath**    Oh no, you're never Fat Keith, you're too thin for Fat Keith, and you're a bit too short for Tall Keith.

**Keith**    Yes, he was tall.

**Kath**    Tall Keith is ever so tall it's almost not natural how tall he is.

**Keith**    Scary Keith though?

*A beat.*

**Kath**    Well, you were scary, Keith.

*A beat.*

In fact we used to say, if a patient wasn't critical in the ambulance they would be by the time they'd seen you.

**Keith** (*amazed*)  I can't believe this!

**Kath**  You were the last thing anyone wanted to see when they arrived at hospital. Enough to scare you to death!

**Keith**  And for two years on and off you called me that behind my back?

**Kath**  Well, we couldn't call you it to your face, could we? That would have been good, 'Hello Scary Keith, have you seen Fat Alan? Yes he's talking to Slutty Jenny on reception and Mr Poppadam's on tonight because Mr Sleep's got the shits.'

*A beat.*

**Keith**  No, fair enough!

**Kath**  Anyway, now you're completely different!

*A beat.*

**Keith**  You never wanted to know me then, and now I know why. Even at Vicky's birthday you body-swerved me and danced with Alan.

**Kath**  You mean Fat Alan?

**Keith**  Does he know what you call him?

**Kath**  I hope not!

**Keith**  I mean that was scary, watching him dance: nearly had somebody's eye out.

**Kath**  Yes, mine!

*A beat.*

**Keith**  Scary Keith, I can't believe it!

*There is magic abroad,* **Keith** *and* **Kath** *are bonding. A small whiff of smog crawls onto the bridge.*

**Kath**   Oh the smog's coming in again and I've no idea where Holly is and she'll never find me!

**Keith**   Smog, perfect for Scary Keith . . .

**Kath**   She's found herself a mime artist, so she might get up to all sorts . . . I just hope she's all right, she's never been out of Hull.

*Music. Puppet theme (sub organ-grinder genre).*

**Hans** *enters from nowhere through the smog. He pushes on a large puppet cart which is old but colourful, grotesque and has huge wheels.* **Hans** *is the puppet master and is dressed accordingly, in outlandishly theatrical costume, which resembles something of an old toy soldier.* **Kath** *and* **Keith** *are suspicious of this.*

**Hans**   Oh yes, very nice peoples. You like nice peoples English?

**Keith**   English yes!

**Hans**   For you, yes in love?

**Keith** (*attempting to correct*)   Oh no . . .

**Hans**   Yes, yes, can tell in love. You like we do show ladies?

**Kath** (*resigned*)   Why not?

**Hans**   Yes, why not, this is good, why not, nice ladies and gentlemens! Sit please yes, to sit please. I no charge you to pay okay . . .

**Hans** *positions the puppet theatre upstage centre.* **Kath** *and* **Keith** *take seats on the downstage wall.* **Kath** *and* **Keith** *nod their approval.* **Hans** *launches into his routine.*

**Hans**   Here tonight famous puppet show! So like life you be amazed. Have been good? If been good get present, if not go to devil and die horrible death! Here for you in Prague tonight nice ladies and gentlemens, I give to you Mik and Kit very good; but at Michaelmas, maybe they very bad. Maybe they story of Christmas, not so good. Okay I give you, Mik and Kit!

*Music plays under the routine. The puppet master pulls open the curtains to reveal* **Mik**, *a clown with a blue face, red nose and a sinister look, and* **Kit** *who has a white face and a wedding headdress with flowers. They are life-size puppets hanging from the roof of the puppet cart with string. The puppet master disappears upstage.* **Mik** *and* **Kit** *make robotic actions with each line and smile inanely at whatever they say.*

**Mik**    Every Christmas it's the same.

**Kit**    Going through the old routine.

**Mik**    Basting chicken . . .

**Kit**    Stuffing birds.

**Mik**    Struggling hard . . .

**Kit**    To find nice words.

*Building tension.*

**Mik**    Me at her.

**Kit**    Him at me.

**Mik**    Me at her!

**Kit**    Him at me!

**Mik**    We watch the Queen . . .

**Kit**    On ITV.

**Mik**    Spending money.

**Kit**    Credit shame!

**Mik**    Nothing left . . .

**Kit**    We take no blame.

*Building tension.*

**Mik**    Me at her.

**Kit**   Me at him.

**Mik**   Me at her.

**Kit**   Me at him.

**Mik**   We have to take it on the chin!

*Happier.*

**Kit**   Oh it's Christmas!

**Mik**   Oh it's Christmas!

**Kit**   Chance to eat and drink . . .

**Mik**   And cook.

**Kit**   Oh it's Christmas!

**Mik**   Oh it's Christmas!

**Kit**   Waiting for my . . .

**Mik**   Annual fuck!

**Kit** *picks up a small blouse and looks at it.*

**Kit**   Oh that's nice!

**Mik**   Just what I wanted.

**Kit**   How did you know I wanted that?

**Mik**   Just what I wanted.

**Kit**   When will I wear it, you useless twat?

*Not responding.*

**Mik**   And at work, the Christmas do!

**Kit**   Another nightmare to get through.

**Mik**   All those people . . .

**Kit**   That we hate.

**Mik**   Saying the party . . .

**Kit**   Has been great!

**Mik**    And back at home.

**Kit**    At the kitchen sink.

**Mik**    Gagging for another drink.

**Kit**    Don't have another . . .

**Mik**    She does scream.

**Kit**    But stop myself . . .

**Mik**    I cannot seem.

**Kit**    Then the red mist descends.

**Mik**    Looks like a man . . .

**Kit**    With nitrogen bends.

**Mik**    And hateful bile . . .

**Kit**    Fills his eyes.

**Mik**    I shout and scream . . .

**Kit**    Rage and rally.

**Mik**    Can even hear me . . .

**Kit**    Down the alley.

*Calling out.*

**Mik**    Keep the noise down!

**Kit**    Keep the noise down!

**Mik**    They shout and scream just like that.

**Kit**    He say 'It's . . .

**Mik**    Christmas, Mrs Macgregor. Don't be such a miserable twat!'

*Happier now.*

**Mik**    Oh it's Christmas.

**Kit**    Oh it's Christmas.

**Mik**    We must be nice to all mankind.

**Kit**    Oh it's Christmas.

**Mik**    Oh it's Christmas.

**Kit**    He's drunk so much . . .

**Mik**    I'm going blind.

*Darker.* **Mik** *hits* **Kit**.

**Kit**    And now the beer has taken hold.

**Mik**    I bash her head for talking back.

**Kit**    That'll teach me, he keeps saying!

**Mik**    And then she gets another crack!

**Kit**    Give it a rest . . .

**Mik**    Give it a rest . . .

**Kit**    Oh you merry gentlemen.

**Mik**    Give it a rest . . .

**Kit**    Give it a rest . . .

**Mik**    He beats me till I won't survive.

**Kit**    Give it a rest . . .

**Mik**    She keeps on calling . . .

**Hans** *now appears with the puppets but wearing a policeman's helmet.*

**Hans**
But just then the police arrive.
Now what's the problem?
What's been happening?
Chimes along this PC Plod!

**Kit**
He's trying to kill me.
Now you've saved me!

You've saved my life.
Oh thank God!

**Hans**
Just doing my duty,
Playing my part,
There's no need to thank me!

**Hans** *disappears from the show.*

**Mik**    And then he's gone.

**Kit**    He's disappeared.

**Mik**    And we end up in A and E!

**Kit**    He's so drunk.

**Mik**    And she starts crying . . .

**Kit**    Whilst all around . . .

**Mik**    There's people dying.

**Kit**    We sit and wait.

**Mik**    We wait in line.

**Kit**    The nurses say . . .

**Mik**    We're wasting time.

**Kit**    My head still bleeds.

**Mik**    My fists are red.

**Kit**    They stick a plaster to my head.

**Mik** *sticks a plaster to* **Kit**'s *head.*

*Softer, touching.*

**Mik**    And I love her.

**Kit**    And she loves me!

**Mik**    And that's the tale.

**Kit**    Our Christmas story.

**Mik**    And Christmas cheer . . .

**Kit**    To you we send.

**Mik**    Now we're off . . .

**Kit**    To drown our sorrows.

**Mik**    We're heading home.

**Kit**    It is the end!

**Mik** *and* **Kit** *draw the curtains and the puppet show comes to an abrupt end.* **Hans** *appears around the side of the puppet show.*

**Hans**    You like good Christmas story, you hear before?

**Kath**    Yes, I'm afraid we've heard that before!

**Hans**    Is what call, all the world has same!

**Keith**    Universal.

**Hans**    Sorry if offend. Puppets in Praha have life of own but never get bad head with Pivo! Ha, ha you like, you like? Puppet never get bad head! I go now, I give you show for free my present for you. Goodbye!

*A musical sting gets the puppet cart and* **Hans** *off stage.* **Kath** *and* **Keith** *come centre stage.* **Kath** *has her bags.*

**Kath**    Is it really the same all over the world, Keith?

**Keith**    The same as what?

**Kath**    People just getting out of their heads for any reason.

**Keith**    I think it probably is.

*A beat.*

**Kath**    Why does everything always turn bad? I like happy endings.

**Keith**    Well, you've got to dream them.

**Kath**    Is that what you did, dream a happy ending?

**Keith**   Well, I couldn't stand watching the waste, every night. Not so much the young, pissed up, drugged up . . . beaten up . . . pregnant . . . It was the old women who'd had heart attacks and had never been anywhere. Lived a life from an estate and never wanted to go off it, for fear of feeling out of place, or thinking it wasn't for them. Or blokes who'd worked hard all their lives with nothing in a pension plan, worried to a stroke about kids chucking stuff through their windows. A health service struggling, people like you trying to help, and people treating you like shit, I couldn't stand watching that . . .

**Kath**   They're not all like that!

**Keith**   Of course not, but too many are, otherwise I wouldn't have had a job!

*A beat.*

**Kath**   Yeh well . . .

**Kath**   And for two years I was a laughing stock on that course. But I met a woman from Halifax who was eighty-six, doing a degree in maths, and I met a bloke from Hull who worked on the bins, just starting out on his education at forty-two! I saw a chance for me to change.

*A beat.*

**Kath**   I don't think I could change now, in fact I don't know if I'd even want to.

*A beat.*

But you're right though, you can get too close to people and before you know it, you're involved.

*Silence.*

**Keith**   Yes, we're just a bag of chemicals.

*A beat.*

**Kath**   You see, I wish I'd said that, that's clever.

**Keith**    Words, Kath, just words.

**Kath**    You can do a lot with words.

**Keith**    You can!

*A beat.*

**Kath**    But you can't bring anybody back . . .

**Keith**    Not in real life you can't!

**Kath** *is confused by her feelings.*

**Kath**    Oh dear this is all a bit of a surprise.

**Keith**    Is it?

**Kath**    I mean it's almost romantic.

**Keith**    Yes, all we need is music.

**Kath**    That would be nice.

**Keith**    Be careful what you wish for.

*Music. Love theme plays softly under.*

I never mentioned it before but . . .

**Kath**    What?

**Keith**    Well, you always imagine it's going to be a lot easier.

**Kath**    Imagine what?

**Keith**    I always liked you.

**Kath**    Did you?

**Keith**    I had a thing about you for years. When you lost Mike, I didn't know what to say. I wanted to be there for you but I didn't know what to say! And I didn't think you wanted to hear anything from me, you hardly knew my name anyway.

*A beat.*

**Kath** *is moved, she can hardly take much more of this in.*

**Kath** *(reflective)*   I don't know, Prague at Christmas, is there anywhere any more beautiful?

*A beat.*

**Keith**   What about Hull?

*A beat.*

**Kath**   Well . . .

**Keith**   There is beauty there.

**Kath**   Not like here.

**Keith**   You just don't see it, too busy living life.

**Kath**   Too busy running away from it, Keith.

*A beat.*

I erm . . .

**Keith**   What?

**Kath**   I'm glad we've met. I'm glad we've met up again.

*A beat. Things are certainly beginning to develop between* **Kath** *and* **Keith**.

**Keith**   Shit, I better go and see the students.

**Kath**   Oh right . . .

**Keith**   I've got to go and meet up and tell them what's happening later tonight.

**Kath**   And what is happening?

**Keith**   Well?

**Kath**   Because . . .

*A beat.*

**Keith**   Well, I was going to take them up to the castle . . .

**Kath**   Well, can't they go on their own?

*A beat.*

**Keith**   Well, they are old enough!

**Kath**   Well, that's good then.

*A beat.*

**Keith**   I'm sure they could.

**Kath**   Well, I just thought it would be nice to see the rest of Prague, and not just this bridge . . .

*A beat.*

**Keith**   Well, why don't I go and tell them, and you wait here? Will you be okay?

**Kath**   On a bridge on my own at night in the middle of Prague? What could possibly happen?

**Keith**   Anything!

**Kath**   Just don't be long!

**Keith**   I'll be as quick as I can.

**Kath**   Before the smog rolls back in.

**Keith** *exits.*

**Kath** *is left alone on the bridge. She is happy for the first time in a long time. She investigates her shoes again as smog rolls over the back wall of the bridge.* **Mike**'s *theme is played low. The eyes in the statues begin to glow once more.*

*Silence.*

**Kath** *is very still, suddenly she is chilled. She senses someone else is on the bridge. She moves downstage.*

**Kath** *(shouts)*   Mike! (*Loudly.*) Is there anybody there? (*Louder.*) Mike? Hello? (*Loudly.*) Hello!

**Mike** *enters amid the smog upstage. He is much smarter now, dressed in what would have been his wedding suit. It is smart but still decaying* *and stressed, though he looks quite good for a dead guy.* **Kath** *is extremely frightened.*

**Mike**    Don't ever forget me.

**Kath**    Mike?

**Mike**    Coz you weren't there for me . . .

**Kath**    I didn't know what to do!

**Mike**    You weren't there for me . . .

**Kath**    Why did you do it?

**Mike**    It was a mistake, Kath.

**Kath**    Eh?

**Mike**    I wanted you to save me.

**Kath**    Please listen . . .

**Mike**    But you worked over.

**Kath**    We were short-staffed. There'd been cut-backs . . .

**Mike**    I needed you to help me . . .

**Kath** *is in tears.*

**Kath**    I am so sorry, Mike . . . I am so, so sorry!

**Kath** *and* **Mike** *hang in space. It is unbearably tender.*

**Mike**    Don't ever forget me, Kath . . .

**Kath**    How can I?

**Mike**    Don't ever let me go!

**Kath**    I can't let you go!

*Musical sting.* **Mike**'s *theme plays as* **Mike** *slowly pulls away from* **Kath**. *She is emotionally torn.*

**Kath**    Mike? Mike! (*Shouting.*) Mike?

*The atmosphere is broken by* **Holly**'s *shrill voice. She enters carrying her carrier bags and balancing on her shoes.*

**Holly** (*from off*)  Oh you're here . . .

**Kath**  Where the bleeding hell have you been?

**Holly**  Where've you been?

**Kath**  You just ran off.

**Holly**  Oh it's Franz, he's crazy!

**Kath**  I thought you might have come back to the bridge.

**Holly**  I did come back to the bridge.

*She points.*

I came back to that bridge!

**Kath**  I meant this bridge, you dodo.

**Holly**  Well I didn't know there were so many bridges. I've been worried sick. We were waiting for you to come us.

**Kath**  I didn't know where you'd gone!

**Holly**  We went busking: it was a great laugh! Anyway if we got lucky every man for himself you said!

**Kath**  I didn't expect it to happen so quick.

**Holly**  I said to Franz, if you got lost should you go to the police, but he said they wouldn't do anything much so . . .

**Kath**  Well that's reassuring!

**Holly**  He said they'd probably lock you up and put your bail up!

**Kath**  For being lost?

**Holly**  For doing anything. He says people go missing here all the time and they end up working in brothels or picking bananas.

**Kath**  Spot the difference!

**Holly**  We're in like a jazz club. He's still there with some of his theatre mates.

**Kath**   Are they miming getting drunk?

**Holly**   Have you been here on your own all the time?

**Kath**   No, I bloody haven't!

**Holly**   Oh well, that's good then.

**Kath**   Is it?

**Holly**   Well I mean . . .

**Kath**   Luckily enough, I met somebody just after you'd gone.

**Holly**   What, somebody you knew here?

**Kath**   Yes, here. Don't sound so surprised.

**Holly**   It isn't that bloke from the hotel with the sad eyes, is it?

**Kath**   No, funnily enough!

**Holly**   Hey, I'm dreading going back there.

**Kath**   Well, I'll have to be drunk to sleep in that prison, I will, honest.

*A beat.*

**Holly**   So who've you met then?

**Kath**   Do you remember Keith?

**Holly**   Eh?

**Kath**   Keith?

**Holly**   Keith who . . . ?

**Kath**   You know Keith, from the hospital.

**Holly**   Which Keith from the hospital? Mr Keith?

**Kath**   No, not Mr Keith.

**Holly**   Not Fat Keith?

**Kath**   (*nervously*)   No, not Fat Keith no.

**Holly**    You've not met Sweaty Keith, have you?

**Kath**    Hey, do me a favour!

**Holly**    Well which Keith have you met then?

**Kath**    Can't you remember him?

**Holly**    Which other Keith was there?

**Kath**    Well, there was another Keith wasn't there, who left.

*A beat.*

**Holly**    Not Scary Keith?

**Kath**    Well yes . . .

**Holly**    What?

**Kath**    I've been chatting to him. Only he's . . .

**Holly**    Scary Keith's here?

**Kath**    Well . . .

**Holly**    What, here in Prague?

**Kath**    Yes, he is but . . .

**Holly**    What the friggin' hell is he doing here?

**Kath**    He's on a course.

**Holly**    For stalkers?

**Kath**    Hey listen . . .

**Holly**    Scary Keith's in Prague and you've met him on your own?

**Kath**    Holly, listen . . .

**Holly**    I mean seeing your dead husband is bad enough, Kath, but meeting scary Keith is just plain dangerous, he'll bore you to death with his wanderings-off!

**Kath**    He's changed.

**Holly**   Into what?

**Kath**   Oh be serious.

**Holly**   I am being serious.

**Kath**   I don't know, he's just different.

**Holly**   That's what makes him scary, coz he is so friggin' different!

**Kath**   He's here for the weekend, and suddenly we've just clicked.

**Holly**   Clicked or cracked?

*A beat.*

**Kath**   Well, to be honest, I think I'm developing a thing about him.

*A beat.*

**Holly** (*outraged*)   Holy shit!

**Kath**   I know.

**Holly**   Holy shit.

**Kath**   I can't help it!

**Holly**   We are friggin' doomed.

**Kath**   He's fantastic!

**Holly** (*frightened*)   I said this: I said we should have never come!

**Kath**   He's funny, kind!

**Holly**   Kind?

**Kath**   Intelligent!

**Holly**   He'd slit your throat for a quid!

**Kath**   I looked but I couldn't see him before, that's what he said.

**Holly**   He's an absolute fascist!

**Keith**   We judge too much by appearances.

**Holly**   This is an absolute nightmare . . .

**Kath**   It's not, he's taking me up to the castle . . .

**Holly** (*shouting*)   Yes, to murder you!

**Kath** (*shouting*)   No, to tell me about it!

**Holly** (*shouting*)   And then to murder you!

**Kath**   You don't know him!

**Holly**   Kath, Scary Keith is scary, that's why we called him Scary Keith and not Pleasant Keith or Sexy Keith. It's like Fat Alan, we called Fat Alan Fat Alan because he's not a size eight. Why couldn't you meet somebody normal?

**Kath**   Oh listen who's talking. Well at least mine hasn't got a blue face.

*A beat.*

**Holly**   Oh I knew you'd have to get personal!

**Kath**   Well, you haven't seen him!

**Holly**   I don't need to, Scary Keith will always be . . .

**Keith** *enters.*

**Holly** *sees him sharply and screams.*

*Silence.*

**Holly**   Keith?

*A beat.*

**Keith**   Hi!

*A beat.*

**Holly** *laughs.*

**Keith**   How are you?

*A beat.*

**Holly**   Who, me?

**Keith**   Yes?

**Holly** *laughs.*

**Keith**   You okay?

**Holly** *laughs.*

**Keith**   Great!

*A beat.*

**Holly** *is smitten by* **Keith**.

**Holly**   So how are you, Keith?

**Kath**   I thought you had a jazz club to go to?

**Holly**   Oh there's no rush!

**Kath** (*suggesting*)   Well, won't Franz be waiting for you?

**Holly**   Eh? Oh yes . . . well, he can wait a bit longer . . .

**Keith**   I like your shoes!

**Holly** (*flattered*)   Oh do you, thanks a lot . . . They just fit on my feet, you know like at the end of my legs.

**Keith**   Yes, I can see that!

*A beat.*

**Kath**   Right well, we don't want to keep you any longer so . . .

**Holly**   Oh it's no problem.

**Kath**   Yes it is!

*A beat.*

**Holly**   Oh right well, I'll get off then. We're at a jazz club. Drop in if you . . .

**Keith**   Well, I think we're going to have a bit of a saunter up to the castle . . .

**Holly**   Oh yes, that'll be romantic.

**Kath** (*almost to herself*)   With a bit of luck!

*A beat.*

**Holly**   Feels like we've been here ages, we haven't been here one night yet.

**Keith**   Prague grows on you.

**Holly** (*loaded*)   Yes, I can see that.

**Kath** (*suggesting she goes*)   Anyway . . .

*A beat.*

**Holly**   I'll see you back at the prison cell, shall I? If I'm not there don't worry . . . Franz will have mimed something up!

**Kath**   Yes, if you're not there I'll have your gruel.

*A beat.*

**Holly**   So, see you then, Keith.

**Keith**   Take it steady.

**Kath**   You going then?

**Holly**   I can stop if you want.

**Kath**   I don't want!

*A beat.*

**Holly**   Right, I'll go then!

**Holly** *exits in her high heels. There is a moment between* **Kath** *and* **Keith**. **Kath** *collects her bags and stands.*

**Kath**   She's smitten with a mime artist who paints himself blue. I just hope he doesn't mime everything or she will be disappointed.

*A beat.*

To tell the truth it's been a funny night, Keith. I don't know how much more I can take.

**Keith**   Yes and we'll catch our death if we stay on here much longer.

*A beat.* **Kath** *drifts on the bridge.*

**Kath**   I don't know what it is about this bridge but I have this overwhelming desire to kiss you, Keith!

*A beat.*

**Keith**   Oh right!

*A beat.*

**Kath**   In fact, I'd like to kiss you all over!

**Keith**   Oh right!

*A beat.*

**Kath**   Would you mind that?

*A beat.*

**Keith**   Well, I think we should start with the lips and see how we get on!

*A beat.*

**Kath**   I mean, after all it is Christmas, isn't it?

**Keith**   Yes. It is Christmas!

*A beat.*

**Kath**   So I wondered if you'd mind?

**Keith**   We don't have any mistletoe though.

**Kath**   We don't need mistletoe for what I've got in mind, Keith.

**Keith**   Don't we?

**Kath** *moves slowly towards* **Keith**. *She still has her shoe bags with her.* **Keith** *and* **Kath** *stand together. She slowly puts the bags down.*

**Kath**    That's it then.

**Keith**    The bags are down.

**Kath**    The shoes are off!

*A beat.*

I just can't believe how much you've changed!

**Keith**    Neither can I!

*Music plays under.*

**Kath** *and* **Keith** *kiss. It is very gentle and very touching.* **Kath** *pulls away.*

**Kath**    Merry Christmas, Keith!

*A beat.*

**Keith**    Merry Christmas, Kath.

**Franz** *appears behind a statue upstage. Eyes light up and watch the action, smog rolls onto the bridge from the Vltava.* **Franz** *with his violin stands on the bridge wall and calls to* **Kath** *and* **Keith**.

**Franz**    Yes, come we go! We wait for you in jazz club. So much to see good disco techno bars yes! Good beer. Come, come we go. Yes, yes, romantic bridge we know, but so much to see only little time. Must come back yes?

**Kath** *and* **Keith** *collect the bags and drift off the bridge.* **Franz** *watches as they do. He then notices the audience, and freezes in his mime style.*

**Franz**    Okay yes you like? Good tour on bridge many ghost! Very good smog tonight many things can happen! Bridge at night very, how you say, scary place? Is very scary place for me at night; no like much on my self! No one like cross bridge at night, can hear the dead yes, can hear dead sing, many think is beautiful. I think they cuckoo! Yes, yes cuckoo! You understand cuckoo? I go castle tour with you tomorrow, tonight we drink and good times with new England friends!

*Snow flakes begin to fall.* **Franz** *notices them.*

Ah snow. Snow! Snow make Praha very nice, you think. Snow make how you think, 'winter wonderful land'. Yes, you like?

*A beat.*

I think it make bridge even more, as you say, scary place. Goodbye!

**Franz** *blows as if to blow out the light, and the stage is plunged into blackout.*

*Music. Crashing, impressive, thunderous.*

# Act Four

*7.25 a.m.*

**Franz** *has used the mime style to reconfigure the set, first the back wall of the A and E and then the fold-out parts of the actual Accident and Emergency department. He is helped in this by other backstage crew dressed in hospital fatigues. Gentle snow still falls, but stops as if it has been a flurry, as the lights come up.* **Keith** *is standing in exactly the same spot as he was in Act One as if nothing untoward has happened. We catch him slightly pursing his lips, with his eyes shut as if he is kissing someone.* **Holly** *enters. It is the end of her shift, she is clearly tired but excited about the possibility of going to Prague. As she enters she puts on her coat and adjusts her handbag. She checks her phone for messages.*

**Holly**   That's it then, Keith, all done.

*No response from* **Keith**.

**Holly**   Please yourself!

*No response from* **Keith**.

**Holly**   It's still cold out here this morning. Are you with us? Keith! (*Louder.*) Keith? Keith!

**Keith** *is shocked into a response.*

**Keith**   Eh?

**Holly**   There's been a fire in there, you know?

**Keith**   Where?

**Holly**   And you were miles away.

**Keith**   A fire?

**Holly**   What if there had been and you'd wandered off?

**Keith**   You finished then?

**Holly**   That's it for me.

**Keith**   Flown this last half hour . . .

**Holly** *checks her phone.*

**Holly**    No messages, Keith, nobody loves me!

**Keith**    Don't worry, nobody loves me either!

**Holly**    I thought Darren might have come crawling back but . . . sod him, the spotty arse.

*A beat.*

**Keith**    Prague then?

**Holly**    I can't believe it!

**Keith**    Like a fairy tale, isn't it?

**Holly**    Four days off and one night in Prague, I can't wait!

**Keith**    You might find somebody out there.

**Holly**    What, in one night, it doesn't usually work like that, Keith.

**Keith**    You never know your luck!

**Holly**    We'll just about have time for a bit of shopping and then we'll have to come back.

**Keith**    Loaded down with shoes!

**Holly**    I wish.

**Keith**    You want to be careful what you wish for.

**Holly**    I know what I wish for!

**Keith**    And me!

**Holly**    What do you wish for then, Keith?

**Keith**    Now that would be telling.

*A beat.*

**Holly**    Have you got time off or will you be stuck here?

**Keith**    There's beauty here you know . . .

**Holly**    Oh yes, where?

**Keith**    You've just got to look for it.

**Holly**    What are you doing for Christmas then, anything special?

**Keith**    Well, I thought I might have a few days away.

**Holly**    Oh that'd be good, anywhere nice?

**Keith**    Well, I was thinking of Prague.

**Holly**    Oh really?

**Keith**    Yes, I thought I'd come and surprise!

**Holly**    Oh Keith, you needn't bother.

**Keith**    You never know!

**Holly**    You'll be watching the Queen on ITV, won't you?

**Keith**    I might do.

**Holly**    And then dealing with the domestics down here.

**Keith**    Probably.

**Holly**    That'll be exciting!

*She is now ready to depart.*

Anyway Keith, I'm going. Don't do anything I wouldn't do!

**Keith**    Like what?

**Holly** *makes her way away from* **Keith** *and out towards the city through the auditorium.*

**Holly**    Like following us to Prague!

**Keith**    Go on, you cheeky sod!

*A beat, as* **Keith** *yawns against morning. As he stands on sentry* **Alan** *enters wearing a party hat and carrying a plastic cup of coffee, and the joke from his cracker.*

**Alan**    Sure you didn't want one?

**Keith**    I don't know how you drink that!

**Alan**   I just put it in my mouth!

**Keith**   It's like mud.

*A beat.*

**Alan**   Jenny pulled my cracker!

**Keith**   That's good then!

**Alan**   It went off like a wet fart like but . . .

**Keith**   All a bit messy then?

**Alan**   Do you know I think I'm in there!

**Keith**   Another one?

**Alan** *reads from the joke.*

**Alan** (*reading*)   What did one reindeer say to the other reindeer?

**Keith** (*dead*)   Go and shoot yourself!

**Alan**   Nearly: 'Will it rain, deer?' Here's another (*Reading.*), 'What did the fish say when it swam into a wall?'

**Keith**   Go and shoot yourself.

**Alan**   Dam!

**Keith**   Oh right!

**Alan**   You never join in, do you?

*A beat.*

**Keith**   I like your hat.

**Alan**   Do you?

**Keith**   Oh aye, it looks very Christmasy does that, I bet that's cheered 'em up in there, hasn't it?

**Alan**   Oh aye!

**Keith**   I bet you've brought some of 'em back to life in there by wearing that?

**Alan** (*sarcastic*)    Oh aye, it's really lifted it in there has this.

**Keith**    I thought it must have, because it's really festive.

**Alan**    Changed the atmosphere altogether. People are singing and dancing!

*A beat.*

**Keith** (*dead*)    They were at twelve o'clock.

**Alan** (*flat*)    Aye I heard!

*A beat.*

**Keith**    Holly's gone!

**Alan**    She's off like shit off a shovel tonight then.

**Keith**    And no Darren to pick her up either.

**Alan**    He was an arse, that kid.

**Keith**    A spotty arse, by all accounts.

**Alan**    That's too much information, Keith.

**Keith**    Well, that's what she said!

**Alan**    You never miss a thing, do you?

**Keith**    It's my job, mate!

**Alan** *sips his coffee. Both men are tired.*

**Alan**    I dunno, we're like vampires on this shift. We start in the dark, finish in the dark, and then sleep all bloody day. We're like vampires.

**Keith**    Blood-suckers, you mean?

*A beat.*

**Alan**    No, I think we're just suckers, to be honest!

**Keith**    I don't mind it, I don't spend as much.

**Alan**    And there isn't a lot to spend, is there?

**Keith**    Tell me something I don't know!

*A beat.*

**Alan**  Mind you, you'll be glued to Open University all morning, won't you? I bet that's interesting. What are you doing at the minute then?

**Keith**  Expressionism!

**Alan**  Oh hell Keith, what's that about?

**Keith**  It's about how artists feel about the world.

**Alan**  I think I should be doing that course. You want to be careful stuck down here all night and then watching that, you'll be jumping off the bridge next!

**Keith**  A lot of it's online now.

**Alan** (*sarcastic*)  'Online'? Bloody hell, beam me up!

*A beat.*

**Keith**  I like doing it!

*A beat.*

**Alan**  Steven Chiko's a lot calmer now he's had his fix! He's still bouncing off the ceiling in there like, but he's calmer.

**Keith**  I'd like to fix him with a kick up the arse.

**Alan**  It'd fix you though, you'd be out of a job! Mind you, if you keep on with your studying you'll be off anyway, won't you?

**Keith**  I can't bear it down here sometimes.

**Alan** *drifts around the forecourt.*

**Alan**  It's just a job, Keith.

**Keith**  I know that.

**Alan**  That clown's got his arm back from X-ray, I think Belkowski had lost it.

**Keith**  You mean Mr Sleep!

**Alan**    Eh?

**Keith**    Mr Sleep.

**Alan**    Mr Sleep!

**Keith**    That's what I call him.

**Alan**    Why?

**Keith**    Have you ever spoken to him?

**Alan**    Yes, he's a nice bloke!

*A beat.*

**Keith**    He sends me to sleep.

**Alan**    You've a lot in common then, Keith.

*A beat.*

Wouldn't you like it on a different site?

**Keith**    Like where?

**Alan**    I don't know: somewhere where there's no people?

**Keith**    Oh no, I like people. I like to watch people, it gives me ideas.

**Alan**    For what?

**Keith**    For nowt, just ideas!

**Alan**    You must be bored to death though!

**Keith**    No, I think about all sorts.

**Alan**    Well I suppose . . .

**Keith**    It's like, if you get a 999 call I imagine what's going on.

**Alan**    Well aye I suppose . . .

**Keith**    Oh aye, I think: I wonder what's happening on Fat Alan's call-out tonight?

**Alan**    You what?

**Keith**   I create a scenario.

**Alan**   No, I'm not on about that.

**Keith**   What then?

*A beat.*

**Alan**   What did you say?

**Keith**   Eh?

**Alan**   What did you just say?

**Keith**   I said I wonder what happens on your 999 calls.

*A beat.*

**Alan**   No, not that bit, the other bit.

**Keith**   What other bit?

**Alan**   What did you call me?

**Keith**   Eh?

**Alan**   What did you call me?

**Keith**   I just . . .

**Alan**   You've just called me Fat Alan . . . that's what you've just called me.

**Keith**   Who?

**Alan**   You, you've just called me Fat Alan!

**Keith**   Have I?

**Alan**   To my face!

**Keith**   Well, it is your nickname.

**Alan**   Since when?

**Keith**   Well . . .

**Alan**   You cheeky bastard!

**Keith**   I've always called you Fat Alan.

**Alan**    To my face?

**Keith**    Well . . .

**Alan**    Don't call me fucking Fat Alan, all right!

**Keith**    Sorry!

**Alan**    Fat Alan?

**Keith**    Sorry!

**Alan**    Fat Alan?

*A beat.*

Okay so I might have weight issues that I've been trying to deal with, but I don't want attention drawing to them here. It's a stress thing. And a lot of it is because I've got a sedentary job. That is bullying in the workplace and we've got a policy about that!

**Keith**    Sorry!

**Alan**    Fat Alan?

**Keith**    Sorry.

**Alan**    Cheeky bastard.

**Keith**    I don't know where that came from.

**Alan**    It came from out your bloody mouth, mate, that's where it came from!

**Keith**    Sorry!

*Silence.*

**Alan**    Bloody Prague then!

**Keith**    Oh aye, that!

**Alan**    I saw Kath with Rojinsky earlier: all over him like a bad case of the shits. It is so obvious he's got them tickets, she was nearly wetting herself.

*He sips his coffee and drifts around the forecourt.*

He's on for a promise there or I'll eat my hat.

**Keith**   Yes?

**Alan**   He's on for a sly one with both of them or I'll eat my own shit!

**Keith**   Why don't you shit in your hat and eat them both at the same time?

*A beat.*

**Alan**   Fat Alan, I can't believe it!

**Keith**   Sorry.

**Alan**   That's how the world works, Keith. He's left them reference numbers and he's going to fettle them both when they get back: sex drive gone mad! He's got it all lined up. He needs doctoring he does, he needs tablets. Mind you, he's probably got tablets, that's why he's like he is. He's going to have 'em both.

**Keith**   Give up!

**Alan**   Don't argue with me, Keith, you don't know anything about how to play a woman, I'm a bloody expert.

**Keith**   Well ar . . .

**Alan**   I'm telling you.

**Keith**   I don't think it's like that though!

**Alan**   Well how do you know?

**Keith**   Well . . . !

**Alan**   He's lining Kath up for a session, whether we like it or not! And we can't do a thing about it! We're just pawns. You don't know what day it is half the time, you just stand there letting life pass you by!

**Keith**   Not all the time.

**Alan**   Well you could have fooled me.

**Keith**    Well obviously I have.

**Alan**    Eh?

**Keith**    Obviously I have.

**Alan**    How have you fooled me then?

**Keith**    Well . . .

**Alan**    Go on, if you've fooled me, how?

**Keith**    Well . . .

**Alan**    Go on?

**Keith**    Well . . .

**Alan**    Keith, get real.

**Keith**    I am getting real.

**Alan**    Rojinksy's playing 'em like a violin! Then he'll be playing sommat else.

**Keith**    No he's not!

**Alan** (*exhausted*)    Well how the fuck do you know?

*A beat.*

**Keith**    Because I left those reference numbers!

*A beat.*

**Alan**    Eh?

**Keith**    I left them.

*A beat.*

**Alan**    Now you are talking bollocks!

**Keith**    Am I?

*A beat.*

**Alan**    Well, you haven't got any spare cash, so how do you expect anybody to believe that?

**Keith**   Well . . . !

*A beat.*

**Alan**   It's a wind-up, mate. I can spot it a mile off.

**Keith**   Please yourself.

*A beat.*

**Alan**   Are you serious?

**Keith**   Please yourself.

*A beat.*

**Alan**   Why?

**Keith**   Because I did!

*A beat.*

**Alan**   Keith, they hate you! They ignore you! They talk about you behind your back. They have nicknames for you, they think you're scary. They're happier when you're not on their shift.

**Keith**   How do you know?

**Alan**   Because they've told me! Kath's told me. You can see it! Everybody knows what they call you.

*A beat.*

They think you're a laughing-stock because of this Open University thing. They're pissing up your back most of the time, mate!

*A beat.*

**Keith**   So what?

**Alan**   So what? You've just lashed out for two tickets to Prague and you haven't got two pennies to scratch your arse with: that's so what!

**Keith**   Well, it's Christmas!

**Alan**    I thought you hated Christmas?

*A beat.*

(*Realising the motive.*) Bloody hell, Keith!

**Keith**    What?

**Alan**    It's Kath, isn't it?

**Keith**    What is?

**Alan**    Bloody hell.

**Keith**    What?

**Alan**    It's Kath?

**Keith**    What about her?

*A beat.*

**Alan**    You've got a thing about her, haven't you?

*A beat.*

**Keith**    I just . . .

**Alan**    Bloody hell!

**Keith**    I dunno I . . .

*A beat.*

**Alan**    Because people don't do that, Keith, people don't give presents out like that without there's more to it! People want pay-back these days.

**Alan** *drifts around the forecourt as* **Kath** *enters. She is putting on her coat and adjusts her belongings. She senses something in the air.*

**Kath**    What's up with you?

**Alan**    Nowt, we were just saying: all done and dusted and going to Prague. You know you could always dump Holly and take me, I'll ask our lass if I can go!

**Kath**    Yeh but what would I do with you?

**Alan**    Oh I could think of a few things.

**Kath**    I bet you could.

**Alan**    You could always take Keith.

**Kath**    Maybe next time eh!

**Alan**    Oh there's going to be a next time. Sounds like you're in there, Keith.

**Kath** *is about to depart.*

**Kath**    Anyway I'll see you, have a nice Christmas . . .

**Keith**    Night!

**Kath** *moves to go away.*

**Alan**    Oh Kath, I meant to tell you sommat about that Prague trip.

**Kath**    What's that?

**Kath** *stops.*

**Alan**    Have a good time!

**Kath**    Don't worry we will.

**Kath** *exits.*

**Alan**    Bloody hell, mate.

*A beat.*

**Keith**    Go and pull another cracker, you fat bastard!

**Alan** (*shaking his head in disbelief as he exits*)    Oh dear, Keith . . .

**Keith** *is alone on the forecourt for a moment. As he stands* **Stevo** *comes out of the hospital. He appears slightly calmer but he is still highly agitated.*

**Stevo**    All right, mate . . . Got a light?

**Keith**    I'm not your mate.

**Stevo**    Eh?

**Keith**    I'm not your mate.

**Stevo**    What's up with you?

**Keith**    You! You shit bag!

**Stevo**    Hey mate!

**Keith**    Do you know I could kick your teeth in and think I'd done nowt, do you know that! I could give you a pasting as soon as look at you!

**Stevo**    Why?

**Keith**    Because reality is shit!

**Stevo**    It is, it's shit reality! What's in your head is better!

**Keith**    We're just a bag of chemicals, aren't we?

**Stevo**    You're not wrong!

*A beat.*

**Keith**    We can't bring people back, mate.

**Stevo**    I'm not your mate.

**Keith**    We can't bring people back!

**Stevo**    What's brought this on?

**Keith**    Christmas!

**Stevo**    Christmas?

**Keith**    What's it all about?

**Stevo**    It's all about baby Jesus! You know in like a manger, and this angel came down, and she like spoke to t' shepherds. And they had to follow a star, and three wise men brought frankincense and stuff. And others gave gifts, like a goat and that, and that's why we give presents. And it's about Mary and Joseph riding a donkey. And it's about that good King Wenceslas (*Singing.*) 'Good King Wensles last looked out, on the feast of Steven. When the snow was all about, deep and crisp and even. Brightly shone the stars that night though the frost was cruel. When a poor man came in sight gathering winter fuel.'

**Lilly** *enters from A and E. She and* **Stevo** *are a dangerous pairing.* **Lilly** *cracks open a can of special brew and shares it.*

**Lilly**   You doin'?

**Stevo**   Carol singing.

**Lilly**   You fuckin' cracked or what?

**Stevo**   He is.

**Lilly**   Yes, he is him.

**Stevo**   Are you cracked?

**Keith**   I must be.

**Stevo**   Reality's shit, isn't it?

**Lilly**   It is here!

**Stevo**   He's cracked, him. His brother does martial arts, doesn't he?

**Keith**   He does, yes.

**Stevo**   He does martial arts, his brother, I might start doing it!

**Lilly**   I'm not doing it!

**Stevo**   Hey has he seen *Kill Bill?*

**Stevo** *and* **Lilly** *drink their can of beer.*

**Lilly**   I'm not having a fucking operation tonight, I've told 'em in there.

**Stevo**   You do right.

**Lilly**   No fucking way.

**Stevo**   I'm not.

**Lilly**   You don't need one, do you?

**Stevo**   No right.

**Lilly**   Got your stuff?

**Stevo**   Yes.

**Lilly**   Come on then.

**Stevo**   See you, mate . . . have a good Christmas, mate . . . Cheers, mate. And have a safe and prosperous New Year.

**Stevo** *shakes* **Keith**'*s hand.*

**Lilly**   Come on you!

**Stevo** *and* **Lilly** *make their way out. They shout abuse to* **Keith** *as they exit the auditorium.*

**Stevo**   Come on then, if you think you're hard . . .

**Lilly**   Tosser.

**Stevo**   Come on, tosser!

**Lilly**   Wanker.

**Stevo**   Kung Fu!

*A siren is heard disappearing into the night.* **Keith** *is once again alone. As he stands* **Len** *reappears outside A and E. He coughs heavily as he looks for another cigarette. He is trying not to cry.*

**Keith**   How we doing then?

**Len**   I can't believe it!

**Keith**   Oh dear!

*A beat.*

**Len**   They've had that Czech to look at her. (*Coughs.*)

**Keith**   Rojinskjy?

**Len**   He's only got her on a ward and got her all wired up. Fucking hell he doesn't mess about, does he?

**Keith**   No, he doesn't mess about.

**Len**   Them Czech lads don't mess about. I can't believe it! She was on her last legs when I saw her, just laid there. He's come in and bloody hell he must be a bloody magician or sommat, he says she's going to be all right.

**Keith**   A nice Christmas present then?

**Len**   It's best I've had!

**Keith**   *You'll* believe in Father Christmas then?

**Len**   Oh aye I do now.

*A beat.*

Why, does tha believe in Father Christmas?

**Keith**   Me?

**Len**   Aye.

*A beat.*

**Keith**   I am Father Christmas me, mate . . . I am Father Christmas.

**Len** *returns to A and E,* **Keith** *stands alone.*

*Music. Slavic.*

*It snows on* **Keith** *as he drifts off once more.*

*Lights fade. Curtain.*

# Crown Prince

## Characters

**Jack Batley**, *former miner and shop-owner, who ages from sixty-one to eighty-one*

**May Batley**, *Jack's wife, sixty-eight*

**Ted Morely**, *former fisherman and carer, who ages from sixty-one to eighty-one*

**Ronnie Carlton**, *former club singer turned actor, who ages from sixty-one to eighty-one*

**Max Haigh**, *delivery man turned groundsman, who ages from twenty-seven to forty-seven*

**Caroline Upton**, *local doctor, who ages from sixty-one to eighty-one*

**Faye Kirby**, *Jack's granddaughter, a green activist, who ages from seventeen to twenty-three*

*Crown Prince* was first performed by Hull Truck Theatre Company in May 2007 at Spring Street Theatre, Hull, with the following cast:

| | |
|---|---|
| **Jack Batley** | Rob Angell |
| **May Batley** | Sarah Parks |
| **Ted Morely** | Martin Barrass |
| **Ronnie Carlton** | Iain Rogerson |
| **Max Haigh** | Jack Brady |
| **Caroline Upton** | Sarah Parks |
| **Faye Kirby** | Hester Ullyatt |

*Directed by* John Godber
*Designed by* Pip Leckenby

# Act One

## Scene One

*2007.*

*The setting is Beech Hill Bowling Club, which comprises a weather-beaten clubhouse, positioned upstage off-centre left, with a small patio and fencing surround. We get the strong impression that the club has fallen into some disrepair in recent years. Downstage of the clubhouse is a tarmac area which is home to a number of garden benches and a small patio-style table and chairs with a parasol. The entire stage is surrounded by a large wooden fence. Upstage right in the fence is a secure gate which is the only means of entry to the outside world. Downstage centre looking out towards the audience is the corner of a bowling green. When the characters bowl towards the audience they have their eye on an imaginary 'jack' which is somewhere out towards the centre of the audience.*

*House lights fade.*

*Music.*

*Lights fade up to reveal **Jack** (sixty-one), in part bowling whites, jumper and grey slacks, **Ted** (sixty-one), dressed similarly and **Ronnie** (sixty-one), more casual, with **Caroline** (sixty-one), wearing all white and a white floppy hat, on stage looking out towards a wood that has just been bowled by **Jack**. In the clubhouse we see a number of ladies sitting chatting, wearing white bowling hats. As the music plays we see the cast follow the wood in absolute slow motion. It is balletic and beautiful to behold. There is not a semblance of histrionics, they are peacefully watching the wood. As the wood falls near the jack **Ronnie** stands up and **Jack** comes towards the mat and picks up a wood. As he does, the lights fade.*

*Blackout.*

## Scene Two

*2007.*

*Lights fade up to reveal* **Jack** *having just sent a wood all the way down the green towards the jack.* **Ted**, **Ronnie**, **Caroline** *and* **Jack** *watch this wood with real interest, then they slowly stand and look at each other.* **Jack** *looks at* **Ronnie** *and* **Ronnie** *walks to look at the potential problem down the green.*

*The lights fade. Blackout.*

## Scene Three

*2007.*

*Lights fade up to reveal* **Ronnie** *feeling a wood as he looks at the potential problem down the green.* **Jack** *and* **Ted** *walk around the green, crouch and stand to try and get a better look at the situation down the green.* **Caroline** *sits and feels the heat.* **Ronnie** *also feels the heat and looks to make another bowl. As he prepares to bowl the lights fade.*

*Blackout.*

## Scene Four

*2007.*

*Lights fade up to reveal* **Ronnie** *willing his wood towards the jack.* **Ted** *and* **Jack** *look on nervously. It is quite tense.* **Caroline** *stands and looks at the wood, as they see the wood kiss the jack there is polite but generous applause from the players.* **Ronnie** *is delighted and he pats* **Jack** *on the back in an ironic gesture of friendship; in truth they hate each other. Lights fade.*

*Blackout.*

**Scene Five**

*2007.*

*Lights fade up to reveal* **Jack** *picking up a wood and looking down the green. The ladies from the clubhouse are now standing on the veranda looking down the green.*

*The music stops. Silence. Nothing can be heard.* **Jack** *is deadly serious as he weighs the wood in his hand.* **Ted** *looks nervous and a little tired.* **Caroline** *sits once more and looks down the green.* **Jack** *takes his time to have a look down the green and at the problem that has been created by the last wood that* **Ronnie** *has bowled.* **Jack** *and* **Ronnie** *look at each other.*

**Jack** (*concerned*)    Oph.

**Ronnie** (*beat that*)    Oph!

**Jack** (*determined*)    Ophh!

**Ronnie** (*stoic*)    Oh.

**Ted** (*worried*)    Oh eh!

**Caroline** (*worried*)    Oh oooh!

**Jack** *walks towards the mat and feels the weight of the wood in his hand. As he gets down to make a bowl there are a number of involuntary grunts.*

**Ted** (*encouraging*)    Oph o ooh!

**Ronnie** (*discouraging*)    Oph . . .

**Caroline** (*worried*)    Ooh!

**Jack** *gets down to make his shot. As he does the lights fade.*

*Blackout.*

**Scene Six**

*2007.*

*Lights fade back up to reveal* **Jack**, *who turns away from the green feeling very despondent, as he shakes hands with* **Ronnie**, *who is once again the winner of this on-going rivalry.* **Ted** *applauds in support and* **Caroline** *also applauds from her seated position. The ladies from the clubhouse applaud and slowly make their way back into the clubhouse.* **Jack** *remains static looking down the green.* **Ronnie** *and* **Ted** *all look down the green.*

**Jack** (*astonished*)    Dear me!

**Ted** (*stoical*)    Well aye!

**Jack**    Dear me!

**Ted**    Well aye!

*A beat.*

**Jack** (*considered*)    Dear me!

**Ted** (*finally*)    Well . . . aye!

**Jack** *is still static.*

**Caroline**    How many is that, Jack?

**Jack**    Too many.

**Caroline**    You should stop playing him.

**Jack**    I'll beat him one day!

**Caroline**    Well, I'd get a move on, you're sixty-two in August.

**Ronnie** *is delighted and moves down the green and begins to gather his woods.*

**Ronnie**    Are we on again next month? I'll pencil it in if we are, but we've got a lot of bookings at the minute.

**Ted**    Where are you tonight then, Ron?

**Ronnie**    The Goodfellowship!

**Ted**    Have you seen 'em, Caroline?

**Caroline**    I'm a groupie, Ted.

**Ted**    Is it still thriving?

**Ronnie**    We're having to travel more, I've got to work around stuff.

**Jack**    I've never liked club acts.

**Ted**    Especially those that beat him at bowls.

**Ronnie**    My agent's getting us work but it's getting thinner locally. Mind you, she reckons there's a telly thing coming up so . . .

**Ted**    A telly thing?

**Ronnie**    Apparently they're looking for somebody to play somebody's dad so she's put me forward. I mean, I've never acted but you never know.

**Jack** (*joking*)    Oh I couldn't bear that, him being on the telly, that would kill my pig, that would.

**Ted** (*lightly*)    He's a miserable sod!

**Jack**    I am when he keeps beating me!

*There is laughter to* **Jack**'s *response.*

**Ronnie**    That's the thing about this business, you never know what's round the corner, do you?

**Caroline** (*floated*)    Just like real life, Ronnie!

**Ronnie**    I've never done any acting but she says they're looking for somebody fresh so . . .

**Caroline**    And you're certainly that . . .

*A beat.* **Ronnie** *is nearly ready to leave.*

**Ronnie**    Anyway, I'm going to have to make tracks. Hard luck, mate! You'll beat us one day.

**Jack**    I'm doing sommat wrong.

**Ronnie**    Yes, you're supposed to get the woods near the jack!

**Caroline** (*lightly*)    He didn't know that, did you?

**Ronnie** *is ready to depart.*

**Ronnie**    I love it when I beat the President. It's always a good win is that, I'll see you then.

**Ronnie** *exits the green.* **Ted** *walks to the gate to close it after him. We hear* **Ronnie** *open and close a car door and pull away.*

**Ted**    He's got a big car and all, hasn't he? That's the thing about Ronnie, he's got to have the biggest of everything! Have you been to their house, his fridge . . . !

**Ted** *moves central.*

**Jack**    Well I'm ready for that sandwich, Ted!

**Ted**    I've ordered them from that Asda Online. Mind you, I've no idea how that works, so they could have gone anywhere. I mean, we only eat fry-up so I didn't know what to order!

**Jack**    Well, I hope you've not ordered fry-up.

*A beat.*

**Ted**    Hey, I've only just got used t' internet. I've probably sent 'em to Hornsea or somewhere. It says just click, so I kept clicking.

**Jack**    Clicking or clucking?

**Ted**    I was clicking and then I started clucking!

*A beat.*

**Caroline**    Well, I'd better make a move, chaps, otherwise I'll be here all night.

**Jack**    The ladies team did well again.

**Ted**    I'm sorry about the teas not turning up, Caroline, I did book them.

**Caroline**   I thought there was going to be a riot with the Middleton lot when you said they weren't coming.

**Ted**   I didn't know they weren't coming until they didn't come.

**Caroline** (*lightly*)   Rather obviously!

*A beat.*

**Jack**   Knowing our luck they'll come tonight and we'll have to eat 'em.

**Ted**   Well, they're paid for!

*A beat.*

**Caroline**   Anyway. I'll see you in a month. I'm up to my neck.

**Jack**   All right, Caroline, thanks for turning out.

**Caroline**   It is hot today, it's a real sun-trap up here. Bye!

**Caroline** *exits.*

**Jack** *moves upstage towards the roller.*

**Ted**   Are we getting off then?

**Jack**   I thought I'd roll this green first.

**Ted**   You want to stop doing that at your age.

**Jack**   In fact I was going to give the clubhouse a coat.

**Ted**   We need to get somebody on to that!

**Jack**   We're dwindling in numbers though, aren't we?

**Ted**   They say there's clubs attracting youngsters, but I can't see it. I mean they're giving 'em money to stop at school now, what chance have we got to get 'em bowling? Giving them money to stop on at school!

**Jack**   What's all that about?

**Ted**   It's about giving 'em money to stop on at school.

*A beat.*

**Jack**    You know, he might be right, I might be compensating for playing all that time on a crown green.

**Ted**    That's the trouble with you West Yorkshire lot, you're bloody crackers. Fancy playing bowls on a hill?

**Faye** *enters,* **Jack***'s granddaughter. She is seventeen, trendy and modern with purple streaks in the front of her hair. She has plenty of attitude.*

**Jack**    Oh look out!

**Faye**    My gran wondered if you'd got lost.

**Jack**    No, I'm still here.

**Ted**    He did lose, but he didn't get lost.

*A beat.*

**Jack**    This is my granddaughter, Ted.

**Ted**    I thought.

**Jack**    Faye.

**Faye**    Hello!

**Jack**    She's seventeen now.

**Ted**    Seventeen!

**Jack**    She's come to collect me.

**Ted**    He wants tagging, doesn't he?

*A beat.*

**Jack**    She's going skiing, aren't you?

**Ted**    Skiing? Oh now then, skiing.

**Faye**    That's right.

**Ted**    Skiing! Well aye they do, don't they?

**Faye**    While I can.

**Jack**    She's one of these who thinks the world's doomed, Ted, she's obsessed with the end of the world.

**Ted**    Oh dear, that's not so good then.

**Jack**    She's a . . . what are you again . . . ?

**Faye**    I don't know, what am I?

**Jack**    She's a Green, Ted.

**Ted**    A green what?

**Faye** *is not impressed.*

**Jack**    Reckons we're all doomed.

**Ted**    Your granddad is, his bowling's all over the shop.

**Faye**    Well, he tells us that he's the best in Yorkshire.

**Jack**    I was.

*A beat.*

**Ted**    Where are you going skiing then?

**Faye**    France, on a glacier with the sixth form.

*A beat.*

**Ted**    France on a glacier with the sixth form!

*A beat.*

We used to go tadpoling and thought it was great. France on a glacier with the sixth form: a trip to Redcar and we thought it was great, Jack. And we once went to Helmsley Castle, I'll never forget that, Rob Jones got appendicitis.

**Faye**    Yes, I've been there.

*A beat.*

**Ted**    France on a glacier with the sixth form.

**Jack**    This is what happens, Ted, you encourage their parents to go away and now their kids are never at home. She wants to be a lawyer and all, don't you?

**Faye**    I'm not sure yet.

**Ted**    Better than me, I was sweeping roads when I left school. Mind you, they needed sweeping.

**Jack**    Aye, she's a prophet of doom is Faye.

*A beat.*

**Ted**    France on a glacier with the sixth form then?

**Jack**    She comes into the bungalow and she's turning lights off right left and centre.

**Ted**    Well, we sit in the dark me and Alice so she'd be struggling with us.

**Jack**    Aye, she wants to save the planet!

**Faye**    Well if we don't do something by 2030, the planet will be two degrees warmer and then we'll all be in a mess!

**Ted**    Be nice in Brid for once though.

**Faye**    Well, daft as it sounds, people won't be able to holiday in Spain.

**Ted**    I've only been once!

**Faye**    The ecosystem's heading for melt-down! Plants can only absorb carbon dioxide up to a certain heat, after that they start to release it. Then global warming becomes self-perpetuating.

**Ted** (*meaningless*)    Well aye!

**Jack**    Oh aye, she's full of this, on about my carbon what's-it . . .

**Faye**    . . . Footprint.

**Jack**    She blames me for being a miner . . .

**Ted**    She does right!

**Jack**    Hey, I'm not like the Chinese, they're burning coal like it's going out of fashion.

**Faye**    Yes, but they have a smaller footprint per person than us.

**Jack**    She's got all the facts.

**Faye**    Everybody thinks the Chinese are the biggest polluter, but it's still the USA. We've offshore industry and then we blame them for their carbon footprint. They've got two hundred million underemployed. Did you know that we lose rainforests the size of Wales every year?

**Ted**    I do now!

**Faye**    The point is we need to look beyond the tribalism of mankind.

**Ted** (*disabling*)    Oh Faye lass, it's too warm!

**Faye**    It will be. The earth's a living thing, but we abuse it, always have!

**Ted**    Hey listen, I make no excuses, I don't get it.

**Faye**    You will when societies start to collapse.

**Jack**    This is all we get, she won't speak to her mother because she lives in Malaga.

**Ted**    Why, what's up with Malaga?

**Jack**    She flies there.

**Ted**    So how are you going skiing?

**Faye**    On a bus.

**Ted**    Oh hell!

**Faye**    If something's worth fighting for, it's worth fighting for, for all of us!

**Ted**    Well aye but . . .

**Faye**    There's so much junk science people don't realise what the truth is.

**Ted**    And what is the truth?

**Faye**   The truth is the big oil companies are funding the misinformation that people are swallowing for their own ends.

**Ted**   I thought it was all a cycle like . . . hey, I'm not an expert but . . .

**Jack**   She's supposed to be doing her A levels but she's on with this. Reckons that that Exxon company are funding all this bloody junk science or whatever it is!

**Ted**   Well, if you don't want to burn energy stay in bed.

**Jack**   She does do some of the time, she's that worried by it.

**Faye**   We're burning more energy, that's a fact! And if we don't do something there'll be no water, higher temperatures, faster spread of disease . . . glacier shrinkage . . .

**Ted**   Hang on Faye, it's tea time.

**Faye**   Yes, every time you fill a kettle or turn on a light you condemn somebody to death somewhere in the world so . . .

*A beat.*

**Jack**   There's no wonder I come up here, is there?

**Faye**   We can't just do nothing!

**Ted**   Well, if that's the future, Jack, it sounds like we've had it.

**Faye**   We have all had it if we don't do something!

*A beat.*

Anyway my gran wanted to know when you're coming back because my mum's going to go to the airport in an hour.

**Jack**   Tell her I'm on my way.

*A beat.*

**Faye**   Nice to meet you.

**Ted**   Well aye, thanks for coming and cheering us up! Have a lovely holiday skiing.

**Faye**   You mean while there's still some snow?

**Faye** *exits.*

*Silence.*

**Ted** *and* **Jack** *look at each other, neither is sure of the other's response.*

**Jack**   It's driving her round the bend, all this, according to her dad!

*A beat.*

**Ted**   Daughter's back then?

**Jack**   We don't get on.

**Ted**   No, you mentioned.

**Jack**   She lives with a woman in Malaga, left her husband for another woman, worked at the hospital. Faye lives with her dad, you bring 'em up and you've no idea what they're going to turn into.

**Ted**   Well, I've only got Alice so . . .

*A beat.*

**Jack**   Bright as a button but she's got this thing about the end of the world. Why are they telling 'em that at seventeen?

**Ted** *has been affected by these thoughts.*

**Ted**   Mind you, you know six years ago there were sixty-two clubs around here and now there's only forty.

**Jack**   What's that got to do with global warming?

**Ted**   I'm just saying that we're an endangered species and all. It makes me wonder how we'll keep going.

**Jack**   Oh don't you start. It's all a load of my arse all that, there's been heatwaves and ice ages on and off for bloody years. I've seen it on telly. It's just the latest fad. It'll be sommat else before you know it!

*There is a knock at the gate.* **Max** *enters. He is a large, powerful man wearing the livery of an Asda delivery employee. He carries a large tray of selected foodstuffs.* **Max** *would be a threatening presence except he is cursed with a slight stammer.*

**Max**   S-S-Sorry! Asda Online!

**Ted**   I told you! I knew I'd ordered sommat!

**Jack**   Aye, it's just a shame it's not a blow-up doll!

**Max**   I g-got lost. I t-thought it said B-Beech H-Hole, I've been down by the ri-ri-river.

**Jack**   You should have been here at half one.

**Max**   I've got twenty-seven pork p-pies, sandwiches . . .

**Jack** (*to* **Ted**)   Twenty-seven?

**Ted**   Aye, I just kept clicking.

**Jack**   Everybody's gone.

**Max**   Well, what shall I do with 'em?

**Jack**   I could tell you.

**Max**   I've got cottage cheese, celery, c-c-cucumber, c-c-coleslaw, c-carrots.

**Jack**   You did the Cs then, Ted?

**Max**   Shall I l-leave 'em?

**Jack**   Well what are we going to do with them?

**Max** *comes centre and looks at the green.*

**Max**   Woooh! N-nice la-lawn.

**Jack**   He's more interested in the lawn than the bloody food.

**Ted**   Do you fancy a go? We're looking for recruits.

**Max**   It's for old men, isn't it?

**Ted**   There you go!

**Jack**   Hey, I was still playing rugby at fifty.

**Ted**   Fifty?

**Jack**   Well, forty-three.

**Ted**   Give up!

**Jack**   I played for Skirlaugh when I was thirty-nine, Ted!

**Max**   No, I'm t-training anyway.

**Ted**   Well, if you're training to deliver you've a lot to learn.

**Max**   I suppose when you get to sixty it's about all you can d-do! My dad does it: mind you, it plagues his b-back!

**Ted**   What do you do then?

**Max**   I th-throw weights about.

**Jack** (*not hearing*)    He does what?

**Ted**   He throws his weight about.

**Jack**   Well he's big enough!

**Max**   I'm n-not on t' team, I'm on t' fringes. I need to make a qualifying weight, and then who knows: Olympics . . .

**Ted**   Well, it'd be no good you going to t' Olympics, you'd never bloody find it!

**Max**   I thought it was B-Beech Hole!

**Max** *appeals to them. It's touching.*

Hey, y-you'll not report me will you? Only I'm h-having some t-trouble with our lass, so I went home and she locked me out and then I lost the keys to the v-van! I've only been doing this a c-c-c-couple of w-w-w-weeks.

**Ted**    Oh it's all coming out now, Jack!

**Jack**    Hey, in a relationship where there are no arguments somebody is getting too much of their own way!

**Max**    Thanks, I t-tell her t-that!

**Max** *refers to the tray of food.*

Shall I take these with me then?

**Ted**    Aye, you and your lass have a picnic.

**Jack** (*sarcastic*)    Yes, there's twenty-seven of everything so you should have enough.

**Max**    It's b-been one of them days to be honest: air conditioning's playing up in t' van and a spring's coming through my seat, and I don't think that's d-doing me any g-g-good.

**Max** *exits.*

*Silence.*

**Ted**    He's not a full jigsaw, is he? I think he's got some corners missing.

*A beat.*

**Jack**    Well, I suppose I'd better go. Will you lock up?

**Ted**    Oh aye.

**Jack**    Dear me!

*A beat.* **Jack** *walks out towards the green.*

**Ted**    How is May then, Jack?

**Jack**    Well, you know.

*A beat.*

They say to keep swimming . . .

**Ted**    Well aye.

**Jack**    Comes when you least expect it!

**Ted**    Aye, I know that!

**Jack** *deflects the conversation.*

**Jack**    This green's looking good.

**Ted**    Aye, it's got a lovely run to it.

**Jack**    It has, I just wish that I could find it.

**Ted**    It's hot today!

*A beat.*

**Jack**    Aye, I just wish I could find it!

*Music.*

*Lights fade to blackout.*


### Scene Seven

*2007.*

*Music. Lights fade up.*

*A month later.* **Ted,** **Jack** and **May** *(sixty-seven), who sits in a wheelchair and despite a terminal illness is bright and stoical, and a number of ladies inside the clubhouse, are watching the bowling.* **Ronnie** *is on the green. He is standing on the mat and the whole ensemble are watching his wood as it lands near the jack and he wins another victory against* **Jack Batley**. **Ronnie** *turns to* **Jack** *and pats him on the back. The whole ensemble applaud. The ladies in the clubhouse are making their way off stage or are packing away buns and the teas which this time have arrived on time.*

**Jack**    I don't believe it! I'm going to get another pork pie.

**Ted**    Are *we* going to have another end then, Ron?

**Ronnie**    Not today, I need to get off.

**Ted** (*disappointed*)   Oh right . . .

**Jack** *makes his way into the clubhouse.* **Ronnie** *and* **Ted** *remain on the green and begin to tidy away their woods.* **Ronnie** *calls to* **May**, *who despite her illness, is loud and brusque.*

**Ronnie**   You should be on here, you know, May.

**May**   Get away with you!

**Ronnie**   You'd be better than him.

**May**   He's always been a bad loser.

**Ronnie**   I'm serious, get yourself up here! It's no good just sitting there, get yourself down here and let's get a game going!

**May** *laughs at the impossible demand.* **Ronnie** *remains on the green and plays to* **May.**

**Ted**   He's going to be a star now, May, got that job on telly! Two-year contract.

**Ronnie**   I keep thinking they've made a mistake.

**May**   I like him best when he's singing.

**Ronnie**   I'm still singing, this is just another string!

**May**   I don't get out like I used to.

**Ronnie**   You should have been at the Goodfellowship last month. We were rocking them in there. Mind you, they were all over sixty . . . At least I'm keeping the osteopaths in work, we've more slipped discs! We had two that died on us at Christmas.

**May** (*disbelieving*)   Give up!

**Ronnie** (*joking*)   I'm serious, they were doing the hokey-kokey and it turned into the chokey-chokey. Absolute honest truth, we can't get insurance now, we don't have bouncers on the door, we have doctors, that's why Caroline comes. You want to get yourself to Spiders you do, I bet you'd love it in there.

**May** (*enjoying this*)    Oh give over!

**Ronnie** (*jokingly serious*)    I'll tell you something, you're twice as healthy as any of the crowds we've played to in the last six months. They don't dance round their handbags any more, they dance round their spare limbs. I'm serious!

**May**    I thought you could have let him win just once!

**Ronnie**    Oh I couldn't do that, not to Jack. He'd never forgive me.

**May** (*effortlessly changing theme*)    Our Faye's been skiing.

**Ronnie** (*enjoying the banter*)    That's what you should be doing.

**May**    She says there's not been much snow.

**Ronnie**    If God had wanted us to ski, May, he wouldn't have given us long feet.

**May** (*from nowhere*)    Jack's got long feet.

**Ronnie**    It's longer arms he needs!

**May** (*from nowhere*)    Are you going to sing then?

**Ronnie** (*effortlessly dealing with her ramblings*)    I will if you want. What do you want? Frankie Vaughan? Johnny Mathis? Elvis?

**May**    I love Johnny Mathis.

**Ronnie**    It's Johnny Mathis then.

**May**    There's nowt on the telly for us, you know. There's nowt on, unless you want to watch ice-dancing.

**Ted**    Alice watches that.

**May** (*changing direction*)    I do.

**Ronnie**    So it's Johnny Mathis then, which one?

**May**    They're all good what he's done.

**Ronnie**    I tell you what, I'll sing if you sing along with me.

**May**    I'm not singing.

**Ronnie**    What's up with you today? You won't sing, you won't get up and play bowls and I bet you wouldn't go bloody skiing either, would you?

**Ted**    Alice reckons there's nowt on the telly if you're over sixty-five.

**May**    Well I'm sixty-eight in August . . . If I ever get there!

**Ronnie** (*avoiding the dangerous territory*)    'If I ever get there'? You'll be here longer than me, you!

**Max** *enters. He is a little less hassled than previously, but still exhausted.* **Ronnie** *and* **Ted** *consider their woods and put a few in their bags.*

**Max**    I've left my t-trays.

**Ted** (*dry*)    I thought you'd be back! There in t' clubhouse.

**Max**    I s-should've have t-taken 'em, they're going mad at me down t-there . . . I forgot about them but I was on t-t-time!

**Max** *makes his way to the clubhouse.* **May** *buttonholes* **Max** *directly.* **Ronnie** *sits to watch.*

**May**    I say, there's nowt on the telly!

**Max**    No?

**May**    Nowt to watch if you're my age.

**Max**    I've just come for t-trays!

**May**    Trays?

**Max**    I've left m-my trays.

**May**    There's no trees in here, this is a bowling club.

**Max**    Eh?

**Ted**    He's a big 'un, May!

**May**    He is.

**Ted**   He's a big 'un!

**Ronnie**   I bet he likes a pie, May.

**May**   Jack's father could eat two pies more than a pig!

**Ronnie**   Could he?

**May** (*to* **Max**)   Mind you, our Pauline's first husband was a big 'un, he was a prison warden, only had one ear, Ted, bad with his kidneys he was.

**Ted**   Aye you've said.

**May**   He was a prison warden with one ear was our Pauline's first husband, and that didn't last. Then she married Mark and they had our Faye.

**Ted**   Smashing!

**May**   And now she lives with another woman. Mind you, I can understand that after living with Jack for forty-three years. I've told him: I wished I'd've lived with another woman, it would have stopped a lot of bloody arguments. I could have just come home at weekends and bank holidays.

**Ted**   He's entering Olympics.

**May**   Who, Jack?

**Ted**   He's entering the Olympics.

**Ronnie** (*to* **Max**)   Are you?

**Max** (*to* **Ronnie**)   Trying to.

**May** *carries on regardless.*

**May**   I say all that money they're spending and they're struggling for members up here.

**Max**   I'll get m-my t-trays!

**Max** *goes into the clubhouse for his trays.*

*Silence.*

**May** (*from nowhere*)   I love Johnny Mathis, always have, I've always liked black men.

**Ronnie**   Have you?

**May**   And they can't swim, can they?

**Ronnie**   They can dance though.

**May**   I've always liked black men. I don't know why I married Jack!

**Max** *returns from the clubhouse with a large tray.*

**Max**   Got 'em!

**May**   Does he know Mary Peters?

**Max**   Eh?

**May**   I went to school with Mary Peters.

**Ted** (*surprised*)   Did you?

**May**   No, it was Audrey Spence: she had a cousin who was Irish and she'd never eat corned beef.

*A beat.*

**Max**   I'll g-get off then!

**Max** *exits. There's a moment's repose.*

**Ted**   Bloody Olympics!

**Ronnie**   All that money!

**May**   Aye and none of it coming to Hull. All that money! I wouldn't care if we were any bloody good!

*A beat.*

**Ronnie** (*energised*)   Right, are you getting up to play or not, because if you're not I'm going.

**May**   I wish I could!

**Ronnie** (*caringly light-hearted*)   Well sod you then, I'm going. I'll see you next time, then we can have a few ends.

**May**   Has he got lost?

**Ted**   He's in the little room.

**May**   We'll be here another five hours then.

**Ronnie** *gathers his bowls equipment, steps off the green up the grass bank and near to* **May**. *He is very tender with her; this belies the joking. He knows she is very poorly.*

**Ronnie**   I'll see you, love, take it steady. Look after yourself.

**Ronnie** *awkwardly hugs* **May**.

**May**   And you take it steady and stop smoking, it'll bloody kill you. I can smell it on your breath, and he's been drinking, Ted, and that's before he's been on the telly. Look at Roy Castle, he was a club act and he never smoked and it killed him.

**Ronnie** (*dry*)   There you go then! (*Upbeat.*) Anyway I'm going, you look after yourself.

**May**   And never let Jack win, it'll go to his head!

**Ronnie** *makes his way to the gate.*

**Ronnie**   No, there's no chance of that!

**Ronnie** *has gone. Birdsong. The odd seagull.*

*Silence.*

**May**   Bloody Ronnie!

**Ted**   Well aye!

**May**   Caroline's not playing today then? I like to talk to her, but she's bloody depressing, I'm glad she's not my doctor.

*A beat.*

**Ted**   Well, I'd better get off.

**May**   Alice all right? I haven't seen her for ages.

**Ted**   She can't get out any more. Somebody has to sit with her so I can come up here!

**May** (*a new thought*)   I haven't seen her for ages.

**Jack** *slowly emerges from the clubhouse.*

**Ted**   He's here look!

**Jack**   I'll see you at the weekend then.

**Ted**   It depends what Alice is like. Doctor's coming to see her again.

**May** (*loudly*)   Does she still do the crossword?

**Ted**   Oh aye, she still does the crossword.

*He exits.*

See you!

**Jack** *walks downstage.* **May** *sits and looks out. It is a very warm day.*

**May**   That grass wants watering, and don't be pushing that roller, it's getting too much for you now that is!

*Silence.*

**Jack**   Peaceful up here at this time.

*A beat.*

**May**   I don't want cremating you know!

*A beat.*

Did you hear me?

**Jack**   I heard you.

*A beat.*

**May**   Our Faye says it's not good for t' atmosphere so . . .

**Jack** *looks down the green, he is moved to tears by the brutal honesty in* **May**'s *approach. She doesn't know this.*

**Jack** (*crying*)   Bloody hell!

**May**   She says bury me under a tree, it's better for t' planet.

**Jack** (*crying*)   Oh dear!

**May**   She says they're having to build bigger furnaces in Hull to get rid of the bodies, she says it's not good for the environment but they've put bigger fires in. It's because there's so many fat folk, there's so many fat folk they won't burn so easy, Jack.

*A beat.*

**Jack**   I don't know why you listen to our Faye.

*A beat.*

**May**   I don't want cremating.

*A beat.*

**Jack**   I've heard you!

*A beat.*

**May**   Ronnie makes me laugh.

*A beat.*

**Jack**   I wish he made me bloody laugh!

*A beat.*

**May**   What'll happen to the shop then?

**Jack**   Shop'll take care of itself.

**May**   Will you sell it?

**Jack**   I don't know.

**May**   Will you ever sell t' bungalow?

**Jack**   No, love.

*A beat.*

**May**   They didn't do what they said they were going to, did they?

**Jack** (*kind*)   Who?

**May**   Labour party, they didn't do what they said they were going to. Hospitals are in a state, Jack, and I should know! And I've always voted Labour, but they didn't do what they said.

*A beat.*

I blame the Queen.

**Jack**   Do you?

**May**   She should have never married Prince Philip.

**Jack**   No, that's right!

**May**   Phil the Greek they called him. Phil the Greek, how did he get a job like that with him being Greek? And the pension funds?

**Jack** *is upset by* **May**'s *ramblings.*

**May**   I mean that was Gordon Brown that, and he's had another baby, and he was playing about with the pension funds and it looks like he's only got one eye, Jack!

*A beat.*

**Jack** (*saddened*)   It does, May lass.

*A beat.*

**May**   Can you remember my dad's allotment?

**Jack**   I can.

**May**   And Mrs Whitton next door?

**Jack**   I can.

**May**   She only had one eye, didn't she, can you remember? I say when you think what we've done, all the way from Barnborough to run a boarding house in Brid and we end up owning our own shop. Who would have thought it?

**Jack**   Nobody, love.

**May**   We've done some daft stuff.

**Jack**   We have.

*A beat.*

**May**   I wonder why they made her marry a Greek, Jack?

**Faye** *enters. She wears Animal and Surf casuals. There is a bond between her and* **May**.

**Faye**   Thought you might be up here.

**May**   Your granddad wanted to get me out of the house.

**Faye**   I'll take you back if you want.

**Jack**   You fill her head.

**Faye**   It's already full if you ask me! All she does is talk about you.

**Jack**   I'll go and lock these windows up.

**Jack** *exits towards the clubhouse.*

**Faye** *can't help but notice that* **Jack** *has been upset. She remains still.* **May** *is upbeat.*

**May**   He's soft is your granddad, Faye, he can't bear the fact that I'm dying. He's pretending I'm not.

*A beat.*

And all that practice and he still lost to Ronnie Carlton.

**Faye**   Did he?

**May**   He'll never bloody beat him, as long as he's got a hole in his arse!

**Faye** *laughs at* **May**.

**May**   You laughing at?

**Faye**    You! You're funny!

**May**    Aye but not funny ha ha! Come on, let's get down that bloody hill!

*A beat.*

Beaten by a club act, I'll never let him live that down.

**Faye** *takes hold of the wheelchair as music plays.*

*Lights fade. Blackout.*

# Act Two

*2012.*

*Music fades.*

*Lights come up to reveal* **Ted** *five years into the future in 2012. He is now sixty-six years old and has aged accordingly, wearing clothes which might suggest that money is tight. He is standing on the green downstage of the clubhouse inspecting the grass. It is an extremly hot day.* **Jack** *can be heard in the clubhouse.*

**Ted** (*to off stage*)   It's not getting any better, is it? We need some rain. No, I've never seen it like this! Bloody heat that is. And there's no sign that it's going to break, is there? I say there's no sign that it's going to break! This is the worst I've seen it in the last five years! (*To himself.*) Five years, bloody hell where does it go? (*Musing.*) It just goes . . .

**Ted** *looks down the green. He is very warm.*

What time are they coming?

**Jack** *enters from the clubhouse. He has aged significantly. He is perhaps less steady on his feet. He has a paintbrush and a tin of Sikkens. As he speaks he begins to paint the veranda of the clubhouse.*

**Jack**   Half ten, leave it any longer and it's too warm. We might get to the point where we're playing at midnight.

*A beat.*

**Ted**   It is warm.

**Jack**   It is for October.

**Ted**   That grass'll not last much longer in the middle.

**Jack**   It might be the only way I'll beat Ronnie: playing him on sand.

**Ted**   It's what the French do!

**Jack**   I nearly got a draw last month when he came back from wherever the hell he was.

**Ted**   He's not changed though, has he?

**Jack**   No, you can take the man out of the club, but you can't take the club act out of the man.

**Max** *appears through the gate with a tray of food covered in tin foil. He too has aged five years.*

**Max**   M-morning!

**Ted**   Hey he's back, look. We've missed you! Your replacement was awful, couldn't rely on him. Hey, he's on time and all, Jack!

**Max** (*referring to the tray*)   Aye I'm b-back. B-back to reality. Here's your ice-c-creams and f-frozen prawns. They're all the rage these, there's a local firm making a killing. M-mind you, I think they've been frozen b-before so . . . And it's bloody f-freezing in that van, I think the air conditioning's gone mad, I'll end up with b-bloody pneumonia the way it's g-going.

**Ted** (*not thinking*)   Well I've had pneumonia, it's not that bad.

**Jack** *is still painting.* **Max** *stands with his tray.*

**Jack** (*calling*)   I didn't see you on t' telly.

**Max**   I didn't g-get the qualifying w-weight. Did you see some of the R-russians?

**Ted**   How many medals did we win?

**Jack**   Two golds. One in the clay-pigeon shooting.

**Ted**   Aye and that's because we're the only country silly enough to do it.

**Jack**   And what was the other?

**Max**   Horse j-jumping, wasn't it?

**Jack**   We did nowt on t' track, except drop the baton!

**Max**   We c-came third in the relay. Twelfth over all!

**Ted**  All that money and all, what did it end up at, did they say?

**Max**  N-no idea.

**Ted**  A hundred billion, wasn't it?

**Jack**  It was never that.

**Ted**  It was sommat.

**Jack**  It was never that, was it?

**Ted**  And how much has come to Hull?

**Max**  I don't know how much it c-cost but that c-complex is brilliant. Did you watch much of it?

**Jack**  There was sod all else on.

**Ted**  Hey there is, there's pornography now on that BBC 4.

**Jack**  How do you know?

**Ted**  Well, I watch it.

**Jack** (*to* **Max**)  I'm watching Olympics and what's he been watching?

**Ted**  I've been watching Olympics!

**Max** *makes his way to the clubhouse.*

**Max**  Well, you say no money's come to Hull but w-we've got casino now, haven't we? W-w've got all that!

**Max** *is passing* **Jack** *and exits.*

**Jack**  Watch this veranda.

**Max** (*off stage*)  I do a lot of d-deliveries there, have you been?

**Jack**  I'm going to no casino.

**Max** *enters.*

**Max**  It l-looks great.

**Ted**   You wouldn't get Jack in a casino, he's no idea how to spend money.

**Jack**   I thought it was a daft idea when they were building it.

**Max**   Oh aye it's all changed down there, you should get yourself off, there's l-lap d-dancing and all s-sorts.

**Ted**   Lap dancing? Oh!

**Max**   L-lap d-dancing! It's like Las Vegas down in Hull now.

**Jack** (*painting*)   Aye and I bet there's a load of bloody social problems!

**Ted** *goes back to considering the grass.*

**Ted**   This grass is a right mess in the middle.

**Max**   They reckon you can get w-whatever you want: it's one of the top t-ten cities.

**Jack**   For what?

**Max**   You w-want to get yourself down, you'd b-be surprised.

**Jack** (*painting*)   No, I've never liked surprises!

**Max**   Hey honestly, t-they've g-got all the t-top shops and all sorts n-now!

**Jack** (*dry*)   They've had Top Shop for years!

**Ted** (*from centre*)   Well there's no need to go into town when you can get everything online is there? I just click now, me!

**Jack**   He's clicking mad is Ted!

**Max**   They've d-done all t' s-schools up and all.

**Jack** (*dry, still painting*)   Have they done the kids up though?

**Max**    M-mind you, they reckon there's still some estates that blokes won't d-deliver to.

**Jack**    They've not done it all up then?

**Max**    They reckon there's some parts you're b-better off keeping out of.

**Ted**    You can get whatever you want online you know!

**Jack** (*dry, still painting*)    Oh aye, he's a whiz on the internet. If you want to know what time the library opens in Rotterdam he's your man.

*A beat.*

**Max**    Got a match on?

**Jack**    Every other Saturday. They're coming from Hornsea and York today.

**Max**    I'm surprised you're still g-going. Are there m-many clubs left?

**Jack** (*dry*)    Oh aye there's clubs opening up all over with money from t' Olympics.

**Max**    Are you j-joking?

**Jack** (*dry*)    Yes I'm joking!

**Max**    Still r-recruiting then?

**Jack** (*dry*)    Oh aye!

**Ted**    Everybody's not off lap dancing and gambling you know!

*A beat.*

**Jack** (*painting*)    No, we'd like to be but we're stuck doing this.

*A beat.*

**Max**    Anyway. I'd better g-go, I'd like to stop and c-catch up b-but our lass if on a s-s-short fuse. Married l-life eh?

**Max** *moves to the exit.*

And I dread getting in that v-van it's f-f-f-f-f-f-f-f –

**Ted**    Careful, don't spoil yourself!

**Max**    F-friggin' freezing!

**Max** *exits.*

*A beat.*

**Jack** *stops painting the veranda. He looks at his work and inspects the brush. He is very hot.*

**Jack**    It's a warm one today, Ted. I'll do the roof another day. I need to bring my ladders, I think there's a few slates lose.

**Ted** (*easily*)    On the roof or in the delivery van?

*A beat.*

**Jack**    Both.

**Faye** *enters. She is now twenty-three and is dressed with a hint of Green activist about her. She wheels an old bike into the bowling club.*

**Faye**    Can I come in or is it members only now?

**Ted**    By gum!

**Jack** (*delighted*)    Now then!

**Faye**    Remember me?

**Ted**    They're all coming out of the woodwork today, Jack. It must be the weather.

**Faye** *places the bike against the fence.*

**Faye**    I've been staying at my dad's for a few days: he said you'd probably be up here!

**Ted**    Hey they're good on petrol, aren't they?

**Faye**    Very good, these, very green.

*A beat.*

**Jack**    Well, look at you!

**Faye**    Twenty-three!

**Jack**    Twenty-three!

**Ted**    I can remember when you were born. Twenty-three, Jack!

*A beat.*

**Faye**    I've just been down to the church . . .

**Jack** (*not wanting to dwell on it*)    Yes!

**Faye**    I don't get there as often as I'd like!

**Jack**    Yes, yes!

*A beat.*

**Ted**    A first-class degree from Oxford then? He tells me everything.

**Faye**    Oh that!

**Ted**    I haven't seen you for ages. You look well.

**Faye**    I've been in Venice for a few days.

**Ted**    Not skiing?

**Faye**    Water-skiing maybe.

**Jack**    Venice eh? We used to be happy with two weeks at Skipsea.

**Faye**    Yes but Venice is so tragic.

**Ted**    So is Skipsea.

*A beat.* **Faye** *laughs.*

**Faye**    It's falling into the lagoon.

**Ted**    We're falling into the sea, coastal erosion up here.

**Faye**    It's happening all over.

**Ted**    We've had no rain for five months.

**Faye**    My dad said.

*A beat.*

**Jack**    Your mother texts me!

**Faye**    I think she's concerned about you.

**Jack**    I've got no idea how to text her back. Anyway I've told her, I'm sixty-six, I'm not going to change my ways now.

**Faye**    Well, you never know!

**Jack**    I don't want to.

*A beat.*

**Faye**    I think she just wants to make sure you have a life.

*A beat.*

**Jack**    Is that why she went to live in Spain?

**Faye** (*caught*)    . . . No comment!

*A beat.*

**Jack**    If you ask me, Faye, this country's getting worse but I'm better off sticking to what I know.

**Faye**    She has invited you out there.

**Jack**    No, I've got my life, I've got my little routine. Besides, if I went to live out there I wouldn't be able to keep my eye on the government, would I?

**Faye**    Well . . .

**Jack**    I mean, you might think we're getting on a bit but we sort the world out, don't we?

**Ted**    Well, we try. I mean, a lot of the time we just sit and talk rubbish but . . .

**Jack**    That's what we do, Faye, any chance to have a moan, we do, do! I mean, we're no better off under a

Labour government than we would be under the
Conservatives, they're all the same!

**Ted**    That's it, now you've set him off!

**Faye**    Well, I only came to see how you were!

**Jack**    It's getting worse, and that's the truth.

**Ted**    Here we go!

**Jack**    Schools, NHS, pensions, private equity firms taking
over everything. There was a fella comes here, wasn't there,
Ted?

**Ted**    I don't know, Jack, I don't know what you're going
to say!

**Jack**    He'd been trying to set up a bereavement group
since he'd lost his wife and he couldn't get any money for it.
We should be catered for when we get older, there should
be better provisions. He couldn't get any money to set a
group up. I mean, it wasn't for his benefit, it was to help
other people. And yet . . .

**Ted**    Here we go!

**Jack**    There's still thousands coming in from Europe and
getting financed. I know this, Faye lass, you can't change the
world and it's a waste of time trying.

**Jack** *takes his paint and brush into the clubhouse.* **Ted** *and* **Faye**
*share a look.*

**Faye** (*calling after* **Jack**)    Well I don't think it is and neither
do a lot of other people!

**Ted** (*advising*)    Did you have a good time in Venice then,
you know, apart from it sinking into t' lagoon?

**Faye** *is being drawn by* **Jack**.

**Faye** (*calling to* **Jack**)    I think Mum's just saying that she
doesn't want life to pass you by.

**Jack** *enters from the clubhouse with a drink of orange.*

**Jack**    What does she want me to do, find another woman? I'm sixty-six, I'll just go out and get one, shall I? Life does pass you by. Everything changes when you get older, and you never know until you're there.

*A beat.*

**Faye** (*friendly*)    Well I didn't come up here to upset you.

**Jack** *drinks his orange. Stoical.*

**Jack**    You'll have to go a long way to upset me.

**Faye**    It's just, I've always believed that we had to do something with our lives. Mum taught me that!

**Jack**    I wanted her to do well, but you never know how it's going to turn out. There's other things, Faye: simple pleasures in life, without worrying about the bloody planet. We die whether you worry or not.

*A beat.*

**Ted**    So what is it you're doing now then?

**Faye**    Well, I'm waiting to hear if I've got a job with the UN in Africa but I think I'd better not mention that.

**Ted**    Oh hell, Africa!

**Faye**    They've got a lot of problems with the heat. People can't live there much longer. They're expecting massive migration.

**Ted**    Oh hell!

**Jack**    This is what I'm saying, why are you bothered?

**Faye**    There's two hundred million who might have to relocate.

**Ted**    Oh hell.

**Faye**    It's a nightmare.

**Ted**    Frightening when you think about it!

**Jack**    Don't think about it, Ted.

**Faye**    They're crossing borders, but where do you put them?

**Ted**    Bloody Africa!

*A beat.*

**Faye**    So you're still up here bowling with your head in the sand?

**Ted**    Aye we're like Drake, we're bowling while the earth burns, Faye. Mind you, if the weather keeps like it is, we might make a sand pit, open a crèche!

**Faye**    That'd be good.

**Ted**    We've thought about it!

*A beat.*

**Faye**    Anyway, Dad says if you want to pop in for a cup of tea any time let him know, he's been phoning but you never answer, he says.

**Jack**    No, I don't answer the phone any more.

*A beat.*

**Faye**    Anyway!

*A beat.*

**Jack**    There's only one person I want to hear from, Faye, and she'll never call me again.

*Silence.*

**Faye**    Anyway, that's what I came up to say, I didn't mean to go on! I'm getting better, trust me! And Mum says take it steady.

**Faye** *approaches* **Jack** *to kiss him. It is slightly embarrassing.*

**Jack**    Yes?

**Faye**    Take it steady!

**Jack**    Does *she* take it steady?

**Faye**    No!

**Jack**    Well, there you go then.

**Faye** *leaves* **Jack** *and goes to collect her bike. She stands with her bike.*

**Faye**    See you!

**Faye** *turns to exit.*

**Jack**    It'll kill you all this global warming stuff!

**Faye** (*icy*)    The point is, Granddad, it'll kill us all.

**Faye** *moves off.*

**Jack**    And watch what you're doing.

**Faye**    That's what my gran used to say.

**Faye** *exits.*

**Jack** *places the empty glass on the veranda and inspects his painting.*

**Jack**    Missed a bit here, look.

**Ted**    Two hundred million on the move she says.

**Jack** (*inspecting*)    I thought I had.

**Ted**    Bet you're proud of her, aren't you?

**Jack**    She comes out with such horseshit at times.

**Ted**    Africa!

**Jack**    First off she was saving the whale.

**Ted**    Bloody Africa.

**Jack**    Then it was the polar bears! Now it's the Africans she's saving.

**Ted**    Sounds like somebody's got to.

*Sound effect.*

*A large four by four can be heard parking up in the distance.* **Jack** *comes centre stage and looks out towards the green.*

**Jack**    That grass is going to be a right mess!

**Ted**    I bet it's warm there, Jack!

**Jack** (*looking downstage*)    You're right about that grass you know!

**Ronnie** *enters, five years older. He has put on quite a bit of weight, is very sunburnt and looks out of shape. He carries his bowling bag and wears a hat. He has an inordinate amount of jewellery on him.*

**Ronnie**    Bloody hell, it's a warm one, isn't it?

**Ted**    Not as warm as Africa.

**Ronnie** (*contradicting*)    I don't know!

**Ted**    There's two hundred million on the move.

**Ronnie** (*lightly*)    You might get some new players then.

**Ronnie** *has lightened the atmosphere.*

**Ted**    Hey he goes down to that casino, don't you?

**Ronnie**    Oph, smashing down there.

**Ted**    Do you have to be a member?

**Ronnie**    I am.

**Ronnie** *comes centre and places his bowling bag on the edge of the green.*

**Ted**    They reckon you can get what you want, don't they?

**Ronnie**    If you want it!

**Ted**    Have they got that lap dancing?

**Ronnie**    And the rest.

**Ted**    I think I'd worry about my heart packing in if I had a go!

**Ronnie**   They're lovely down there, Romanian a lot of them. If you get lucky you never know . . .

**Ted**   Why, do they . . . ?

**Ronnie**   They'll do anything for money, Ted, let's just say that . . .

**Jack**   I think it'd put years on me.

**Ronnie**   Well, it takes years off of me.

**Ted**   Hey, there's even pornography now on BBC 4, you know. If you look for it.

**Ronnie**   How do you know?

**Jack**   He looks for it!

**Ronnie** *makes his way to the clubhouse.*

**Ronnie**   We'll go down one time if I get a chance to take you. Is there a drink, I'm parched?

**Ted**   There's ice-creams and all sorts in there.

**Jack**   If they've not melted.

**Ronnie** *enters the clubhouse.*

*A beat.*

**Ted** (*whispers*)   He lives down there according to Dennis at the post office.

**Jack**   How does Dennis know?

**Ted**   Graham told me, Dennis goes down there all the time, apparently he's lost a fortune.

**Jack**   He didn't have a fortune, did he?

**Ted** (*dry*)   Well he's lost one.

**Jack**   The problem with Ronnie is you don't know what's true and what isn't!

**Caroline** *enters, she is still refined but is slightly aged. She carries a small bag and wears an expensive tracksuit.*

**Caroline**    Are we getting earlier?

**Ted**    It's breakfast bowls next month.

**Caroline**    I tried to make it on my bicycle, you know, keep the old legs going but I couldn't get up the hill. Luckily Ronnie gave me a lift. New car, very nice: four by four. You could play tennis in the boot.

**Caroline** *comes centre, looks at the green and reacts to the heat.*

What time are the ladies coming?

**Jack**    Eleven.

**Caroline**    I didn't know if I was going to be early or late. I'm getting awful with time, I am honestly. Some days I arrive at work an hour early and another time I'm an hour late. Thank God I don't do the rotas. As you get older, my word . . .

*She winces at the state of the green.*

Oh that looks scorched, my word!

**Ted**    There's ice-creams and frozen prawns in there, Caroline, I'd get one before Ronnie eats 'em all.

**Caroline**    Yes, the food firms are on to every angle! Talk about making the best of a bad job, frozen prawns and ice-creams in the middle of winter. It doesn't bear thinking about, where have they got the prawns from, the seas are bubbling . . . my word, Jack, that green looks poor.

*She moves towards the clubhouse.*

And I think that the fence is flat-lining! It needs a bit of life if you ask me!

**Caroline** *disappears into the clubhouse.* **Ted** *and* **Jack** *drift together on the edge of the green.*

**Ted** (*whispers*)    There's sommat going on there.

**Jack** (*whispers*)    How do you know?

**Ted** (*whispers*)    She said he gave her a lift up the hill.

**Jack** (*whispers*)    So what?

**Ted** (*whispers*)    Well, he usually comes the other way round, he doesn't have to come up the hill, does he? If he comes up the hill he comes past her house!

**Jack** (*whispers*)    Bloody hell.

**Ted** (*whispers*)    What?

**Jack** (*whispers*)    Get a life, Ted!

**Ted** (*whispers*)    I've got one, Jack, it's shit!

*A beat.*

**Jack** (*whispers*)    Well, I've never played away so it doesn't interest me!

**Ted** *has a weather eye on the clubhouse.*

**Ted** (*whispers*)    And you know that he's had a heart scare? Caroline told me; nobody's supposed to know about it.

**Jack** (*whispers*)    Sounds like you've been spending a lot of time with her, Ted. Are you sure it's you that's not having t' affair?

**Ronnie** *enters from the clubhouse. He is eating an ice-lolly. He stands on the veranda.* **Ted** *and* **Jack** *busy themselves with the bowls equipment.*

**Ronnie**    I was just on about property shooting up again, Ted.

**Ted**    Land's at a premium, if we could ever sell this we'd make a fortune.

**Ronnie**    Well, you're t' Treasurer, aren't you, why can't you sell it?

**Ted**    It doesn't belong to us. We have to pay a rent, it belongs to the village.

**Ronnie**    Well, I never knew that!

**Jack**    Oh aye, this'll only ever be a bowling club no matter what!

**Ted**    I mean, nobody'll be able to play here like because of the membership dwindling, we'll not even be able to pay t' rent.

**Ronnie** *stands on the veranda and holds court.*

**Ronnie**    There's a bloke in our village sold his garden off for one point five million. Not half the size of yours, Jack.

**Ted**    Well aye, people need cash, because of the pension lark!

*A beat.*

**Ronnie**    There's a cameraman working with me who's taken a loan out to pay off the interest on a loan he's taken out!

*A beat.*

**Ted** (*stating*)    Gordon Brown borrowed too much. And Cameron?

**Jack**    He's got no idea, has he, which is odd because his wife's got money.

**Ronnie**    They're making a film of his book, aren't they?

**Ted**    Who?

**Ronnie**    David Cameron, they're making a film of his autobiography. Mind you, I hope it's better than the film they made about Tony Blair's, I was up for a part in that: Charles Clarke. I didn't get it, did you see it? They skipped over Iraq, didn't they? It's bloody chaos out there now, we were supposed to be going out there with Peter Kaye to do a show but it's too dangerous, they say.

**Ronnie** *sucks his lolly.* **Ted** *and* **Jack** *look at the green.*

**Ted**   Bloody politicians, they're all tarred with the same brush.

**Ronnie** (*sucking his lolly*)   They reckon that more people voted for *X-Factor Eight* than voted in the last election!

**Ted**   I didn't vote for either.

**Ronnie**   They're on about making you vote. They reckon you'll be able to vote by text the next time. One of the runners was telling me that with artificial intelligence you'll be able to think what you want to vote and it'll be registered.

*A beat.*

**Jack**   Well, I hope they never register what Ted's thinking or it'll be a prison job!

**Ronnie**'s *mobile phone rings. The tune is over the top.* **Ronnie** *struggles to get out his mobile. It is minute. He struggles to get a clear signal.*

**Ted**   What the bloody hell is that?

**Ronnie** (*to the phone*)   Sharon! Yes, fine! Yes, last week, Gozo. Oh yes, really lovely . . . as a berry. How are you? Yes? Just hang on, love, you're really not good here . . . No, I'm with some old boys, bowling . . . I can't.

**Ronnie** *moves around trying to get a better signal.*

You're not. Sharon? Can you . . . If you can hear me I'll call you back from the car, I've got a booster signal on the hands-free. Sharon, if you can hear me I'm going to call you back!

**Ronnie** *clicks the phone away.*

My agent!

**Ted**   Bloody hell!

**Ronnie**   No rest . . . I'll show you the car later if you want. I'll just give her a quick call.

**Ted**    Well aye.

**Ronnie** *exits.*

*Sound effect of car doors opening and closing.*

*A beat.*

**Ted**    Gozo!

**Jack**    Sharon!

**Ted**    Another bloody advert, I bet.

**Jack**    I wondered where he'd got that tan from!

*A beat.*

**Ted** (*dry*)    You'd get one like that in Brid today though, Jack!

**Jack**    So we know what we are now, Ted.

**Ted**    What's that then?

**Jack**    We're old boys.

**Caroline** *enters eating, and stands on the veranda looking out onto the green and finishes her prawn.* **Ted** *sits near the small table.* **Jack** *is on the green.*

**Caroline**    Lovely those.

**Ted**    He plays in York now most of the time, doesn't he, Ronnie?

**Caroline**    With the Yorkshire singles champion on and off. Where's he gone?

**Ted**    Phone call!

**Caroline**    Yes, he hobnobs now. Lovely prawns, Jack! He plays at the Sessy club.

**Jack**    That's a good green.

**Ted**    I mean we're lucky he still comes here.

**Jack** (*dry*)    Aye, coz he's such a lovely man.

*A beat.*

**Ted**    He's reinvented himself, hasn't he. I wish I could do that.

**Jack**    What would you reinvent yourself as though, Ted?

*A beat.*

**Ted**    Do you know, I'm not sure.

**Jack**    You need to get that worked out first.

*A beat.*

**Caroline**    I don't think I've ever known it so hot.

**Jack**    It was this hot in 1972. We had that long spell. I was still at Barnborough pit, that was hot.

**Caroline**    Not in October. I can remember that summer but it wasn't like this.

**Ted**    Maybe the world's trying to tell us sommat?

**Jack**    Yes, we've just had my granddaughter telling us that Venice is sinking.

**Caroline**    Three millimetres a year. And the water's rising.

**Jack**    Earth's been changing for years, it's bound to run out of resources one day, but we'll be long dead, so there's no need for us to worry about it.

**Caroline**    We should be doing something about it though, that's why I came on my bike, well I did try . . . unfortunately I couldn't negotiate the hill but . . .

**Ted**    Oh don't set him off, Caroline, we've had this already this morning.

**Jack**    Well, I don't give a toss.

**Caroline**    Oh you can't say that.

**Jack**    I've just said it!

**Caroline**    But you don't mean it, do you?

**Jack**    I do. We didn't ask for what happened to May.

**Caroline**    No, I know but . . .

**Jack**    The world can rot for me!

**Caroline**    Well, I understand how loss can make you feel, Jack, but . . .

**Jack** (*rising*)    Do you?

**Caroline**    Of course . . .

**Jack**    I keep thinking that it was all a dream, and she'll come back and I'll see her sat there.

**Caroline** (*easy*)    I know it's awful . . .

**Jack**    How did she get to that? How did May get to be in a chair?

**Caroline**    It was very quick.

**Jack**    That's why I'm not bothered about global warming. It doesn't mean that . . .

*He clicks his fingers.*

to me . . . In fact I wish I was dead sometimes! And then we get Ronnie going on about his series and his new car, and he's going to give us a ride in it! I mean why was it May? Can you answer me that?

*No one can answer.*

**Caroline**    Life isn't fair, Jack.

**Jack**    I know that!

**Jack** *is frustrated. He looks down the green.*

**Ted**    There's a hundred and fifty channels now.

**Jack**    And still nowt to watch.

*A beat.*

**Caroline**    I don't watch much really so . . .

**Jack**    And the bloody Olympics! All that money, and none of it spent up here. I mean what is it with us, we're lucky if we've got an Englishman in the national football team. And now everybody wants to be famous.

*A beat.*

**Ted** (*kindly*)    That's it now, Jack, I think you've covered everything!

**Jack**    Sod the bloody planet!

*A beat.*

**Caroline** (*lightly*)    Well, we're only designed to live to be about forty anyway, so anything after that is a bonus.

**Ted**    You see, that's why I've never liked doctors: they always tell you sommat you don't want to know.

**Caroline**    They say the summer ice-caps have already melted.

**Ted**    Oh aye, they'll all want to come up here if Hull floods. So every cloud has a silver lining, Jack.

**Jack** (*easily*)    Aye, if Hull floods, them lap dances Ronnie goes to see'll be mermaids.

**Ted** *laughs at this indiscretion.*

**Ted**    Well aye!

**Caroline** (*slightly concerned*)    What's that?

**Jack** (*uncaring*)    Ronnie: he's casino happy. Goodness knows what his wife thinks he's doing down there.

**Caroline** (*alert*)    I didn't know he even went!

**Ronnie** *enters with his phone, he seems a little vacant. He drifts towards the clubhouse.*

**Jack**    Here he is, look, the man from Lapland!

**Ted** (*interested*)    Is it diesel then, Ron, or . . . ?

**Ronnie** (*vacant*)    Diesel.

**Ted**    Third new 'un in as many years, isn't it?

**Ronnie** (*easily*)    Well, if you've got it, you know!

**Ted**    We were just saying, what's it like playing at Sessy?

**Ronnie** (*not interested*)    It's a good club!

**Ted**    They've got the county champion there, haven't they.

**Jack** (*bitter*)    Well I've been county champion, so that's nowt to go on about.

**Ronnie** *feels aggravated by* **Jack***'s bile.*

**Ronnie**    That's it, if anybody's done something Jack's done it twice over.

*A beat.*

**Jack**    What do you mean by that?

**Ronnie**    I was only saying, you've done a lot of things. Why, what do you mean?

**Jack**    I was only saying, I've been Yorkshire champion.

**Ted** (*lightly*)    Jack, it was twenty years ago.

**Ronnie**    Well, I was only saying.

**Jack**    And I was only saying.

*A beat.*

**Ronnie** (*worriedly*)    Listen I've got high blood pressure, I don't want to get into an argument.

**Jack** (*easy*)    I've had high blood pressure all my life, and it's never stopped me doing owt!

**Ted** (*easily*)    It has, it stopped you playing rugby.

**Ronnie** (*making a point*)    Well, I'm on tablets for it if you must know.

**Jack**    I've been on tablets for it for years!

**Ronnie** (*panicking*)    Look, I've not to get stressed, Jack, so . . .

**Jack** *regardless of the consequences.*

**Jack**    I should keep away from that casino then.

**Ronnie** (*uneasy*)    That's nowt to do with you that, that's my private life!

**Jack**    Private life, who do you think you are?

**Ronnie**    That's nowt to do with you!

**Jack**    You'll always be a club act to me, Ronnie, whether tha's on the bloody telly or not.

**Ted** (*confused*)    Where's this come from?

**Caroline** (*keen*)    Can we park this and move on?

**Ronnie**    I'm not going into it, I don't want the stress.

**Jack**    There's no wonder you've got stress if you're down there with some nineteen-year-old wriggling about in your lap and God knows what else.

**Caroline** (*forcefully*)    Why don't you just start the game?

**Ted**    Aye, I think I'd have that stress, Ron!

**Ronnie** *is rising to the bait.*

**Ronnie** (*to* **Jack**)    If you must know I had an angina do last month. (*To* **Caroline**.) Didn't I? (*To* **Jack**.) So now you know!

**Jack**    Ronnie, I've had angina for twenty years!

**Ted** (*easily*)    Aye, that's why he took up bowls, isn't it?

**Ronnie**    There you go, look. If you get a cold Jack's got pneumonia!

**Ted**    Mind you, I've had pneumonia, Ronnie, it's not that bad!

**Ronnie**    I've not got to get stressed, that's all!

**Jack**    Tha' doesn't know what stress is.

**Ted**    Hey, he's a younger wife, Jack, he might do!

**Caroline** *is annoyed by these antics, and upset by the revelation about* **Ronnie***'s lap-dancing antics.*

**Caroline**    Can we park this?

**Jack**    He's been a lucky sod all his life!

**Caroline**    Can we park this?

**Jack**    I don't know who he thinks he is!

**Caroline**    Can we park this please?

**Jack**    Aye, park it by his new four by four. His carbon footprint's bloody terrible!

**Ronnie**    What do you know about that?

**Jack**    More than you bloody do!

**Caroline**    This is not the place for this, it's too warm. I didn't come all the way up here to hear this, my word, life's too short.

**Jack** (*piqued*)    Aye, it is, tell me about it!

**Caroline** *comes down from the veranda and makes her way towards the gate.*

**Ted**    Caroline?

**Caroline**    Little boys . . .

**Ted**    Are you going?

**Caroline**    I'm going to get some cigarettes.

**Jack**    Yes, get some for Ronnie, that'll calm him down.

**Caroline** *exits.* **Ted** *follows her to the gates.*

**Ted**   Nay Caroline, no need to go off t' deep end!

**Caroline** (*off stage*)   The deep end? Please!

**Caroline** *has gone.* **Ted** *exits.*

*A beat.*

**Ronnie**   Now look what you've done.

**Jack**   It doesn't bother me! It's nowt to what I've been through.

**Ronnie**   She's bloody prickly as it is this morning!

**Ronnie** *is clearly under stress.* **Jack** *watches as* **Ronnie** *finds a seat. He is clearly not very well. He is worried about many things and this hasn't helped.*

**Ronnie**   I've had an earful all the way up here. I should've put a stop to it years ago!

**Ted** *enters enthused by* **Ronnie**'s *car.*

**Ted**   Nice car, Ronnie! What do the young uns call 'em? A babe magnet, isn't it? What does it do to the gallon?

**Ronnie** (*in the throes of a stress attack*)   Oh when I think about what I've been doing!

**Ted**   I like the number plate: Ron One. (*Laughs.*)

**Ronnie** *is beginning to develop into quite a state.*

**Ted**   Which way did you come up?

**Ronnie** (*with slight difficulty*)   I've pains in my chest now.

**Jack** (*lightly*)   I've pains in my chest all the time, it's called loss.

**Ted**   Mind you, I've pains with bowling, I pulled right across my shoulder last week.

**Ronnie** *is becoming uncomfortable.*

**Ronnie**   Oh hell!

**Ted** *looks at* **Ronnie**, *then* **Jack**.

**Ted**   Is he all right?

**Jack** (*sure*)   He's bloody milking it.

**Ted**   The thing is, you never know the truth with him!

**Jack**   Are we going to have a few ends?

**Jack** *begins to gather his woods together.*

**Ronnie** (*in pain*)   Oph!

**Ted** *looks at* **Ronnie** *from the green.*

**Ted** (*whispers*)   I'll tell you sommat, if he is acting it though, he's bloody good.

**Jack** *and* **Ted** *watch* **Ronnie** *in the throes of having a heart attack. It is both unsettling and amusing. They hate* **Ronnie**'*s success and here it shows itself fully.* **Ted** *gets to his knees to inspect the woods.*

**Jack**   He's better sat there than he is on that series to be honest.

**Ted**   I don't watch it. Isn't that awful? How long have I known him and I can't bring myself to watch it.

**Ronnie** (*painful*)   Oph!

**Ted**   Alice can't stand it, she shouts out when he's on so . . .

**Ronnie** (*agony*)   Oh!

*They watch him as he struggles in agony.*

**Ted**   No, I don't watch it, I wait till Alice drops off and then I switch over . . .

**Jack** (*dry*)   To BBC 4?

**Ronnie** (*appealing*)   Oh . . . !

**Ted** (*oblivious*)   Well, when I say I don't watch it I've seen it once.

**Ronnie** (*coughing*)    Oh!

**Ted** (*oblivious*)    In fact I might have seen it more than once . . .

**Ronnie** *is now having a heart attack.*

**Ronnie** (*shouting*)    Oh somebody . . . !

**Ted** (*oblivious*)    Do you know, I can't think how many times I've seen it . . .

**Ronnie** (*in agony*)    Get somebody . . .

**Jack** (*easily*)    I thought tha' was joking, Ronnie.

**Ronnie** (*screaming*)    I'm not bloody joking! I think I'm having a bloody heart attack!

**Jack** (*to* **Ted**)    Get Caroline, Ted!

**Ted** *attempts to get up quickly but can't.*

**Ted**    I'll get her! (*Agony.*) Oh I can't get up! I'm going to have to get sommat done with this knee. (*Agony.*) Ooh I can't get up!

**Jack**    Is it bad?

**Ted** (*agony*)    This one is!

**Ronnie** (*agony*)    Oh!

**Ted** *is slow to get moving.*

**Ted** (*panic*)    I'll get Caroline and then I'll have to have a tablet!

**Jack**    Do you take tablets?

**Ted**    For my knees I do!

**Ronnie** (*agony*)    Oh!

**Ted**'*s rising is pure tragi-comedy.*

**Ted** (*still slow*)    I can't make my bloody legs go!

**Ted** *hobbles towards off stage calling after* **Caroline**.

**Ted** (*calls*) Caroline? (*To himself.*) Look at me, I'm a bloody old man. (*From off stage.*) Look at my legs! Oh, a lovely motor that Ron.

**Jack** *holds the wood he has in his hand.*

**Jack** (*jokingly*)    I bet I'd beat you now, Ronnie!

**Ronnie** (*agony*)    Opphhh!

*A beat, as **Ronnie** stumbles from his seat.*

**Jack** (*icy*)    I bet I'd beat you today!

**Ronnie** (*in pain*)    I'm not bothered, just get me a bloody ambulance!

**Jack** *bends to make a shot.*

**Jack** (*to his shot*)    Oh yes, look at that!

*Music plays.*

*Lights fade. Blackout.*

# Act Three

*2022.*

*Music.*

*Lights fade up to reveal* **Caroline** *at seventy-six. She is standing on the green and is slowly gathering together a number of woods. She is clearly older but still smart in her whites, with glasses, a hat, and she also has a stick which she reluctantly uses. It is extremely warm.* **Jack** *eventually enters from the clubhouse. He too is seventy-six and age is taking its toll. He moves slowly over the veranda in his grey trousers and his white shirt. He has a new pair of glasses and seems slightly glazed. He responds to the heat.*

**Jack** (*groans*)   Oh!

**Caroline** (*the heat*)   Oph!

*A beat.*

**Jack**   Can I give you a hand?

**Caroline**   No, no . . . nearly done.

**Jack** *stands on the apex of the green.*

**Jack**   Won again, Caroline.

**Caroline**   Well, I'm getting used to it now after thirty years.

*Takes a big breath.*

But I must say I think we're depleted on the ladies front.

**Jack** (*groans*)   Opph!

**Caroline**   Still no new members.

**Jack**   Yes, I'm beginning to think that that's not going to happen!

**Caroline** *pauses in the heat.*

**Caroline**   It's nearly unbearable, isn't it?

**Jack**    Well, we can't play any earlier. They tell me that there's a club in Skipton who play under floodlight.

**Caroline**    Floodlight?

**Jack**    They reckon the council are going mad, but they're still playing.

**Caroline** *looks at* **Jack**.

**Caroline**    Are you all right?

**Jack**    Me?

**Caroline**    You're ever so red.

*A beat.*

**Jack**    Well, to tell you the truth I've just had a smoke, Caroline.

**Caroline**    Oh dear!

**Jack**    Yes, yes, just a few puffs on that stuff Ronnie's been going on about.

**Caroline**    Oh dear!

**Jack**    They say it's good for arthritis, and I'm crippled by it!

**Caroline**    Well, they do say that, I don't know how true it is!

**Jack**    I'll try anything once!

**Caroline**    Where are they?

**Jack**    They're still in there, it's like a Turkish bath at the minute! Ted's on another planet.

**Caroline**    Oh dear, drugs hits bowling.

**Jack**    At last!

**Caroline**    Alert the media.

*She begins to gather her woods into a group.*

Well, we've no rain now for three months, Jack.

*She makes her way to the clubhouse to pick up her trolley which has been pre-set there. When she walks we notice she really is becoming older.*

(*Reaction.*) Oph I can smell it, what are they smoking?

**Jack**    I've no idea, I only had two goes, it makes me dizzy taking deep breaths so . . .

**Jack** *stands sweltering in the heat.*

**Caroline**    Mind you, when it did rain! It was like a monsoon. I think it's clear things are changing.

**Jack**    We've had weather like this before though.

**Caroline** *has her trolley and brings it onto the green.*

**Caroline**    I can't remember when. We used to blame the Russians but . . .

**Jack**    We did.

**Caroline**    We did.

**Jack**    We used to blame the Russians for everything.

**Caroline**    And now we blame everyone for everything. Especially the Chinese.

**Jack**    It's not their fault though, we're all in it together now according to my granddaughter.

**Caroline** *bends slowly to pick up a wood.*

**Caroline**    How's she doing, Jack?

*A beat.*

**Jack** (*sad*)    Not so good at the moment!

**Caroline** (*sad*)    Oh dear.

**Jack**    No, not wonderful from what I can gather.

**Caroline**    Oh I'm sorry.

*A beat.*

**Jack**   They've admitted her for some treatment.

**Caroline**   Dear me.

**Jack**   Mental exhaustion, I think they call it.

**Caroline**   I'm really sorry for you.

**Jack**   All that talent!

**Caroline**   Dear me!

**Jack**   First-class honours, grade eight piano! Her mother had wanted her to be a barrister. Absolutely dead set on saving the planet she was, even as a kid! A complete non-conformist, all her life, anti everything, war, police, government!

**Caroline** *puts another wood in her trolley.*

**Jack**   Obsessed with it. I think it must be the frustration, people not listening.

**Caroline**   Governments, Jack, not people.

**Jack**   I thought she'd grow out of it.

**Caroline**   Sounds like a bright girl, Jack!

**Jack**   I mean, what can we do about it? I don't know if we're causing it or it's destined or what.

**Caroline** *slowly places another wood in her trolley.*

**Caroline**   Oh we're causing it: we've been raping the planet for too long! And it might be too little too late! Did you ever read James Lovelock's work?

**Jack** (*easily*)   What do you think I am, Caroline? I used to read the racing page of the *Yorkshire Post* and that's about it!

**Caroline** *places another wood in her trolley.*

**Jack**   The worrying thing is that you never know what's around the corner.

**Caroline**   You don't.

*A beat.*

**Jack**   No, you don't!

**Caroline**   But we can't go back, Jack!

**Jack** (*echoing*)   No, we can't go back!

**Caroline** *has completed packing her trolley. She adjusts her white jumper and hangs it over the trolley.*

**Caroline**   Well there we are, all done, my word, the effort!

**Caroline** *laughs at her breathlessness.*

**Jack**   We've ordered some food, I don't know if you want to wait for it or . . . We've gone for a butcher's in Hessle, that online stuff was driving Ted mad!

**Caroline** *has gathered herself and is ready for off.*

**Caroline**   No, I think I've had enough.

**Jack**   I mean, I don't know what they'll come up with but . . .

**Caroline**   No, I think I've had enough.

**Jack**   Well, I thought I'd mention it, because it's a long walk back.

*A beat.*

**Caroline**   No, I think I've had enough altogether, Jack, thanks!

**Jack**   Oh right?

*A beat.*

**Caroline**   In fact I think I've had enough of the club.

*A beat.*

**Jack** (*shocked*)   Oh well . . . !

*A beat.*

**Caroline**    Well, I can't stay here for ever.

*A beat.*

**Jack**    Well, I'd have to agree that the recruitment's been a bit of a disappointment over time.

**Caroline**    Now that is an understatement! In the twenty-five years I've been playing here, Jack, we haven't attracted a single new player, have we?

**Jack**    Well . . .

**Caroline**    I think the answer you're looking for is 'No'!

**Jack**    Well no, you're right, no we haven't, but it's not through a lack of trying. I don't know what *you* do!

*A beat.*

**Caroline**    So anyway!

*A beat.*

**Jack**    Well, we've done well today, another victory thanks to you. I mean I'm still struggling with my form . . . and my eyesight's in a bit of a mess . . .

**Caroline** *looks around the clubhouse site.*

**Caroline**    Well, it's not just the club.

**Jack**    Oh right.

*A beat.*

**Caroline**    I've had enough of everything, the village, the city, the club, the hospital, and even the country . . .

*A beat.*

**Jack**    Oh hell.

**Caroline**    Yes! I know!

*A beat.*

**Jack**    You're not going to do something stupid though, are you?

*A beat.*

**Caroline**    Do you know what, I think I might.

**Jack**    Oh hell . . .

*A beat.*

**Caroline**    I think I just might.

**Jack** (*aghast*)    Dear me!

*A beat.*

**Caroline** (*serious*)    I have been thinking about it! I've been thinking about it for a long time, Jack, for a long time.

*A beat.*

**Jack**    Well, I don't know what to say!

**Caroline** *stands with her stick. She is confident and proud.* **Jack** *animates and is concerned.*

**Caroline**    And I haven't felt this sure about anything for years.

*A beat.*

**Jack**    But you're only seventy-six.

**Caroline**    Seventy-seven in March.

**Jack**    It's no age.

**Caroline**    I know, that's what I keep telling myself.

**Jack**    So why are you thinking it?

**Caroline**    Well . . .

**Jack**    It's outrageous, you're a fine attractive woman, I mean I've always thought of you like that, good grief, Caroline, if I had my time again, I can tell you, for what it's worth, I . . . you know, well . . . you know . . . ! And I'm sorry I've said it but I have thought it on and off for the last twenty-five years, and if that stops you from doing something stupid well so be it!!

**Caroline**   Well, I'm flattered.

**Jack**   Well, all right, I've said it . . . but if it'll stop you killing yourself . . .

**Caroline**   . . . I have no intention of killing myself, Jack!

*A beat.*

I've just decided I'm going to do something else.

*A beat.*

**Jack**   Something else?

**Caroline**   Yes, I'm going to do something different.

*A beat.*

**Jack** (*astonished*)   Something different? You're seventy-seven in March!

**Caroline** (*elated*)   Haven't you ever thought of doing something else?

**Jack**   There is nothing else, this is what I do! I'm retired, so are you, we hang around and we wait!

**Caroline**   For Godot?

**Jack**   Who?

**Caroline**   No, I've been thinking about it for a long time.

**Jack**   So where are you going?

**Caroline**   Abroad!

*A beat.*

**Jack**   To live?

**Caroline**   To help, to work. I'm giving myself five years, and then I'll come back, all being well! Like they say, we don't know how long we've got left. My cousin's eldest daughter is fifty-nine and she's still in the Gulf, she only went there for three years! I mean you never know what you're starting, do you? So who knows . . .

**Jack**   Bloody hell!

**Caroline**   And that was a waste, wasn't it? They've all gone now, haven't they? The men who took us into that! Bush, Blair, Rumsfeld. She tells me that Tony Blair has a radio programme on Radio Five Live. I didn't know that was still going, how funny don't you think?

*She is slightly excited.*

Yes, I sat there one night and I thought, Caroline, what next? Turn again, Whittington. My word, why not?

**Jack**   Well, I'm afraid I'm here for the duration.

*A beat.*

**Caroline**   Well, good luck!

**Caroline** *appears to be preparing to depart.*

**Jack**   You were one of the best doctors we've ever had around here.

*A beat.*

**Caroline**   Yes, but what have I really achieved?

**Jack**   People relied on you, they still do!

**Caroline**   Well I'm going to re-invent myself.

**Jack**   Not like Ronnie?

**Caroline**   Well, he's had a colourful life, from club land to TV stardom!

**Jack**   Yes, and back again!

*A beat.*

**Caroline**   He's been lucky with everything.

**Jack**    Five heart attacks and he's still here!

*A beat.*

**Caroline**    You see, I think we make our own luck, Jack!

**Jack**    Well, I have never been lucky.

**Caroline**    You were lucky with May, lucky she didn't suffer for too long, and lucky you met her!

*A beat.*

**Jack**    No, I'm not lucky, I want her back. That's what I want.

**Caroline**    I know!

*A beat.*

**Jack**    No, my chance to change has been and gone!

*A beat.*

**Caroline**    So I'm going after Xmas.

**Jack**    That's the week after next!

**Caroline**    I don't know where the months go!

*A beat.*

You'll get by without me.

**Jack**    The ladies team won't: you're it!

*A beat.*

I don't know, since I lost May everything's been up and down . . . It's never the same it's just wave after wave!

**Caroline**    It's about how you ride them!

*A beat.*

**Jack**    She loved Johnny Mathis you know.

**Caroline**    I know she told me.

*A beat.*

**Jack**   Loved Johnny Mathis.

**Caroline**   We used to talk about him.

*A beat.*

**Jack**   In fact she loved all black men. Pele, Eusabio, Charlie Williams. She loved black men. I don't know why she ever married me!

**Caroline**   She told me that as well.

*A beat.*

**Jack**   I think she preferred me in my pit muck, to be honest. Did I ever tell you that I was a miner?

**Caroline**   Every time we met for the first twenty-five years, Jack.

*A beat.*

**Jack**   I was proud of that, and that's all gone, and I've sold the shop so that's gone. I'm a dinosaur, Caroline.

**Caroline**   Maybe.

*A beat.*

**Jack**   I used to come home in my pit muck and have a bath in the kitchen. And that's not so long ago!

**Caroline**   I know it's not.

**Jack**   When our Pauline went to college we didn't have a fridge. When you think! We didn't have a phone, then May wanted the kitchen sink moving. We used to keep the milk in the grate in the shade at the back of the house. I mean that's not fifty years ago.

**Caroline**   Things change so quickly.

**Jack**   I think that's why I've always liked it up here. I know I'm living in the past.

**Caroline**   That's because from the first wood ever bowled the rules have been set, they haven't changed for five thousand years, there's some comfort in that.

*A beat.*

That's why I'm going, Jack, I want to break the rules.

*A beat.*

**Jack**   They do say it's getting worse, I mean I don't go into Hull if I can help it. I haven't been in for years. Don't they reckon Spurn Point's going? And a lot of the front at Hornsea has gone! It sounds like people are just starting to waken up to it . . .

*A beat.*

**Caroline**   People only understand politics when it's happening to them, Jack!

**Jack**   That's true!

**Caroline**   Things change and not always for the better.

*A beat.*

**Jack**   They do! I mean I've finally succumbed to cannabis.

**Caroline**   Just cut out the dairy stuff.

**Jack**   I'd rather hang myself.

*A beat.*

**Caroline**   Well it's always an option.

*A beat.*

Anyway, all the best! You're not a bad old stick, you've never really adapted to the flat lawn, but there you go!

**Caroline** *kisses* **Jack**. *It's quite touching.*

**Jack**   Aren't you going to say goodbye to Ted and Ron?

*A beat.*

**Caroline**    Forty years ago Ron said he was going to leave his wife, I think he knows how I feel about him. And I don't think he's ever going to leave her now, do you?

*A beat.*

Just tell them I've gone to play for another club, they'll hate me for that!

*A beat.*

**Jack**    They will do, you know that!

*A beat.*

**Caroline**    May was a good player, Jack. Do you know I think that she was the best bowler I've ever seen.

**Jack**    A pig to live with though.

**Caroline**    But you loved her.

**Jack**    How did she get to be in that wheelchair? How did she ever get to losing her mind, Caroline! What kind of disease is that?

**Caroline**    Vicious, absolutely!

*A beat.*

**Jack**    There was never a woman loved so much. But I was a bastard to my daughter.

**Caroline**    Yes, she told me that.

*A beat.*

**Jack**    Especially when she got married.

**Caroline**    She told me that as well.

*A beat.*

**Jack**    You reap what you sow! She never comes to visit me, and I wanted everything for her!

**Caroline**    Take care.

**Caroline** *grabs her trolley and her stick and slowly makes her way out of the bowling club.* **Jack** *stands and watches her leave. He is sad and follows around to look at the clubhouse roof. We hear birdsong.*

**Jack**    Bloody hell, look at them slates! The whole bloody thing's falling to bits.

*As* **Jack** *stands we hear a car pulling up in the distance.* **Jack** *turns around and looks at the green. He winces as he looks at the state of the grass in the middle. As he does,* **Max** *enters.* **Max** *wears a traditional butcher's apron and has aged considerably. He is now forty-one, and quite nervous. He has a few pork pies and a couple of bread rolls.*

**Jack**    We've finished! Everybody's gone before they fry!

**Max**    I'm doing my b-best, this v-van I've got is f-f-f-ffriggin' d-dreadful, this is all I could get, four pork p-pies and six b-baps. People are panic-buying because of the w-weather, they reckon there's to be no rain for another two-two-two months. Some r-roads are cracking b-by all a-accounts. M1 is split right across North-North-Northampton! And petrol prices have gone mad again! London's a m-m-madhouse. Hey you know they're still doing stuff on-on-online if you . . .

**Jack**    Yes, but the price . . .

**Max**    You get what y-you p-pay for though, don't you?

**Jack**    What's it like at the butcher's?

**Max**    Chaos this m-morning. There's hundreds with n-nowt to live on in Hull! Cars on fire! They reckon the Humber's not got long before it bursts its banks.

**Jack**    Bloody hell!

**Max**    Oh aye it's c-c-c-c-c –

**Jack** (*helping*)    Crap?

**Max** (*continuing*)    Kak down there!

**Jack**    How's that casino doing?

**Max**    D-dunno, I've stopped delivering. I think a lot of people wished that they'd not spen-spen-spent up! There's parts of the east coast that's under water. Nobody knows what to do! They reckon there'll be a lot of them trying to get on high-high land. The funny thing is I always thought the world wou-wou-would end in my lifetime!

*A beat.*

Well, it looks like I'm going to be right for once!

**Jack**    Well, you're bloody cheery!

**Max**    Well, they've been going on about it for l-long enough. Fire and ice they said, looks like they were wrong though, it l-looks like it's going to be w-water!

**Jack**    I felt all right and now you've depressed me! I don't know if it's the prospect of the end of the world or the thought of those bloody pork pies and baps.

**Max**    Yes, they look a b-bit ropey!

*A beat.*

**Jack**    You're not still training are you?

**Max**    Me, y-yes.

**Jack**    What for?

**Max**    Life!

*A beat.*

**Jack**    What do you weigh anyway?

**Max**    Twenty-one stone.

**Jack**    What's heaviest tha's ever lifted?

**Max**    Thirty-two stone.

**Jack**    Why though?

*A beat.*

**Max**    Because I can!

*A beat.*

**Jack**   Are you going to have a go or does your lass want you back?

**Max**   No, you're my last d-delivery today.

**Jack**   Have you ever felt one of these? Go on have a feel!

**Jack** *bends to offer a wood to* **Max**. **Max** *holds it in his large hand.*

**Max**   Heavy . . .

**Jack**   Surprising, isn't it?

**Max** *weighs the wood.*

**Max**   Oh aye, there's a n-nice line to 'em!

**Max** *holds the wood up to inspect it.*

**Jack**   Beautiful . . . When you let it go it's poetry. When you get a wood kissing the jack . . . ooh . . . !

**Max**   Aye?

**Jack**   That's freedom that . . . It's like it's a part of you . . . You get a sense of the green and you become an extension of the wood and the line. It's like you can put yourself into the wood, I know it sounds daft but it feels completely natural.

**Max**   Aye you're right, it does sound d-d-daft!

**Jack**   Aye, I said it did!

**Max** *steps forward with the wood, he is sensing it, sensing his movement with the wood. He looks down the green.*

**Max**   Feels good.

*He looks around the clubhouse location.*

I always t-thought you'd got your own little w-world up here. I mean you're about fifty ye-yea-years b-behind time but it's so peaceful. All the high land is at p-premium now, they r-r-reckon good high ground is as s-scarce as rocking-horse sh-sh-sh-sh-she-she . . .

**Jack**   Yes, I know what you're saying!

**Ronnie** *and* **Ted** *emerge from the clubhouse. They are both in their mid seventies.* **Ronnie** *looks older and is a little unsteady on his feet.* **Ted***'s clothes look the worse for wear. He has a stick. Both have been smoking cannabis and are very mellow. They stand on the veranda and notice* **Max** *and* **Jack***.* **Max** *has no idea what they have been doing in the clubhouse.*

*Silence.*

**Max**   All right?

**Ted**   All right.

**Ronnie**   All right.

**Ted**   All right, Jack?

**Jack**   I'm all right, are you?

**Ted**   I'm all right, Jack!

**Ted** *chuckles. They find a seat and sit.*

**Ronnie**   Hot.

**Max**   It is!

*Silence.*

**Ted**   Did you want us?

**Max**   No.

*A beat.*

**Jack**   Pork pies are here.

**Ronnie**   Oh pork pies are here then?

**Max**   Aye, the p-p-pork p-p-pies are h-h-here, s'all I could get. Is that all right?

*A beat.*

**Ronnie**   All right.

**Ted**   All right then?

**Max**   I'm all right!

**Ted**   That's good then.

**Max** (*offers the wood*)   I was just having a feel.

*A beat.*

**Ronnie**   Urm . . .

**Jack**   He says Hull's in a mess.

**Ronnie**   Urm.

*A beat.*

**Ted** (*from nowhere*)   I'm in a bungalow now, you've to ring to get in. There's a warden who comes round, you have to ring to get in!

**Max**   Where's that then?

**Ted**   Just off Boothferry, there's a warden who comes round.

**Max**   Oh right!

**Ted**   You have to ring to get in!

*A beat.*

**Jack**   They're building on high land he says.

**Ronnie**   Urm.

**Max** *still has the wood.*

**Max**   I was just having a feel.

**Ronnie**   Urm.

**Max**   Anyway, here's t' pork p-p-pies!

**Max** *puts down the wood and indicates the pork pies and baps.*

**Ted** (*to* **Ronnie**)   What's he say?

**Ronnie**   Pork pies are here?

*A beat.*

**Ted** (*mishearing*)   Pork pies got ears?

*A beat.*

**Max**   Do you still play on this?

**Ted** (*of the pork pie*)   I hope they haven't!

*A beat.*

**Jack**   We have to play in the mornings coz of the heat.

**Max**   I might g-give it a g-go. But I don't think I'm ready for it y-yet.

*A beat.*

**Ted**   Aye, we all think we're never going to be ready for bowls and t' next thing you know it's all you've got!

*A beat.*

**Max**   I'd b-better get off, this van has got no air c-c-c-c! If I don't get finished before one o'clock it's hell in the cabin. See you. Su-su-see you!

**Max** *exits.*

*Silence.*

**Jack**   I don't know about you but that stuff's not touched me. Has it you?

**Ted**   Who?

**Jack**   Has it touched you?

*A beat.*

**Ted**   Well, we've had another two.

**Jack**   Bloody hell.

**Ronnie**   Mmm.

*A beat.*

**Ted**   Has Caroline gone?

**Jack**   Yes.

**Ronnie**   Urm.

**Jack**   She's gone for good.

**Ted**   Eh?

**Jack**   I say she's left!

**Ted**   She's left?

**Jack**   That's it!

*A beat.*

**Ted**   What's she left?

**Jack**   She's left here.

*A beat.*

**Ted**   Her left ear?

**Jack**   She's gone to help . . .

*A beat.*

**Ted**   With the sandwiches?

**Jack**   She said she'd had enough.

**Ted**   Sandwiches?

**Jack**   No, she's going abroad.

**Ted**   Will she not want a pork pie?

**Jack** *finds this amusing and laughs.*

**Jack**   She said you'd understand, Ron.

**Ronnie**   Blame me!

*A beat.*

**Jack**   She was a lovely woman.

**Ted**   Well aye.

**Jack**   A lovely woman.

**Ted**   Well aye.

*A beat.*

**Jack**   She was, you know, in all the time I've known her a lovely person. I mean it's not any of my business, Ron, with all what's gone off, but I don't think it was fair on her. She was a lovely woman.

**Ted**   She was!

**Jack**   She was.

*A beat.*

**Ronnie**   Aye, she was.

*A beat.*

Mind you she was a mucky sod, you know.

**Jack**   Eh?

**Ronnie**   I say, she was mucky.

*A beat.*

**Ted**   She was.

**Ronnie**   She was.

**Ted**   She was.

*A beat.*

**Jack**   Was she?

*A beat.*

**Ted**   Oh aye, she was!

**Jack**   How do you know?

**Ted**   Well . . .

*A beat.*

**Ronnie**   Well, she was making them dodgy films with Help the Aged for a start, wasn't she?

**Jack**   She never.

**Ronnie**   She was making dodgy films with Help the Aged in Hull for a long time.

**Jack**   Well, how do you know?

*A beat.*

**Ronnie**   Well, I was in some of them.

**Jack**   What?

**Ronnie**   Only one or two like!

*A beat.*

**Jack**   Well, I wasn't.

**Ronnie**   Well, I was.

*A beat.*

**Ted**   And I was and all!

*A beat.*

**Ronnie**   Didn't you know?

**Jack**   I bloody didn't.

**Ronnie**   I thought we all knew but nobody was saying!

*A beat.*

**Jack**   Well, I wasn't saying because I didn't bloody well know.

**Ted**   Well aye.

*A beat.*

**Jack**   Aren't we all right with you two?

*A beat.*

**Ted**   He's not happy with that, Ron.

**Ronnie**   He's not happy!

**Ted**   No, he's not happy with that!

**Ronnie** *stands to go back inside the clubhouse.*

**Ronnie**   He's not happy with that, but I'll tell you this, when I had my first heart do he wasn't bloody bothered, so do you know what?

**Ted**   What?

**Ronnie**   Sod him! I'm glad he wasn't in on it!

**Jack**   I didn't know what to do, I thought it was all a bloody act like it normally is with you.

**Ronnie**   Sod him!

**Jack**   Well, when we went to Brid with you on that fishing trip we had to turn back because you didn't like water.

**Ted**   Well aye, that's true.

**Jack**   He ought to have told us that before we got on the bloody boat.

**Ted**   Well aye, that's true and all.

**Jack**   And then he makes that series and he's on a cruise in one episode!

**Ted**   Well aye, that's true . . . mind you, I didn't see that.

**Ronnie**   I thought you didn't watch it.

*A beat.*

**Ted**   I watched it once.

**Ronnie**   More than bloody once!

**Ted**   Aye I did, I enjoyed it to be honest!

*A beat.*

**Jack**   You don't know where you are with him.

*A beat.*

**Ronnie**    I'd better get myself a tablet, or there'll be bother. Oh hell, stiff.

**Ronnie** *hobbles towards the clubhouse.*

**Jack** (*bitter-sweet*)    Go on, you silly old sod.

**Ted**    Aye, that's what we are now, Jack!

*A beat.*

**Jack**    I don't know, you try and live a good life but we've got him with his cars, you with air travel, bloody drugs! If it wasn't bad enough him having a fling with Caroline now it turns out you've both been at it!

*A beat.*

I hope to goodness you both weren't at it at the same time because that would turn my stomach.

**Ted** *comes down from the veranda. He is pathetic but animated.*

**Ted**    I've been a carer most of my life, Jack!

**Jack**    Aye, I know that.

**Ted**    Most of my life.

**Jack**    Both of 'em at it.

**Ted**    Alice was twenty-eight when she took bad. And I nursed her every day, washing her, changing her. Two of us just watching the telly: nowt to talk about. Nobody bothering about us: social services, doctors, what could they do? I wanted to be there for her, but I'd just look at her and wonder why. I'd wonder why she was taken, and we'd watch about AIDS and HIV and about millions on the move and we felt for 'em but part of me thought sod 'em! Where were we living? Across t' hall there were druggies; next-door flat there were bits of lasses selling thessens. Where were we living eh? It wasn't until I started playing up here . . . can you remember the first time?

**Jack**    I can.

**Ted**  I came up here with the Dockers' Club and it was a different world. And I went back to the flat and I could have cut my bloody throat, Jack. Where were we living, in a flat no bigger than your clubhouse! I thought I'm having some of that. And when I was made Treasurer I was so proud, and you and May wanted to come around but I couldn't let you, I couldn't let you see where we lived. I was so touched that I'd come up here to play for you and nobody had asked me where I'd come from. I used to hate you bastards on the hill before that!

**Jack**  I know you did.

*A beat.*

**Ted**  I've been a carer for forty-five years, Jack, a few flights to Bangkok are nowt, are they?

**Ronnie** *enters from the clubhouse. He is a little more together. He has a drink and pops in a tablet.*

**Jack**  Well, I've always tried to live by the book, Ted.

**Ted**  Whose book though, Jack, that's the question.

*The bird of sadness has flown over them.*

He's like the six-million-dollar man now is Ron, aren't you?

**Ronnie**  There isn't one organ I've got that I'm not taking tablets for.

**Ted**  Join the club.

*A beat.*

**Ronnie** (*reflective*)  Eight years at the top of TV: that's not bad, is it? And then they drop you! That's what they do.

*A beat.*

**Ted**  There's pornography now on BBC 1 if you look for it!

**Ronnie**  How do you know?

**Ted**    I look for it, you bloody idiot. I can't fly like I did.

*A beat.*

**Ronnie**    And I wish I'd've done some things different, you know.

*A beat.*

**Ted**    I wish I'd've had a better diet!

*A beat.*

**Ronnie**    The thing is though, you never know what might turn up, Ted.

*A beat.*

**Ted**    You've been saying that for the last fifteen years though, Ronnie, and nothing has. I don't know how long we can wait though, cock!

**Ronnie**    You never know they might invent a pill that'll let us live for ever!

**Ted**    Well, I wouldn't take it, bad eyesight or not!

*A beat.*

**Ronnie**    Well, my agent says never say never!

*A beat.*

**Jack**    Aye, she must be the only optimist left on the bloody planet, Ronnie!

*A beat.*

**Ronnie**    Well, she's got me on the holiday circuit. It's not bad, to be honest . . . I mean, no bugger listens to what you're playing but think of all the skirt.

*A beat.*

**Jack**    Bloody hell!

*A beat.*

**Ted**  What's the youngest you've been with then, Ron?

**Ronnie**  Eh?

**Ted**  I say, what's the youngest you've been with?

**Ronnie**  Youngest what?

**Ted**  Aren't we blessed? Woman, what's the youngest?

**Ronnie**  Youngest, oh now you've got me.

*A beat.*

I could tell you the oldest.

**Ted**  Could you?

**Ronnie**  I could.

**Ted**  You see, there's some things you never forget.

*A beat.*

Go on then!

**Ronnie**  What?

**Ted**  Tell me the oldest.

*A beat.*

**Ronnie**  Seventy-nine!

**Ted**  Seventy-nine!

**Ronnie**  Seventy-nine!

**Jack**  Oh hell.

*A beat.*

**Ronnie**  A great-grandmother from South Shields.

**Jack**  Hellfire!

*A beat.*

**Ronnie**  I said to her are you sure, and she said yes!

*A beat.*

**Ted**   Seventy-nine!

*A beat.*

**Ronnie**   I'm not sure every bit of her worked like but . . .

*A beat.*

Mind you, not every bit of me works, so we were a good match.

*A beat.*

Aye, after we'd both had our tablets we got cracking.

*A beat.*

**Jack**   Don't you ever worry about Julie finding out though, Ronnie?

**Ronnie**   No, not at this age, what's she going to do, find somebody else?

*A beat.*

**Ted** (*pained*)   Forty-two years a carer!

*A beat.*

**Ronnie**   A great-grandmother from South Shields she was. She couldn't get enough of me!

*A beat.*

She only had one breast but you know what . . . I wasn't bloody bothered, she was just . . . just . . .

*A beat.*

**Jack**   Just what?

**Ted**   Just breathing by the sounds of it.

*A beat.*

**Ronnie**   She was just right!

*A beat.*

**Ted** (*drifting*)   Forty-two years a carer. I'm owed a wank somewhere in the world for that, Jack, surely?

*A beat.*

**Jack**   What are you asking me for, Ted?

*A beat.*

**Ted**   When I was forty-five I thought it would go away, you know, my sex drive.

**Jack**   What are you telling us this for?

**Ted**   But it doesn't, does it?

**Jack**   Well, mine has.

*A beat.*

**Ronnie**   Well, mine hasn't!

**Jack**   No, we know that! Bloody Help the Aged? I didn't think they'd want that kind of help.

**Ronnie**   Well, you never know you see, do you!

*A beat.*

**Ted**   Then you're sixty wishing you were fifty, but you're still able to put your socks on stood up.

**Ronnie**   Just!

**Ted**   Then you're seventy, wishing you were sixty.

**Ronnie**   And you can't put owt on stood up!

*A beat.*

**Ted**   But it's there deep inside, pulsing away. And some mornings you go out for a walk and there's a brisk wind and you know what . . . ?

*A beat.*

**Jack**   You get earache!

*They break into laughter.*

**Ted** (*keen*)    Look at the state of grass.

**Ronnie**    Aye, we'll be smoking that before too long!

*The three of them enjoy laughter once more.*

**Ted**    We're a dying breed! That's what we are, things are changing!

*A beat.*

**Ronnie**    There's a place in America where you can have a heart operation while you wait now.

*A beat.*

**Jack**    Well it'd be a bit difficult having it while you were doing sommat bloody else, wouldn't it?

*The three of them roll into laughter.*

**Ted**    Come on, Ron, I'll give thee a game . . .

**Ronnie**    No, I'd beat you with pneumonia, Ted, in fact blind Jack of Knaresborough would beat you in the fog.

*The three of them find this funny.*

**Ted**    Aye, you're right. Sometimes I'd only come up here to see if Jack'd ever beat you!

**Jack**    And the only chance I had he had a bloody heart attack.

**Ronnie**    I did and all.

*A beat.*

**Jack**    And he did that on purpose.

*They laugh once more. It is infectious.*

**Ronnie** (*crying with laughter*)    Oh dear when you think!

**Jack** (*laughing*)    The three bloody stooges!

**Ted** (*amused but sad*)    Well aye . . .

**Ronnie**    Oh dear!

*A beat as they compose themselves.*

**Ted**   We're doomed up here.

**Jack**   Do you reckon?

*A beat.*

I reckon a couple of months.

**Ronnie**   It could be weeks.

**Ted**   We've no young 'uns.

**Ronnie**   And you've the rent!

**Ted**   And t' bloody weather!

*A beat.*

**Ronnie**   That lawn'll not last, it needs re-setting!

**Ted**   We're an endangered species. I mean, I'll just be left.
I can't drive any more with my eyes. And I don't want
people trailing round for me! I'll just be sat in t' bungalow
. . . What shall I do if I can't come up here? I may as well be
dead!

**Ronnie**   Give up!

**Ted**   Well tha's all right, tha's still clubbing. I mean there's
all sorts happening in t' world and we're bottom of the
bloody pile again, aren't we, Jack, miners and fishermen.

**Jack**   Aye, I don't know what I'd do without this place.

**Ronnie**   They were right, you know, them advertising
lads, they said the future was bright, the future was orange!

**Ted**   The future is bloody black, Ronnie!

**Ronnie**   I did one of them adverts!

*A beat.*

**Jack**   What we need is a kick up the bloody arse.

**Ted**    Well, I'd happily kick you up the arse, Jack, but I can't get my leg up that high, not any more . . .

*A beat.*

**Ronnie** (*dryly*)    It would be a waste of time anyway, Ted, especially now Caroline's gone!

*The three of them start laughing, then ice.*

**Ted**    We're bloody doomed, aren't we?

**Ted** *goes back into the clubhouse.*

**Jack**    Aye, it's all finished up here now Ted.

**Jack** *makes his way to the clubhouse.*

It's all bloody finished!

**Jack** *exits.* **Ronnie** *comes onto the green, slowly begins to kick the woods as the lights fade to blackout.*

*Music.*

# Act Four

*2027.*

*Music.*

*Lights. Birdsong.*

**Max** *enters. He is five years older, greying but massive, with a facial tattoo. He is wearing a casual shirt and some overall bottoms even though it is extremely warm. He carries with him a roll of barbed wire and a hammer. He takes a battered old pair of step ladders and proceeds to attach some of the barbed wire to the top of the fencing. He takes his time. When he has completed his task he puts the step ladder at the side of the clubhouse. Then he takes the hose which is at the side of the fence near the clubhouse and tries to water the grass. Very little water comes from the hose, but he still endeavours to shake a little out. As he does this we hear a taxi pull up close to the bowling club, a door can be heard opening and closing and as the taxi pulls away we hear* **Ted**.

**Ted** (*off stage*)   Pieman!

**Max** (*loudly*)   I've got you.

**Max** *walks to the gate and opens it slowly and guardedly, revealing* **Ted** *who is now eighty-one. He has aged considerably and wears dark glasses, shorts, flip-flops, a shirt and a dinner jacket. He also has a hat and has a blind man's stick.* **Ted** *is almost blind and can make little progress alone.* **Max** *helps him into the bowling club. Despite his condition* **Ted** *is ebullient and energised.*

**Ted**   How we doing?

**Max**   Good, we're doing good!

**Ted**   That's what we like to hear.

**Max**   How are you doing?

**Ted**   Excellent, couldn't be better.

**Ted** *hobbles across the stage on the arm of* **Max**.

**Ted**   I'm looking forward to today, I was a bit off-colour yesterday with a dose of the shits but I'm a hundred and ten per cent.

**Max**   Cooler today, I think.

**Ted**   Just, Pieman, just!

**Max** *assists* **Ted** *with the veranda step.*

**Max**   Steady.

**Ted**   Steady? What do you think I am, an old man?

**Max**   Are you there?

**Ted** *slowly makes his way to sit on the bench on the veranda.*

**Ted**   What's it look like?

**Max**   Lush.

**Ted**   Is it?

**Max**   Lush today.

**Ted** *gets settled.*

**Max**   Hey, I've got sommat for you.

**Ted**   It's not two young women, is it?

**Max**   You wish it was?

**Ted**   I do.

**Max**   It's better than two young women.

**Ted**   Nowt's better than two young women, Pieman!

**Max**   This is!

**Ted**   It must be sommat special then.

**Max**   It is . . .

**Max** *disappears behind the clubhouse.*

**Ted** (*loudly*)   I say it must be sommat special then!

**Max** *produces a long iron wood carrier which will prevent* **Ted** *from having to bend. He places it in* **Ted**'s *hand.*

**Max**   Here you go!

**Ted** (*feeling*)   You haven't?

**Max**   Told you!

**Ted** (*feeling it*)   Oh smashing, where did you get it from?

**Max**   Well, you know.

**Ted**   You never made it, did you?

*A beat.*

**Max**   Well, no, I didn't make it!

**Ted**   I was going to say, if you can make sommat like this, Pieman, you're in the wrong job.

**Max**   It wouldn't b-be the f-first time! Let's just say I've b-borrowed it.

**Ted**   Are you taking it back?

**Max**   I don't think they want it b-back.

**Ted**   Oh well that's lucky, then.

**Max**   That is lucky!

**Ted**   How did you know that they don't want it back?

**Max**   I just know.

**Ted** (*feeling it*)   Oh it's just the job is this.

*A beat.*

**Max** *continues to tidy away the ladder and the hammer.*

**Max**   A good ride up?

**Ted**   Aye, he says we came through a bit of water, but it wasn't too bad he says. Once you get up by the bridge it's all clear. He says there's some parts you can't go to, you have to get a boat, he says.

**Max**    Is he on time?

**Ted**    Well aye, I mean I think he is. I can't see much of the clock unless I get up close. Aye, I think he's on time.

**Max**    Otherwise I'll have to have a word with him.

**Ted**    Oh aye, he's on time, I don't want to get him into any trouble. I mean we had that with the other one and you had to have a word with him, and he'd not been long out of prison, had he?

**Max**    I just had a w-w-w-word with him.

**Ted**    Came out of prison and ended up in hospital, well aye but he was late, wasn't he?

*A beat.*

**Max**    There's a beer if you . . .

**Ted**    A beer, oh aye, a beer . . .

**Max**    He's got a fridge now . . .

**Ted**    A fridge, he hasn't has he? A fridge and all now, where did he get that from?

**Max**    We've b-b-borrowed it.

**Ted**    Aye, borrowed it, that's good then, do they want it back?

**Max**    I don't think s-s-s-so! Hey, don't tell anybody, it's his only luxury.

**Ted**    Well aye, you need a luxury item.

**Max** *exits into the clubhouse.*

**Ted**    I'm in the shade, aren't I? I'm in the shade. I don't want to fry . . . am I in the shade?

**Max** (*from off*)    Yes, you're in the shade.

*A beat.*

**Ted** (*calling*)    Time are we on?

**Max** *re-enters with a can of beer.*

**Max**   Ten o'clock! (*Handing the beer.*) Here you are!

**Ted**   That's cool. We'll get shot if they find out.

**Max**   It's the only thing he's got.

**Ted**   We'll get shot having a fridge up here.

**Max**   We'll be all right. I'll have a w-w-w-ord with them!

**Ted**   Everything gets sorted out when you have a word with 'em! How big are you now, Pieman?

**Max**   Twenty-four stone!

**Ted**   Aye, I'd like to see it when you have a word with 'em.

**Max**   I bet you w-w-w-would!

**Ted** *opens his can of beer.*

**Ted**   I listen to the radio now, you know, I don't watch telly much, well I can't, I listen to the radio, they're stopping people having stuff. They're on about that march and all, oh aye, it's all on radio.

**Ted** *drinks his beer.*

**Max**   Are you going away again then, Ted, or . . . ?

**Ted**   No, that was my last one last year, he made me promise.

**Max**   Oh right.

**Ted** *drinks.*

**Ted**   Reduce it or lose it he says, so I says well aye! I'm going to miss it like but, you can't have everything. I mean I've got taxi, so that makes it easier: comes when I want. And all my bulbs have been changed. Mind you, it's freezing at night. And didn't we have some bad rain last week?

**Max**    There's snow forecast.

**Ted**    Thank God! I hope we have about four foot of it!
You don't know where you are, do you, with the weather?

*He drinks.*

No, no more air travel! I mean, I wish but . . . but no . . . no
I've been there! I've done that! I've got the T-shirt.

*A beat.*

Mind you, I've got that many T-shirts, I've got a bloody
wardrobe full.

*A beat.*

I lost my wife you know . . .

**Max**    I know you have, Ted.

*Silence.*

**Ted**    Aye, I lost my wife . . .

**Max**    I know you did, cock.

*A beat.*

**Ted**    Are you playing today?

**Max**    Oh yes!

**Ted**    Getting better Ron said. Is he here?

**Max**    Not y-yet.

**Ted**    He's not here yet then?

**Max**    Not yet.

**Ted** *drinks.*

*Silence.*

**Ted**    You been here long?

**Max**    About an hour, just been getting s-sorted.

**Ted**    I heard some banging.

**Max**   Putting some wire up.

**Ted**   Well aye, you've to put wire up!

*A beat.*

**Max**   Keep the d-dogs out.

**Ted**   Well aye, keep the dogs out! We don't want them ruining the grass.

**Max**   That's it.

**Ted**   You sound a lot better, Pieman, your stammer sounds a lot better.

**Max**   Well, I'm not as stressed out, am I? I mean I've got n-no financial worries now, have I!

*A small car pulls up outside and blows its horn.* **Ted** *drinks.*

**Ted**   He's here. Ronnie!

**Max**   Trouble.

**Ted** *rambles aimlessly.*

**Ted**   Well aye, there's that, always has been, nowt but trouble! A younger wife you see: bloody hell the stories . . . Oh dear, a younger wife, I wouldn't have that, sucked him dry she has, always after sommat, oh aye, no, I wouldn't have that! Aye, nowt but trouble that!

**Ronnie** *enters. He is eighty-one. He is looking smart in his grey slacks and a light blue shirt. He wears a hat and carries a small bag. He also has a large dinghy paddle with him from a small boat. He places his bag on the floor and holds the paddle.*

**Ronnie**   Getting worse, isn't it?

**Ted** (*loudly*)   Is it?

**Ronnie**   It's getting worse, Ted!

**Ted** (*to* **Max**)   What's he say?

**Max** (*to* **Ted**)   He says it's getting worse.

**Ted**   So they say!

**Ronnie** *makes a paddling motion.*

**Max** (*laughing at* **Ronnie**)   Bloody hell!

**Ted**   What's he doing?

**Ronnie** *makes paddling actions.*

**Ronnie**   The water's getting worse, Ted. Most of Hull's gone under now. I've had to leave my car and come by boat.

**Ted**   We heard you pip!

**Ronnie**   That was the coastguard pulling me over for speeding. I've rowed all the way up here, feel this. I've got backache and my arms are killing me.

**Ronnie** *gives* **Ted** *the paddle to feel.*

**Ted**   What's he got there?

**Ronnie**   I've come up by boat, hey, York's gone.

**Ted** (*feeling*)   It's an oar, isn't it?

**Ronnie**   This is what I'm saying, Leeds has gone, and Sheffield. Meadowhall's a swimming pool!

**Ted**   He's brought a bloody oar with him!

**Ronnie** *takes his paddle back and leans it against the clubhouse.*

**Ronnie**   London's the south coast now! They reckon Brighton and Hastings are French now, Ted.

**Ted**   He's a bugger, isn't he?

**Ronnie**   It's not far from the truth.

**Ted**   What tha brought an oar for?

**Ronnie**   It's a birthday present for Jack, coz he likes stirring it. I couldn't find a spoon big enough!

*He stands stage centre.*

(*Loudly*.) So how are we doing?

**Ted**   What?

**Ronnie** (*to* **Max**)   He only hears when he wants. (*To* **Ted**.) I said how are we doing?

**Ted**   Pieman's got me a present, where is it?

**Max**   At the side of you.

**Ted** *feels and demonstrates the bowling tool at his side.*

**Ted**   Save my back.

**Ronnie** (*to* **Max**)   Did you make it?

**Ted** (*sharply*)   Course he made it, do you think he'd pinch a thing like that, what do you think he is?

*No comment from* **Ronnie**.

**Ronnie**   That barbed wire looks nice.

**Ted** (*loudly*)   Keep the dogs out!

*A beat.*

**Ronnie**   Oh aye, you'll keep the dogs out with that. You'll keep a lot of things out with that.

**Max**   That's the idea!

*A beat.*

**Ronnie**   Where is he anyway?

**Max**   Training.

**Ronnie**   On his birthday?

**Max**   Every day!

*A beat.*

**Ronnie**   He'll kill his bloody self, that daft sod.

**Ted** (*loudly*)   He's crackers!

**Ronnie**   Has he been practising?

**Max**   Every day.

**Ronnie**   Well, I keep giving him chances but I promised May that I'd never let him beat me.

*A beat.*

**Ted** (*loudly*)   I say it's a bit cooler, Ron.

**Ronnie**   Only a bit.

**Ronnie** *wanders and stands near the veranda.*

**Ted**   I can't believe Jack's eighty-one.

**Ronnie**   Eighty-one!

**Ted**   The West Yorkshire bastard.

**Max** (*easily*)   Some things never change, do they?

*A beat.*

**Ted** (*loudly*)   We used to argue who worked t' hardest, miners or fishermen. We used to argue who worked t' hardest.

*A beat.*

**Ronnie** (*patronising*)   Aye I know, I was there, Ted.

**Ted**   We were both silly sods working for nowt! But he changed, he left t' pit, opened a boarding house with May, then the shop. He changed! He can do that, his daughter helped him, he can say he's wrong the bastard! I'll give him credit for that, the miserable sod! Aye, we always used to argue.

*A beat.*

**Ronnie**   We've all worked like hell and nobody thinks any better of you, Ted.

*A beat.*

**Ted**   Well tha's never worked hard, Ronnie.

**Ronnie**    Hey, I'm still working! My agent reckons there's a film I might have a chance at.

*A beat.*

**Ted**    His agent must be as old as Methuselah!

**Ronnie**    She's only eighty-eight!

*A beat.*

Hey she's not bad for eighty-eight.

**Ted**    Look out!

*A beat.*

**Max** (*to* **Ronnie**)    Still working then, Ronnie?

**Ronnie**    Just charity dos now! My drummer's only got one arm he can use, and Kenny my bassist can't stand up for long so it does limit you.

*A beat.*

Have you bowled a few?

**Max**    Aye, it's holding up, that middle's a lot better now we've re-set it.

**Ted** (*loudly*)    And they water it, Ron, I could smell it when I turned up, all fresh, lush he said!

**Ronnie**    You'll be shot for that!

**Ted**    That's why he's put the bloody wire up.

**Max** *stands and moves stage centre. He looks at the green.*

**Max**    He says we're going to dig that bottom end out. He wants to set some stuff, and make an allotment along that bottom edge.

**Ted** (*loudly*)    Aye, and he's going to keep pigeons, isn't he?

**Ronnie** (*loudly back to* **Ted**)    Self-sufficiency, Ted, it's all in!

**Ted** (*loudly*)    He's bloody barmy that West Yorkshire bastard!

**Ronnie**    He's on about keeping dogs, isn't he?

**Ted** (*loudly*)    He thinks we're at the bloody Alamo!

**Max** *considers the green.*

**Max**    All that wants ripping out. He says he used to be a ripper but he's going to let me do it.

**Ronnie**    That's good of him, ground's like rock.

**Max**    Like he says: you don't have a dog and bark yourself.

*A beat.* **Ted** *drinks.*

**Ted**    How's it going then, Ronnie, got married again, haven't you?

**Ronnie** (*easily*)    Bloody jungle drums!

**Ted**    Jack told me!

*A beat.*

**Ronnie**    Aye well. You never know which way the cookie's going to crumble, Ted.

**Ted**    You don't.

**Ronnie**    You don't.

*A car pulls up in the distance.*

**Ted**    He said it was to that great-grandmother you'd met in South Shields! I told him not to be so bloody soft.

*Silence.*

**Ronnie**    Aye, it is!

*A beat.*

**Ted**    Well aye.

**Ronnie**    Aye, it is actually.

**Ted**    Well, whatever floats your boat!

**Caroline** *enters gingerly. She is dressed smartly and carries a distinctive stick.*

**Caroline**    My word! I can't believe you're still here!

**Ronnie**    What's left of us.

**Caroline**    I thought you would have closed, but I saw a car and . . .

**Ted**    Is that Dr C?

**Caroline**    It is.

**Caroline** *kisses* **Ted** *awkwardly.*

**Caroline**    How are you?

**Ted**    Better for seeing you.

**Caroline**    Still playing?

**Ted**    Well aye! We should have a decent game now. No more ladies, I'm afraid, not since you left.

**Ronnie** (*dryly*)    In more ways than one.

*A beat.*

**Caroline**    I can't believe you're still here. I've got some friends who play at Sessy and they're flooded out. They've had to sell up, no membership, nothing to keep them going. I just came up to have a look. I've been back six weeks . . . I thought I wonder if there's any chance of a game, or a chat or, well the company . . .

**Caroline** *vaguely recalls* **Max**.

**Caroline**    Now don't tell me, I know the face. Weren't you?

**Max**    Yes, I used to b-bring the pies!

**Caroline**    And the frozen prawns . . .

**Ronnie**    He's the groundsman now, Caroline.

**Ted**   Yes, he's the Pieman! Simple Simon met a pieman! He's our pieman!

**Max**   My name's Max but . . .

*A beat.*

**Ronnie**   This is the only place you can play round here now.

**Caroline**   Well, nobody can get insured.

**Ted** (*loudly*)   Insurance companies are bastards! Always have been!

**Ronnie** (*dryly*)   Yes, thanks for that!

**Caroline**   Well, how have you kept it going when everyone else has gone under?

**Ted**   It's that daft West Yorkshire sod.

**Max** *approaches* **Caroline**.

**Max**   There's beer or beer if you'd like one!

**Caroline**   Could I have a beer?

**Ronnie**   I'll have one and all.

**Max**   You can't.

**Ronnie**   That's part of my promise.

**Max** *goes to enter the clubhouse.*

**Ted**   We've got a fridge, don't tell anybody, it's the only luxury.

**Caroline**   Yes, they're quite keen on your emissions.

**Ted** (*rambling*)   Well aye, I've limited my emissions, but if we have a problem, Pieman has a word.

**Max** *enters.*

**Max**   A beer.

**Caroline**   Well, here's to us. Cheers!

**Caroline** *and* **Ted** *drink.*

**Ted**   Cheers!

**Ronnie**   Cheers.

**Ted**   Ronnie married again. She's eighty-eight but she's a cracker by all accounts.

*A beat.*

**Ronnie**   Nothing's changed here, Caroline, global warming, war, terrorism, famines, death and migration but as you can see it's just the same here.

**Ted** (*sarcastically*)   I mean, I can hardly see a bloody thing like but . . .

**Caroline**   Well, something must have changed because you're still here.

**Max**'s *phone rings.*

**Max**   Hello! Yes! Hang on . . . Hang on . . . Yes, when is it for? Hang on! Let me check the book, hang on!

**Max** *enters the clubhouse.*

**Caroline**   So what about Jack?

*A beat.*

**Ted**   Haven't you heard?

**Caroline**   I haven't heard a thing. Is he still around?

*A beat.*

**Ted**   Sold up. Everything, bungalow. Everything!

**Caroline**   He sold his bungalow?

**Ted**   They had bidders, didn't they, Ron?

**Ronnie**   Nearly five million!

**Caroline**   My word!

*A beat.*

**Ronnie**    Oh aye, he said he'd never sell but . . . five million! I mean it's not worth what it was but . . .

**Ted**    They're building a refuge on it, aren't they!

**Ronnie**    Aye, for folk who they've had to move out of Hull!

*A beat.*

**Caroline**    So where does he live now?

**Ted** *and* **Ronnie** *laugh.*

**Ronnie**    Tell her!

**Ted**    You tell her!

*A beat.*

**Ronnie**    Here! He lives here. Him and Pieman.

**Ted**    And he's not got the money in a bank! It's buried all around the green.

*A beat.*

Oh aye, he's gone mad! Absolutely mad! And did you know that Faye was back?

**Caroline**    No . . .

**Ted**    Well aye, you see that's what did it, her coming back . . .

**Ronnie**    She helped him do it, she's a hundred and ten per cent now is Faye, had a baby girl, hasn't she?

**Ted**    He's a great-granddad now! Did it for the future of the planet he says. He's bloody crackers that West Yorkshire bastard. He's got no carbon footprint he says. But we know he's got that bloody fridge, don't we, Ronnie?

**Caroline** (*drinks*)    Thank goodness!

**Ted**    He pays for my taxi, and my rent. He bought Ron his house after Julie left, and he pays Pieman to live here!

And they've got me onto global warming. I listen to the radio, Caroline, it gives me sommat to do! We're going on a march next month, aren't we, Ron? Against the American bastards. They're still not doing enough Faye says!

**Ronnie**   No, they're not, and that's right is that!

**Jack** *enters. He is eighty-one but looks younger. He wears tracksuit bottoms and a pyjama top. He wheels his bike into the clubhouse.*

*Silence.*

**Jack**   Oh, the helper's back then . . .

**Caroline**   I was just hearing all about you!

**Jack**   You don't want to believe a word they say, they're clinically insane them two, Caroline, look at 'em!

**Caroline**   Well, I understand congratulations are in order.

**Ted** (*loudly*)   We've told her all about little May, your great-granddaughter, Jack! We've told her all about it!

**Caroline**   That's great news!

**Jack** *is unhappy.* **Max** *enters from the clubhouse.*

**Max**   There's a load wanting to coming from Wakefield for a game next weekend, while they can still get across M62 they say. I said I'd try and put some pies on for 'em. Men's doubles and ladies singles they're after! I said I'd have to ask you first.

**Ted** (*keenly*)   That'd be nice, Jack, wouldn't that be nice, Caroline?

**Caroline**   Oh it would be nice, wouldn't it?

*Silence.* **Jack** *is unsure which way to play it. He has absolute power over the bowling club.* **Jack** *nods to* **Max***, who returns to the clubhouse.*

**Jack**   Tell 'em yes!

**Ted** (*excitedly*)    Oh aye, tell 'em yes! For God's sake, tell 'em yes, let's keep swimming while we can, Jack! Oh aye, tell 'em yes! Bloody hell, Pieman, tell 'em yes!

**Jack** (*dryly*)    Right, are we having a few ends or what? (*Shouts.*) Pieman, get my woods! Come on then, Ronnie, I'll give you a game before it gets too bloody warm!

**Jack**, **Ted**, **Caroline** and **Ronnie** *animate.* **Max** *enters the clubhouse and returns with a carrier of woods.* **Ronnie** *grabs a mat and begins to get ready, all manner of activity slowly evolves as the game starts to take shape. Johnny Mathis's 'Wonderful Wonderful' can be heard and plays out as lights fade to blackout.*

*Curtain.*

# Sold

# Characters

**Ray**, *a journalist*
**Caz**, *his wife, a teacher*
**Amy**, *a student, Caz's daughter*
**Jack**, *a journalist*
**Gemma**, *his wife*
**Les**, *a pub landlord*
**Pat**, *his wife*
**Kate**, *a madam*
**Anja**, *a prostitute*
**Sonja**, *a trafficker*
**Elena**, *a police woman*
**Vlad**, *a trafficker*
**Actor 1**
**Actor 2**
**Actor 3**
**Actor 4**
**Actor 5**

*Sold* was first presented as a co-production between Hull Truck Theatre Company and Liverpool Hope University as part of the Wilberforce celebrations. It was first performed in November 2007 at Spring Street Theatre, Hull, with the following cast:

| | |
|---|---|
| **Ray** | Josh Richards |
| **Caz** | Julie Higginson |
| **Amy** | Anne-Marie Hosell |
| **Jack** | Gordon Kane |
| **Gemma** | Kate Baines |
| **Les** | Gordon Kane |
| **Pat** | Julie Higginson |
| **Kate** | Kate Baines |
| **Anja** | Kasia Halpin |
| **Sonja** | Julie Higginson |
| **Elena** | Anne-Marie Hosell |
| **Vlad** | Gordon Kane |
| **Actor 1** | Josh Richards |
| **Actor 2** | Gordon Kane |
| **Actor 3** | Julie Higginson |
| **Actor 4** | Kate Baines |
| **Actor 5** | Anne-Marie Hossell |

*Directed by* John Godber
*Designed by* Pip Leckenby

# Act One

*Essentially an empty stage. The set is suggestive of a number of rooms which can be any of the many rooms that the scenes take place in. The entire set is treated in a design motif of euros which indicates the importance of money, which the play is predicated upon. Upstage there are a number of entrances, some are raised and some are at stage level.*

*House lights. Pre-set fade.*

*A state is established. Singly each actor enters and takes position. They sing an unaccompanied version of 'Amazing Grace'. As each actor takes up the song the power of the song strengthens until all five actors are singing the final two verses.*

**Actor 1**
Amazing grace,
How sweet the sound
That saved a wretch like me.
I once was lost and now I'm found
Was bound but now I'm free.

**Actor 2** *enters.*

**Actor 2**
'Twas grace that taught my heart to fear
And grace my fears relieved.
How precious did that grace appear
The hour I first believed.

**Actor 3** *enters.*

**Actor 3**
Through many dangers, toils and snares
I have already come;
'Tis grace hath brought me safe thus far,
And grace will lead me home.

**Actor 4** *enters.*

**Actor 4**
The Lord has promised good to me,

His word my hope secures;
He will my shield and portion be,
As long as life endures.

**Actor 5** *enters.*

**Actor 5**
Yea, when this flesh and heart shall fail,
And mortal life shall cease,
I shall possess within the veil
A life of joy and peace.

**All**
The world shall soon dissolve like snow,
The sun refuse to shine.
But God, who called me here below,
Shall be for ever mine.

When we've been there ten thousand years,
Bright shining as the sun,
We've no less days to sing God's praise
Than when we'd first begun.

**Actor 3**    Some estimates claim there are eight hundred thousand people trafficked across international borders each year.

**Actor 4**    Some say there are six hundred thousand.

**Actor 5**    Some reports say that the business is worth twenty-five billion.

**Actor 1**    Some say it's worth five billion.

**Actor 2**    Some reports claim that there are four thousand women trafficked in the UK alone.

**Actor 3**    Some reports say there are eight thousand women trafficked in the UK alone.

**Actor 4**    Some say the business is now the most profitable in the world.

**Actor 5**    But some say it is second only to the arms trade.

**Actor 1**    The truth is, nobody knows the truth . . .

**Actor 2**    Nobody can say just how bad this is . . .

**Actor 3**    But they all agree on one thing . . .

**Actor 4**    The trafficking of humans across the world is growing . . .

**Actor 5**    And there are so many stories.

**Actor 1**    Who knows how many of them are true?

**Actor 2**    Let's say that this is one of those stories . . .

**Actor 3**    And let's say that this story is true.

*Music.*

*All exit.*

*Lights.*

**Ray** *enters. He is late for a meeting. He is putting on a tie and has a light-weight mac with him. He speaks directly to the audience.*

**Ray**    And let's say that my name's Ray. Let's say that I'm a journalist looking for a story and let's say that I'm late for a train.

**Caz** *enters,* **Ray**'*s wife, a teacher. She is as harassed as* **Ray** *and hobbles in one shoe.* **Ray** *plays the scene in an imaginary mirror.*

**Caz**    You're going to be late for that train.

**Ray**    I know that.

**Caz**    Did the alarm go off?

**Ray**    Well, I didn't hear it.

**Caz**    Where's my other shoe?

**Ray**    Has the dog had it?

**Caz**    I don't think so. I've taken him out, by the way.

**Ray**    Well done!

**Caz**    Again!

**Ray**    Maybe the rabbits had it?

**Caz**    Where the bloody hell is it?

**Caz** *looks around the stage.*

**Ray**    You in late again?

**Caz**    There's a staff meeting. They reckon we're going into special measures.

**Ray**    Again?

**Caz**    That's what I said.

**Ray**    They should bring the police in.

**Caz**    Do you know what our teenage pregnancy rate is now?

**Ray**    Top of the league, aren't you?

**Caz**    Oh aye, we're good at that, it's the only thing the little sods want to know about.

**Ray**    You love 'em really!

**Caz**    I did!

**Ray** *is almost ready. He puts on his coat.*

**Ray**    Right!

**Caz**    You know Amy's got a band practice tonight, don't you, she's expecting a lift back.

**Ray**    Tonight?

**Caz**    You did promise.

**Ray**    Did I?

**Caz**    You know you did.

**Ray**    Is she up yet or what?

**Amy** *enters, she is tired and wearing a skimpy dressing gown.*

**Amy**   Morning.

**Caz**   Can you get some milk, darling . . .

**Amy**   Urgh . . .

**Ray**   How's the band going?

**Amy**   All right!

**Ray**   That's good then!

**Amy**   'Cept I've got nothing to write about.

**Ray**   Join the club!

**Amy**   My life's so dull.

**Ray**   I thought it was never dull in Hull?

**Amy**   Bollocks!

**Caz**   Have you seen my other shoe?

**Amy**   Why have I seen it?

**Amy** *drifts off stage.*

Are there any clean knickers?

**Caz**   She's in a good mood.

**Ray**   As usual.

**Caz**   What's it for this time then?

**Ray**   *Observer*, colour supplement.

**Caz**   Oh nice!

**Ray**   I haven't got it yet! It's just a pitch. But I'm meeting Jack at the station, he's going down as well.

**Caz**   Why, what's he doing?

**Ray**   He's pitching for a documentary on Channel Four.

**Caz**   On what?

**Ray**   Sex trafficking.

**Caz**    I thought that was your idea?

**Ray**    It was but he reckons telly does it better!

**Caz**    Hasn't it been done?

**Ray**    Not to death. You have to do it to death, anyway he reckons sex will always sell.

**Caz**    And he should know, that's all he ever talks about.

**Ray**    Well, it pays the mortgage!

**Caz**    And we need that!

**Ray**    Tell me about it!

**Caz**    I am doing.

**Ray**    We need to have a talk about this house, it's bleeding us dry!

**Caz**    I don't know why you don't do sport.

**Ray**    Cause there's only one story, somebody wins, somebody loses.

**Caz**    That's called life, Ray.

**Ray**    I know that!

**Caz** *begins to exit.*

**Caz**    I'll see you later. Will you eat?

**Ray**    I'll have something on the train.

**Caz**    Well, be careful, you never know what you're eating!

**Caz** *has gone.*

**Ray**    So let's say that I'm ready and let's say I'm heading for the train. Now there's a story: whether you book a seat or not it's always bedlam, and what are they charging for it these days? Bloody ridiculous! So let's say I get the train and I meet Jack, and let's just say that the train is packed.

*Music.*

*Lights.*

**Ray** *and* **Jack** *are on a busy train, which is signified by having them positioned centre stage. They are joined by the remainder of the cast who wear coats, hold newspapers and crush together.* **Jack** *eats, drinks a coffee and speaks to* **Ray**. *They rock as the train speeds along.*

**Jack**   You can say what you like though, it's never going to go away.

**Ray**   It was my bloody idea though!

**Jack**   You brought it up over supper, mate, all ideas are in the ether.

**Ray**   Bollocks!

**Jack**   I was thinking about it anyway. You only came up with it because you thought somebody would buy it, be honest.

**Ray**   Caz reckons it's been done.

**Jack**   Not to death!

**Ray**   That's what I said.

**Jack**   Hey, immigration: borders coming down, terrorism, what do you want to write about, under-elevens football? Good luck, mate, but that doesn't do a lot for me!

**Ray**   No, I know!

**Jack** *still eats, and drinks a coffee.*

**Jack**   It's all over at the moment, there was a discussion last week on Radio Four about Nuts TV. They're even making a TV version of that.

**Ray**   Nuts TV?

**Jack**   It's a TV version of that wank mag!

**Ray**   It's not a wank mag, is it?

**Jack**   It is when I read it.

**Ray** (*sarcastic*)    Very good, mate!

**Jack**    It's on the hard drive though, isn't it? Men are interested in women, always will be.

**Ray**    Yes, but are women interested in men?

**Jack**    Probably not as much in all honesty.

**Ray**    No, I think you're right there!

**Jack**    Sadly.

**Ray**    I used to think we'd grow out of the page three stuff.

**Jack**    We might have, but there's a whole new generation. That's all about selling papers, and these commissioners don't want Cinderella Ray, they want Bad Detective. Good news is no news, mate, lesson one.

**Ray**    And that's still true.

**Jack**    If they go for this I'm laughing, do you know what they'll pay for an hour's documentary?

**Ray**    So is this a camera strapped to your chest and all the rest of it?

**Jack**    Strapped to my chest, up my nose, I'll stick one up my arse if I get a commission.

**Ray**    That sounds nice!

**Jack**    You know they reckon in Turkey you can buy a girl in a car park.

**Ray**    'kinnel.

**Jack** *still eats.*

**Jack**    I've seen some footage on the internet, you can buy an eastern European girl in a car park, what's that all about?

**Ray**    In a car park?

**Jack**    In a car park!

**Ray**    What like a car boot sale?

**Jack** *still eats.*

**Jack**    What is that all about?

**Ray**    Power and money, mate.

 **Jack** *still eats.*

**Jack**    Sex, power, and money, mate! Triple whammy!

**Ray**    Nothing changes, does it?

**Jack**    You need to get in the field if you're going to write about it!

**Ray**    What with a pen up my arse?

**Jack**    You need a source!

**Ray**    Dangerous though!

**Jack**    Well yes, but . . . how else are you gunna get material? It's one thing getting a commission, it's another thing getting the source.

**Ray**    So how are *you* going get material?

**Jack**    I've got a source, mate!

**Ray**    What, a girl?

**Jack**    I've got a source.

**Ray**    How did you get that then?

**Jack**    I get about, mate.

**Ray**    Does Gemma know?

**Jack**    Hey, this is research, what do you think I am? You know they reckon most of the girls working in the London brothels are foreigners, eighty-five per cent of them! What must they think of us?

**Ray**    But it's probably better than where they came from, that's the point! That's the root of the problem.

**Jack**    It's globalisation, mate!

**Ray**    It makes you want to do something about it.

**Jack**    We are doing something about it . . . we're giving it coverage.

**Ray**    Well yes but . . .

**Jack**    If I get this commission we're laughing. I think Gemma wants the kitchen re-doing.

**Ray**    Who's using who though, mate?

**Jack**    That's democracy, Ray, it's fucking complicated!

**Ray**    Aye I know that!

**Jack**    And now she's on about a loft conversion. I need to work, mate, my mortgage is killing me!

**Ray**    Join the club!

**Jack**    Do you want a bite of this?

**Ray**    What is it?

**Jack**    I have no idea, mate, I just pointed at the picture, the lass selling it didn't speak much English but it tastes all right!

**Ray**    No, I think I'll leave it, I usually like to know what I'm eating! I'm funny like that!

**Jack** *completes his meal.*

**Jack**    You need a source, mate, that's what you need! Get yourself a source and you're laughing!

*Music.*

*Lights.*

**Kate**, *a native Londoner, who speaks directly to the audience.*

**Kate**    Oh yes, we get 'em all in here, Mr Smith, Mr Jones, we get a lot of Joneses in here. I don't mind 'em, I mean it's a living innit. Bloody cold in the winter though, down here.

I mean I'm just surprised how they find us because the
council are always cleaning those booths out. We get a lot of
Nigerians, yes I'm surprised and all. Nice big black blokes,
like I say, we get all sorts. Fucking students, bankers,
wankers, groups, tourists. And the girls are all right, I mean
they don't say a lot, know what I mean? I mean it's not
*Woman's Hour* down here! But the Europeans are all right, at
least they try and speak fucking English which is how it
should be. Some of them South Americans, moody fuckers
they are, I don't know what's wrong with them some days I
don't honest. They don't know when they're well off. When
I was working I was glad not to get a thick ear, I can tell
you.

*Lights.*

*Music.*

**Ray** *enters the brothel. He is rather sheepish.*

**Kate**    All right, darling, you signed in?

**Ray**    That's right.

**Kate**    Mr Smith, is it?

**Ray**    That's right.

**Kate**    What you looking for then, darling?

**Ray**    Well . . .

**Kate**    Got a lovely girl on today.

**Ray**    Yes?

**Kate**    You'll like her, she don't speak much English but
she does all the services.

**Ray**    Oh right.

**Kate**    Oh yes, lovely she is. Better than the South
Americans, darling, you don't want any of that, they don't
stop talking. That'd be like being the wife that would,
wouldn't it?

**Ray**    That's right!

**Kate**    This your first time?

**Ray**    Yes.

**Kate**    Oh well, you let Katie look after you! We'll get you sorted, darling! You wanna see this new girl then or what?

*A beat.*

**Ray**    No, I think I've made a mistake to be honest.

**Kate**    No, you'll be right, you're here now aren't you, you'll be all right when you get settled.

**Ray**    No I . . .

**Kate**    Oh leave it, you're all right aren't you?

**Ray**    Well what . . . ?

**Kate**    You can discuss the terms with the girl, darling, all right.

**Ray**    Well . . . actually . . .

**Kate**    Hey you ain't a time-waster are you, coz we get enough of them! No, you'll be all right, you'll like this girl, she'll get you sorted. Where you come from then, darling?

**Ray**    Leeds.

**Kate**    Leeds, oh I ain't ever been to Leeds.

**Ray**    Well, not actually Leeds but . . .

**Kate**    I got a sister lives up there.

**Ray**    It's actually not Leeds!

**Kate**    You'll be all right, darling, I'll get the girl for you, shall I? You just relax, make yourself at home, I'll get the girl for you!

**Kate** *exits.*

**Ray** *is lost on stage. He looks around the room.*

**Ray**   Let's say that you find yourself in a brothel in London, in a damp basement apartment, and you feel that you are on the brink, on the brink of some excitement.

*A spotlight picks out* **Jack** *who is still eating.*

**Jack**   You've got to get a story they want, mate. I mean look at Hugh Grant, he was dying until he got a blow job. I mean think about it, he gets sucked off on Sunset Strip and suddenly he's an interesting bloke!

**Jack** *freezes.*

**Ray**   And let's say for some reason my mind turns to Abi Titmus, to her sex tape, to her career, to Jordan, to Bill Clinton.

**Jack** *animates and eats.*

**Jack**   It's got to sell! Morals? Leave them at home, coz morality starts at home, mate, just pay your mortgage.

**Jack** *freezes.*

**Ray**   And my mind races to Paris Hilton, to the money, to the celebrity, my mind jumps to the little bed waiting, waiting for something, the little table lamp, the bedspread, the mirror, the big walled mirror, what's the mirror for?

**Jack** *animates and eats.*

**Jack**   I mean these commissioning guys don't want a story about caravanning in Brid; they want arse-fucking and roasting and dogging, just give 'em what they want! Hey, you should try one of these, mate, (*The food.*) I don't know what they are but they're great!

**Jack** *exits.*

*Lights.*

**Ray**   And suddenly I'm back in a dingy flat in Brid before I was married, before I met Caz! Why am I thinking about Caz? If I didn't have Caz would I feel different? Is it because of her that I'm nervous? And what am I going to say to this girl, that I'm looking for a story? Can she help me find a story? What will she say to that? And what will Jack be doing now? Pitching his deal, going deep undercover with a wire up his arse? I'm deep in the shit here, that's what it feels like! Outside around Soho Russian women sell Polish students in peep-shows! It's what we used to do as kids, showing each other our bits, playing doctors and nurses on the side of the railway and this is a business! Bits of kids taking their knickers down, is this all it is?

**Anja** *enters, at once innocent and attractive in a plain way. She stands looking at* **Ray**.

*Silence.*

**Anja**    What you like?

**Ray**    Eh?

**Anja**    What you like?

*A beat.*

**Ray**    What's your name?

*A beat.*

**Anja**    You like massage?

*A beat.*

**Ray**    Listen, I think I've made a mistake here.

*A beat.*

**Anja**    What you like?

**Ray**    Listen . . .

**Anja**    Anal is extra.

**Ray**    Listen . . . I'm sorry!

**Anja**    Without condom is extra.

**Ray** *is very uncomfortable.*

**Ray**    I think I've made a real mistake here!

**Anja**   You give money.

**Ray**   Hey?

**Anja**   You no give money I am bad girl.

**Ray**   How much?

**Anja**   Fifty!

**Ray**   Fifty pounds?

**Anja**   I massage.

**Ray**   No no . . . I'll give you fifty pounds.

**Ray** *searches for the money.*

**Anja**   Why you come?

**Ray**   To talk . . . I dunno, I've made a mistake. I saw a number and . . .

**Anja**   You fifty, now you go!

**Ray** *hands the money to* **Anja**.

**Ray**   Where are you from?

**Anja**   Now you go! Thank you, good time.

**Ray**   Yes . . . thank you! Good time.

**Anja** *turns from* **Ray** *with the money and he watches her exit. As he does,* **Kate** *enters from an upstage door and watches him.*

**Kate**   All right, darling? A good show was it? She do a good show? She's popular she is, she don't say much but she's ever so popular. We'll see you again then, shall we? We'll see you again for another good time?

**Kate** *exits.*

**Ray**   That's right, for another good time!

*Music.*

*Lights.*

*Jack and **Ray** have copies of the* Evening Standard, *and they stand as if they are on a train.* **Jack** *has a can of beer. A tight spotlight picks them out.* **Jack** *is laughing.*

**Jack**   Bloody hell, mate! I can't believe you came out!

**Ray**   Well I did!

**Jack**   Didn't you get a lead?

**Ray**   I didn't get anything.

**Jack**   Oh well done, mate! That is deep undercover.

**Ray**   It's so pathetic, and it cost me fifty quid!

**Jack**   You didn't pay her, did you?

**Ray**   I kinda thought she'd be . . .

**Jack**   What?

**Ray**   I don't know what I thought, I think I'd gone down the Abi Titmus route.

**Jack**   Which is what?

**Ray**   Well, that she'd be clean and washed and . . .

**Jack**   Welcoming? It is a business arrangement!

**Ray**   I'm aware of that.

**Jack**   You'll just have to go back!

**Ray**   Why?

**Jack**   Well, please yourself, mate, but where's the fucking story?

**Ray**   I dunno if it's right though.

**Jack**   Well, they've commissioned me.

**Ray**   Oh aye, they would do!

**Jack**   It's the new slave trade, the editor said. Most of these girls have got fuck all and they're coming over here!

**Ray**    I know that, I told you all about it!

**Jack**    And it's all under the radar, mate! Nobody has got a clue about how many there are in the country!

**Ray**    I think this lass was new to London.

**Jack**    Well, that's perfect. You'll just have to go back, mate!

**Ray**    I don't know if it's right though!

**Jack**    You'll just have to go back, mate, get your fifty quid's worth!

*Music.*

*Lights.*

**Jack** *and ensemble exit.* **Ray** *remains on stage and is joined by* **Caz** *who is wearing an apron and carrying a steaming pan of pasta.*

**Caz**    Well, you knew she wanted a lift, I told you this morning. She's going mad because you said you'd promised, you did say . . . and you said you'd listen to her songs.

**Ray**    I have been to London and back!

**Caz**    So what? Try having thirty fifteen-years-olds who don't want to be there, and then being at a meeting till nine. You took the car.

**Ray**    I just went for a drink with Jack . . .

**Caz**    And how is he, full of it as usual?

**Ray**    He's got a commission for Channel Four, he's going under cover.

**Caz**    And what about you? How did you get on?

**Ray**    Not bad.

**Caz**    Did they commission you?

**Ray**    They want some more detail.

**Caz**    And what does that mean?

**Ray**   Well, as yet I haven't got a story, that's what it means. I haven't even got a source.

**Caz**   Well, there's a statement in there from the bank, have you seen that? That might make you get a story!

**Ray**   I haven't had my tea yet, it might ruin my appetite.

**Caz** *is calling as she exits.*

**Caz**   Well, I'll save you some of this, you can have it microwaved when you get back!

**Caz** *has exited.*

**Ray**   And let's just say that he had his cold pasta later, watching Jeremy Paxman roast a politician. And let's just say that he went down to the Grapes to see Amy try and be famous and to listen to her song!

*Music.*

*Lights.*

**Amy** *enters. She is singing a song to a backing track.* **Ray** *positions himself upstage where he can listen to her singing.* **Amy** *has brought a mike on stage. She is acting out a career fantasy.*

**Amy**
   Cool chicks in magazines
   Everyone wants to be nineteen.
   Dressed in their best
   We're so impressed
   Film stars, rock stars
   Give it a rest.

   What about me, what should I be?
   Grateful or hateful
   For setting me free.
   What about me?
   Where do I fit?
   Not here, not there, not anywhere.
   Is this it?

Hot girls in cut-off jeans
Everyone wants to be nineteen.
Big photographs
And autographs
Coke-heads, slap-heads
What a laugh.

What about me, what should I be?
Grateful or hateful
For setting me free.
What about me?
Where do I fit?
Not here, not there, not anywhere.
Is this it?

Clever girls full of beans
Every wants to be nineteen
Get a degree in history
B.A., M.A
M.Sc.

What about me, what shall I be?
Grateful or hateful
For setting me free.
What about me?
Where do I fit?
Not here, not there, not anywhere
Is this it?

**Ray** *applauds encouragingly.*

**Ray**   Sounded good.

**Amy**   It's not right though.

**Ray**   Sorry I missed you, I was . . . got behind.

**Amy**   Mum tried to call you, she gets worried.

**Ray**   I was in a meeting, I had to have my phone off.

**Amy**   So it sounded all right?

**Ray**   Well . . . to me but . . .

**Amy**   You thought it was shit, didn't you?

**Ray**   I didn't say that.

**Amy**   I can tell by the look on your face.

**Ray**   Not at all.

**Amy**   I'll get this lot sorted out.

**Amy** *begins to dismantle the mike stand.*

**Ray**   I can't win, can I?

**Amy**   If you tried.

**Ray**   I've been trying for five years, Amy.

**Amy**   Really!

**Amy** *exits, taking the mike stand with her.*

**Ray** *looks to the audience.*

**Ray**   Shall we just say that Caz is not the first wife. Shall we just say that the first wife and me didn't work out? And shall we say that the landlord at the Grapes, Les Sutton, is one of the creepiest bastards I've ever met?

**Les** *enters. He is indeed a creepy man, half-cut and vicious. He has a number of empty beer crates with him and a chair that he will leave on stage. He is breathless from climbing up to the pub's attic room.*

**Les** (*wheezing*)   Those bastards stairs! If you slip you're fucking history. She getting any better?

**Ray**   Well, that's debatable!

**Les**   We get 'em all in here, you know, all the students, oh aye we get 'em all in here. I might have to put the rent up though, Ray, I mean I can't just be letting the room go for nothing not since the smoking ban.

**Ray**   No, right!

**Les**   I mean, we're struggling to make ends meet.

**Ray**   It's hit you, has it?

**Les**   And we don't see you as much as we'd like.

**Ray**   Well . . .

**Les**   I've still got my snakes, you know.

**Ray**   Have you?

**Les**   Oh aye, I've still got my snakes.

**Ray**   That's good then.

**Les**   I'll tell Pat you're here, she'd love to see you would Pat. She's always talking about you!

**Ray**   Is she?

**Les**   She loves you!

**Ray**   Smashing!

**Les**   You remember Pat, don't you?

**Ray**   Of course I do!

**Les** *moves off stage and calls to his wife.*

**Les**   Pat! Look who's here, we haven't seen him for ages! Pat, come and look who's here!

**Pat** *enters. She is clearly drunk and is all over the place. A woman in her early fifties, she has seen better times and is a real lush, with too much lipstick. She too is breathless with the stairs.*

**Pat**   Argh! My fucking breath! Argh stranger!

**Ray**   Hello!

**Pat**   Argh sexy!

**Ray**   Hiya!

**Pat** *confronts* **Ray**.

**Pat**   Oh he's here look, bloody hell he's here, not seen you for ages, have we? I say, she's in here though, isn't she, Amy always in here making a racket!

**Ray**   It's not too noisy, is it?

**Pat** *kisses* **Ray**.

**Pat**   Oh, I could eat him. All man that, Les.

**Les**   Aye!

**Pat**   All man. Oh feel him, Les, solid.

**Pat** *is all over* **Ray**, *who is uncomfortable.*

**Les**   No, I'll leave it!

**Pat**   And he doesn't look any different, does he. I say you don't look any different.

**Ray**   A bit greyer.

**Pat**   Greyer? Give over, a bit greyer, did you hear him? I tell you sommat the greyer the better for me!

**Ray**   Smashing!

**Pat**   At least they know what they're doing.

**Les**   That's what she says.

**Pat**   They might not last as long but . . . the greyer the better.

**Les**   I don't last as long, Ray, I'll tell you that much!

**Ray**   Well, there you go!

**Les**   Still on the writing lark?

**Ray**   That's it!

**Pat**   Going to write a book, wasn't you?

**Ray**   That's had to wait.

**Les**   We don't see much of him now, do we?

**Pat**   No, that's right, we don't see much of him now.

**Les** *and* **Pat** *freeze.*

**Ray**   Let's just say that they didn't see much of me because they were the two creepiest bastards I'd ever come across.

**Les** *and* **Pat** *animate.*

**Les**   We still have some fun in here though.

**Pat**   We do, we get up to all sorts in here!

**Les** *and* **Pat** *freeze.*

**Ray**   When I first moved to Hull I stopped upstairs in the
Grapes for a few months. They used to have lock-ins and
watch all kinds of filth, and Pat was the worst one, she was
right out of the bottom draw was Pat. Somebody told me
once that she'd sell herself for a scotch and soda. I used to
wonder how Amy got on down there, but part of me
thought that Amy was big enough to look after herself: let's
just say that, shall we?

*Music.*

*Lights.*

**Pat** *and* **Les** *exit.*

**Kate** *enters through an upstage portal and smokes as she addresses*
**Ray**.

**Kate**   You all right, darling?

**Ray**   Yes!

**Kate**   You signed in, lover?

**Ray**   That's right.

**Kate**   Mr Smith?

**Ray**   Jones. Mr Jones.

*A beat.*

**Kate**   This your first time?

**Ray**   That's right.

**Kate**   I got a good girl for you, what you after, anal?
Hand-relief, what you after?

**Ray**   Not sure.

**Kate**   Well, you deal with the girl, darling! And this one'll do all the services.

**Ray**   Yes?

**Kate**   Where are you from, darling?

**Ray**   Bradford.

**Kate**   Bradford?

**Ray**   That's right!

**Kate**   Isn't that the north? I got some family up there, never see 'em. I'll get the girl for you, darling. Lovely girl this one, eastern European she is, I mean there's a Spanish girl on but you never know what you're getting with the Spanish, do you?

**Ray**   No, I suppose not!

**Kate**   No, you never know what you're getting with the Spanish!

**Kate** *exits leaving* **Ray** *on stage.*

**Ray**   And let's say that I needed a lead, a story, and let's say that she fascinated me, the whole world fascinated me, and I found myself in a shitty Paddington basement looking for a girl who's name I didn't know . . .

**Anja** *enters.*

**Anja**   Anja.

**Ray**   Anja!

**Anja**   My name is Anja!

**Ray**   My name is Ray!

**Anja**   I remember!

**Ray**   You do.

**Anja**   No sex.

**Ray**   Yes. That's right.

**Anja**    No sex!

**Ray**    Sorry!

**Anja**    No sex! I remember!

**Ray**    You remember men who have no sex.

**Anja**    I remember you.

*A beat.*

**Ray**    Is that a good thing?

*A beat.*

**Anja**    Today want sex?

**Ray**    No.

**Anja**    No sex today!

**Ray**    But I will give you fifty pounds.

**Anja**    For no sex?

**Ray**    To talk.

**Anja**    To talk sex?

**Ray**    No, just to talk!

**Anja**    You can talk for fifty pounds?

**Ray**    I give you fifty pounds to talk.

**Anja** *sits on a solitary chair.*

**Anja**    What can I say for fifty pounds? I talk dirty for you?

**Ray**    Your story . . .

**Anja**    My story.

**Ray**    I give fifty pounds for your story.

**Anja**    Is worth more.

**Ray** *laughs as he gets out his wallet.*

**Ray**    I should have seen that. Okay, I give you more.

**Anja**    How you know is true?

**Ray**    Why wouldn't it be?

**Anja**    For more than fifty I say anything!

**Ray**    I suppose!

**Anja**    You like see my tits?

**Ray**    No thank you!

**Anja**    Are you police?

**Ray**    No . . .

*A beat.*

**Anja**    Police come but I not say.

**Ray**    The police come here?

**Anja**    They look for men, I not say. I not know.

**Ray**    How did you get here?

**Anja**    I cannot say . . .

**Ray**    Why, why not?

**Anja**    I need money!

**Ray** hands **Anja** *a hundred pounds.*

**Ray**    Okay, is this good, is this good?

**Anja** (*counts the cash*)    Good money!

**Ray**    I'd like to try and help.

**Anja**    Why?

**Ray**    If I can.

**Anja**    You not know me!

**Ray**    Can I do anything?

**Anja**    For one hundred pounds I say good story for you.

**Ray**    No, not a story, the truth!

**Anja**   For two hundred pounds I tell very good story.

**Ray**   Yes?

**Anja**   Make you come real good!

**Ray**   No, no . . .

**Anja**   I can tell story good!

**Ray**   How did you get to be here?

**Anja**   Am like many!

**Ray**   Where are you from?

**Anja**   Moldova.

**Ray**   Moldova?

**Anja**   My family owe. At school I am not interesting.

**Ray**   Not interested . . .

**Anja**   Yes.

**Ray**   I wasn't interested in school.

**Anja**   I am like you?

**Ray**   I think you might have been.

**Anja**   Is many years!

**Ray**   How old?

**Anja**   Am twenty-one years.

**Ray**   I have a daughter, she is about the same.

**Anja**   She is pretty?

**Ray**   I think so.

**Anja**   I am sixteen when Elena tell me about job in Romania.

**Ray**   Elena?

**Anja**   She tell me that things are very bad in Moldova.

**Elena** *enters. She is a young Moldovian girl dressed in simple western clothes. She begins to speak to* **Anja***.* **Ray** *observes the developing story.*

**Elena**    My brother tell me he knows woman who had to pay for bedpan for his mother in hospital.

**Anja**    A bedpan?

**Elena**    He had to pay nurse so his mother could have bedpan. There is no work here, Anja. There is nothing! My friend has gone Italy, she is working. She is working a good job. Many girls are leaving.

**Anja**    Why are they leaving?

**Elena**    We must have dreams.

**Anja**    I have dreams. I would like to dance. Like on TV, I have seen films, *Flash Dance*.

**Elena**    My friend Natasha has gone to dance in Italy. She has work as a waitress, she is like you she want to sing. In Italy she can work and she can have lessons to sing.

**Anja**    She has gone?

**Elena**    From the next village.

**Anja**    It will be expensive.

**Elena**    Natasha tell me woman who can help.

**Anja**    How can it?

**Elena**    You go, get job and then you pay, Natasha is making good money in Italy, she is paying back, is no problem.

**Anja**    But my mama?

**Elena**    Natasha is paying for her mama.

**Anja**    How?

**Elena**    She is helping pay for operation. Natasha is sending money for her mama, so she can have operation.

You could do that! If your mama need operation, Anja, you can pay, you can save money!

**Anja**    So she is making money?

**Elena**    She is making good money, many girls are leaving for Italy, Spain, there are many girls who like in UK. You like Robbie Williams?

**Anja**    Yes! I like!

**Elena**    Natasha she like see Robbie Williams. Many girls are.

**Anja**    And they are making money?

**Elena**    For their mama!

**Anja**    And it is okay?

**Elena**    Anja, of course it is okay. Why do you think I am not saying it is okay?

*A beat.*

**Anja**    Okay.

**Elena**    I will take you. In eight days, you have passport and I will take, you will meet lady who helped Natasha.

**Anja**    What is name?

**Elena**    I don't know but is good!

**Anja**    You don't know?

**Elena**    She help Natasha and is making real money! Why must you not trust me?

**Anja**    I do trust you!

**Elena**    You must think about it, she is making real money and is helping her mama and papa. You know what it is like here, you must pay for everything. A doctor here earns nothing, why you think you have big ideas, okay I tell you, forget it Anja! Forget it, you do not deserve to have the chance! Forget this!

**Elena** *exits.* **Ray** *has been watching and listening as* **Anja** *picks up the story with* **Ray**.

**Anja**    For some in Moldova who work for state very good. For me not good.

**Ray**    So you said yes to Elena?

**Anja**    I say yes to Elena, and I meet woman who help Natasha.

**Ray**    What was her name?

**Anja**    I never know her name!

**Sonja** *enters, an attractive Russian woman with lush hair and very well dressed.* **Ray** *drifts upstage to watch the action.*

**Sonja**    So Anja okay, very good! We have minibus, you have passport?

**Anja**    Yes, I have.

**Sonja**    Good! We have minibus, you go sit with other girls and we will go. Not long, we will go soon.

**Sonja** *exits at an upstage portal.*

**Anja** (*to* **Ray**)    She told me go to minibus, I sit with twelve girls. And then I see my cousin come and talk.

**Ray**    Your cousin?

**Anja**    Elena is my cousin.

**Elena** *enters. She is now dressed in police uniform. She and* **Sonja** *are in conversation.*

**Sonja**    She is good girl?

**Elena**    Yes.

**Sonja**    Fit?

**Elena**    Yes, she fit.

**Sonja**    Virgin?

**Elena**    I not ask!

**Sonja**    Why not?

**Elena**    She is my cousin.

**Sonja**    Five hundred dollars.

**Elena**    She is my cousin.

**Sonja**    Five hundred. She virgin one thousand.

**Elena**    Okay.

**Sonja**    We have many girls like this, five hundred is good price for you. You know family?

**Elena**    There is no problem.

**Sonja**    Yesterday in Chisnua I have girl for two thousand dollars.

**Elena**    She virgin?

**Sonja**    She twelve!

**Elena**    Eeech!

**Sonja**    She is young, but very fit and virgin, very good price. You get me fucking virgin I pay you real.

**Elena**    Two thousand dollars?

**Sonja**    Okay now we must go. We have cross to Romania. I see you next time.

**Sonja** *and* **Elena** *exit.*

**Anja**    We take in minibus.

**Ray**    Across the border?

**Anja**    We drive and we are taken border.

**Ray**    You were taken to Romania?

**Anja**    We have run to some light, the woman she say run to headlight.

**Ray**   To another vehicle?

**Anja**   Some fall, some are bleeding but we go to headlights and we are in van, just in van little sheep.

**Ray**   And where did they take you?

**Anja**   Italy.

**Ray**   So it was Italy?

**Anja**   They say Italy. We are taken to villa. In room there are many girls, some are bleeding, they are cut on ankles, knees. They are crying! They say they have passports so can get visa for job. Then she enter and she talk to me.

**Ray**   The woman with no name . . . ?

*Lights.*

**Sonja** *enters and comes to* **Anja**.

**Sonja**   You like Berlin?

**Anja**   I do not know.

**Sonja**   Berlin is good for you!

**Anja**   Where is passport?

**Sonja**   Have trouble with visa, no problem.

**Anja**   Where is passport?

**Sonja**   They are getting visa. Is okay! You like Berlin?

**Anja**   For job?

**Sonja**   Yes, for job!

**Anja**   I like good work for money.

**Sonja**   Yes Berlin?

**Anja**   In Berlin I work as waitress? And pay for lessons?

**Sonja**   You like suck cock?

**Anja**   Please?

**Sonja**   In Berlin you like suck cock?

**Anja**   Please?

**Sonja**   You have pretty mouth.

**Anja**   In Berlin I work yes?

**Sonja**   Yes, I think you like good sex in Berlin?

**Sonja** *exits.* **Anja** *takes up the story with* **Ray**.

*Lights.*

**Ray**   Where was the villa?

**Anja**   I don't know.

**Ray**   But you think it was in Italy?

**Anja**   I think was Italy, and then a man come into room . . . We are taken to room, and then men can come . . .

**Vlad** *appears upstage, he is wearing a leather jacket and a T-shirt. He simply stands and looks at* **Anja**. *He slowly reaches for his thick leather belt.*

**Ray**   What did he do?

**Anja**   Many men come.

**Ray**   Did he hit you?

**Anja** *reacts violently to* **Ray***'s questions.*

**Anja**   No please!

**Ray**   What happened?

**Anja** *reacts as if she is being hurt.*

**Anja**   Argh!

**Ray**   What happened to you?

**Anja** *reacts violently.*

**Anja**   Argh!

**Ray**   Did he rape you?

**Anja** *responds as* **Vlad** *unlocks his belt.*

**Anja**   Please, please!

**Ray**   In the villa did he rape you, did he hit you, what happened?

**Anja**   Yes, yes!

**Sonja** *enters and stands upstage looking at* **Anja** *on the floor. A light picks her out.*

**Sonja**   So some men will come, you must be good to them.

**Anja**   No, please!

**Sonja**   You must be good!

**Anja**   Where is my passport?

**Sonja**   Be good and they will not hurt you!

**Anja** *plays towards* **Ray**.

**Ray**   Did he rape you?

**Anja**   I say no please, but then they come, the men come.

**Ray**   How many?

**Anja**   I don't know.

**Ray**   How many were there?

**Anja** (*anxious*)   I don't know!

**Anja** *has to play* **Sonja**.

**Sonja**   Is time to go: have your visa!

**Anja**   Please let me go.

**Sonja**   You owe money for transport, you owe fifteen thousand dollars for transport, you must work.

**Anja**   No please!

**Sonja**    Is good news, they have a job for you, they have job!

**Vlad** *is caught in a spotlight.*

**Vlad**    Sometime with strong girls they are hard to break. Sometime we need hundred men! With strong girl we need to have maybe hundred times. We have to teach lesson.

**Sonja**    Some girls it is not enough, they will not break. For most one hundred is enough!

**Vlad**    Sometime we film and we put online. We put on video, one hundred!

**Sonja**    With one hundred she is broken.

**Vlad**    We make video. It is okay maybe, but not for Dubai, or for the East. For her I think football, you know football! For tourist I think.

**Anja** (*angst*)    Please no!

**Vlad**    It like breaking dog, you must learn! Yes, she must learn sit, stay, it like a dog, you must learn sit and stay, most girls learn this way in Italy, always in Italy, very good!

*Lights fade on* **Sonja** *and* **Vlad** *and they exit.*

**Anja**    Is not a good story . . .

**Ray**    Is it true?

**Anja**    Is a true story, but a sad story.

**Ray**    Were all the girls treated the same?

**Anja**    Sometimes I think have dreamed.

**Ray**    Is it all true, Anja?

**Anja**    I think must have dreamed. Why am I here, where am I? I think am London, I think am Italy! Sometimes I think am dreaming all day!

**Ray**    Did you see any of the other girls again?

**Anja**   They take me and I not speak language.

**Ray**   They took you somewhere else?

**Anja**   They take I think is Antwerp.

**Ray**   From Italy.

**Anja**   I meet with Katja, from my village. I meet in house, she is from my next village, she would be dancer, she would like be dancer. But she leave and they take her. She say she go Germany, with many others.

**Ray**   When was this?

**Anja**   Is last year!

**Ray**   She went to Germany to work?

**Anja**   Is World Cup she say many are taken to work . . .

**Ray**   At the World Cup?

**Anja**   She say many are taken. Thousands of girls go to work at World Cup football.

**Ray**   Fucking hell!

**Anja**   Yes, she say fucking good time in World Cup!

**Ray**   Girls went to Germany to work at the World Cup?

**Anja**   Yes, yes, she say there are thousands of girls! Forty sixty thousand.

*Music.*

**Ray**   So during the World Cup between forty and sixty thousand prostitutes were imported into Germany? Nobody knows the actual figures, but between forty and sixty thousand. She said that they reckoned three million men paid for sex during this time! And all of the women paid taxes. She said it was a good time for her friend Katja and that the German government made four and a half billion dollars. She told me that her friends were looking forward to the Olympics in London: she said she knew a lot of girls who were looking forward to that!

**Anja**    I tell good story for a hundred pounds?

**Ray**    Well, it's not a fairy tale!

**Anja**    Everyone has story.

**Ray**    They do!

**Anja**    Do you have story?

**Ray**    Oh yes, I have a story!

**Anja**    What is your story?

*A beat.*

**Ray**    Would you like to leave here?

**Anja**    I tell good story?

**Ray**    Would you not like to get out?

**Anja**    I owe much. I cannot go back!

**Ray**    If someone got you out?

**Anja**    I cannot go back to family, Elena and my brother they are together, I cannot go back.

**Ray**    What about the woman here, the maid, whatever she is?

**Anja**    She doesn't know my name!

**Ray**    Doesn't know any of the girls?

**Anja**    She take money for herself. We come we go, some girls never come again. Already I say too much. I tell good story but now you must go. I need two hundred for more.

**Ray**    But is it true?

**Anja**    Why I lie? All things are true, people only believe what they think.

**Ray**    So this is all true?

**Anja**    All true, you think I lie make you feel horny?

**Ray**    No . . . I just . . .

**Anja**    I need two hundred pounds for a very good story.

**Ray**    Two hundred?

**Anja**    Two hundred is very good!

**Ray**    It is!

**Anja**    Two hundred is very good!

**Kate** *enters from an upstage portal. She is suspicious.*

**Kate**    Everything all right, darling?

**Ray**    Yes, yes.

**Anja**    Yes, is good. I make good money today, thank you!

**Ray**    Yes, thank you!

**Anja** *exits.*

*There is an icy moment between* **Ray** *and* **Kate***.*

**Kate**    Everything all right then?

**Ray**    Yes, thanks.

**Kate**    Good show was it, you been in here long enough.

**Ray**    Yes, thanks, just . . .

**Kate**    She all right then, not blabbing on, some of 'em do! I got a lovely girl across the way, she just come in, great figure if you fancy . . .

**Ray**    No, I'm . . .

**Kate**    Where you from again is it? Leeds?

**Ray**    Leeds, Bradford, somewhere up there.

**Kate**    We had a pregnant girl in last week, from Peterborough she was, broken arm she's got you know. I thought she ain't going to make a go of it!

**Ray**   Really?

**Kate**   Funny isn't it, but you know, they brought her in, a Latvian I think, and she had a real good go at it, you know what I mean, she had a real go! I mean who the hell wants to go with a pregnant girl with one arm but you just never know do you?

**Ray**   No, I don't suppose!

**Kate**   I had a mute once, couldn't speak or say nothing, a bleeding mute I ask you. Great rack she had, what a figure, I think she'd been a bleeding athlete or summing, I don't know, you learn not to ask too much, don't you?

**Ray**   I suppose you do.

**Kate**   Human frailties, darling, human frailties! I mean they come in here, they do what they have to. And I'll tell you this, lover, I ain't got no idea what they're thinking! And I don't suppose they have: nothing in their heads but shit and chicken's feathers these girls we're getting now! I tell you, they're not a patch on what they used to be. But you just can't get the staff, can you?

*Music.*

*Lights.*

**Anja** *is illuminated behind a bar on stage.*

**Anja**   If you could see me now, Mama, what would you say? I am not your little Anja. Anja is dead, Mama. She died when she went to Italy. Mama, do you miss me? Do you ever think of me? I think of you. I think of you many times. I could smell you, I could smell the house, I could smell the cooking, Mama. I could smell when you were making the soup. But now with each day the smell goes, I can't smell you too good. I can't dream you. I don't dream any more, Mama, I dream now only in English. I hope you are well, Mama, I hope you are well.

*She is in tears.*

I want to be home!

*Music.*

*Lights.*

**Gemma**, **Jack**, **Caz** and **Ray** *are seated at four chairs. A small chandelier is flown in, there is no table, they are at the end of a long evening supper, the atmosphere is sophisticated and pleasant. There is much laughter and we get the impression they are in a conservatory of some description.* **Caz** *is pouring refills of wine, everyone has a drink of wine.* **Gemma** *is refined but shallow, and* **Caz** *is on the brink of the wine taking a hold.*

**Gemma**    So is this conservatory all new then, Caz?

**Caz**    Yes, but don't get carried away, Gemma, we're still paying for it!

**Ray**    Yes, through the nose I think, it's either that or my blood pressure's up!

*A ripple of laughter.*

**Caz**    Eight weeks the man from the firm said. Nine months it eventually took them.

**Gemma**    Well, we're having the loft done!

**Jack**    All being well.

**Gemma**    And the kitchen.

**Jack**    Again!

**Gemma**    Well, you promised!

**Jack**    If I make fifty it'll be a miracle.

**Ray**    I thought you were fifty?

**Jack**    It's a miracle!

**Caz**    Yes, we had every European national working on it. It was like Brussels in here of a morning! And he's no use, he gives them the odd *guten Morgen*, *bonjour* and he's off for a coffee or wherever he goes. He's been in London again today!

**Jack**   I'm back down tomorrow to watch a court case.

**Gemma**   I don't think they should prosecute these girls, I think they should prosecute the men.

**Jack**   They've started doing that in Sweden.

**Gemma**   And what?

**Jack**   Prostitution's dropped.

**Ray**   Yes Sweden, the country that brought you sex in schools, teaching girls to put condoms on at ten, how the pendulum swings.

**Jack**   Well it's the oldest profession and it'll never go away, not as long as men are men . . .

**Caz** *is prickly around* **Jack**.

**Caz**   Yes, good old men, Jack!

**Jack**   Hey, I'm a feminist! Don't get at me!

**Caz**   You're a feminist?

**Jack**   I am!

**Caz**   Well, you must be the only feminist with balls!

**Jack**   Well, I don't think that's true! I've been to some of their rallies!

**Ray**   Have you come across that stuff about the World Cup?

**Jack**   What, that we played like a sack of shit?

**Ray**   There was a brothel in Cologne that dealt with over six hundred men a day during the World Cup!

**Gemma**   Good grief!

**Ray**   Eleven thousand square metres it measured.

**Jack**   I hope you're talking about the brothel here, mate?

**Ray**   State controlled.

**Gemma**   Absolutely awful when you think about it!

**Ray**   Forty thousand girls they brought in!

**Jack**   I didn't know that!

**Ray**   That's one nil then!

*A ripple of laughter.*

**Caz**   So where's all this come from?

**Ray**   Hey? Oh a source I'm developing!

**Jack**   Not the internet, don't trust it, mate, the facts and figures are all over the place.

**Ray**   No, it's not the internet!

**Caz**   So where is it then?

**Ray** *takes a drink.*

**Ray**   Eh?

**Jack**   And now he's being cagey look . . .

**Caz**   So what source was this then?

*A beat.*

**Ray**   Well . . .

**Caz**   Go on, what's the source?

**Ray**   I went to see that girl again!

**Jack**   I knew it.

*A beat.*

**Caz**   What girl is this then?

**Jack**   Didn't you tell her?

**Ray**   I'm telling her now!

**Jack**   Mate . . . I tell Gemma everything, you have to!

**Caz**   So what girl is this?

*A beat.*

**Ray**   Well . . . I went to a brothel . . . today.

**Caz**   Eh?

**Ray**   . . . to talk, just to talk . . .

**Caz**   To talk about what?

**Ray**   To try and get a lead.

**Jack**   Hey fair enough, Caz, it's my fault in all honesty, I told him to get under the skin of it when we went down there last time.

**Caz**   Oh well, thanks for that, Jack, and you a feminist!

**Gemma**   He tells me all this stuff, I mean I don't believe him half the time but . . . I'm not bothered as long as I get a new kitchen!

**Gemma** *laughs on her own. It is empty.*

**Ray**   It was just research . . .

**Caz**   Of course it was.

**Ray**   Here we go!

**Jack**   And did she talk?

**Ray**   A bit.

**Jack**   And?

**Gemma**   I think it's just sick what they're doing with these girls.

**Jack**   Yes, and we're trying to expose it!

**Caz**   It's all about men, if the boot was on the other foot there wouldn't be trafficking.

**Gemma**   It's just horrible, turns my stomach.

**Jack**    Well, they were jumping all over the place when the Berlin Wall came down and what have they got out there now? Next to nothing.

**Ray**    Did you know that in 2001 half the Russians had no jobs?

**Jack**    Well, we're buying their coal now, mate.

**Ray**    And their oil.

**Caz**    And that's all driven by men, so don't set me off on that one.

**Gemma** *drinks.*

**Gemma**    Men, honestly!

**Caz**    I haven't met a good one yet to be honest!

**Ray**    Hey please?

**Jack**    Well, you're getting through 'em, Caz.

**Caz** *is offended.*

**Caz**    What do you mean by that?

**Jack**    Well, Ray's number three, isn't he?

**Ray**    Jack?

**Caz**    What?

**Jack** *is defensive.*

**Jack**    I'm only saying.

**Caz**    Yes, but what are you saying?

**Jack**    It was a joke, darling, it was just a joke, you can laugh now and again, Caz! I know teaching's hard work but you can laugh! Try it, darling, you'll feel a lot better believe me!

**Caz**    You're pathetic.

**Jack** *stands from the chair.*

**Jack** Oh well cheers, I think that sounds like our taxi arriving, Gemma.

**Caz** Good.

**Gemma** Hey come on!

**Jack** No, no, fine, time to go. I know when I've overstepped the mark.

**Ray** Jack, sit down and have another drink.

**Jack** No . . . I just get a bit fed up of everything being the fault of men, okay? Wars, famine, rape, trafficking, it's always the fault of men; half these girls are sold by women as it happens! Did you know that? Cousins, aunts, mothers sometimes.

**Ray** Jack, calm down!

**Jack** It's so nineteen-seventies anyway! And when you try and do something about it, it looks to some like you're in it for what you can get out of it!

**Ray** Jack!

**Jack** No, no, time to go. I know when I've crossed the line, mate.

**Gemma** Are we going?

**Jack** Yes, we're going sweetheart, get your things, we'll phone for a cab outside the premises.

**Ray** Jack!

**Caz** Oh let them go, Ray.

**Jack** *stands to leave.*

**Jack** Don't worry, love, this man is leaving!

**Gemma** I'm sorry, Caz.

**Caz** Are you, I'm not?

**Jack** Good luck, mate! I'll see you around.

**Gemma** *stands and* **Jack** *makes to exit.*

*Silence.*

**Caz** *stands upstage, she has a glass and bottle and things are indeed icy.*

**Ray**    I don't know . . .

**Caz**    That wasn't my fault.

**Ray**    No? Whose fault was it then?

**Caz**    Why did you have to bring it up?

**Ray**    What?

**Caz**    That you'd been to a brothel?

**Ray**    You asked me. It's my job, it's why we're in this house. I can't see what the problem is. And anyway they are our friends, well they were.

**Caz**    They're your friends, Ray. Jack's your friend. I tolerate Gemma, she's a cheap public-school airhead with nothing to talk about but wallpaper colours and bathroom fittings.

**Ray**    That is not fair!

**Caz**    You're exploiting these girls just as much as they're being exploited.

**Ray**    That's not true.

**Caz**    Of course it is!

**Ray**    I'm paying her for it!

**Caz** *finds this extraordinary.*

**Caz**    Oh bully for you!

**Ray** *stands and becomes animated.*

**Ray**    Hey, if I could pay our way on the kind of stuff I want to write I would do! If I'd've got my novel off, I wouldn't even be thinking about this shit!

**Caz**    So it is tokenism?

**Ray**    Hey, I've done match-fixing in the under-elevens league in Goole and it won't keep your gas on!

*A beat.*

**Caz**    But why didn't you tell me?

**Ray**    I was going to tell you!

**Caz**    Were you?

**Ray**    I was going to tell you!

**Caz**    When?

*A beat.*

**Ray**    It's just that I started scratching and . . .

**Caz**    And what?

**Ray**    And the more I found out, the more I wanted to find out.

**Caz**    Pandora's box, Ray!

*A beat.*

**Ray**    Okay, we think we've got problems here, don't we?

**Caz**    We have got problems, Ray, we've got serious problems in this city and you know we have!

**Ray**    Yes, yes, I know that! I don't want the lecture.

**Caz**    Well, I'm getting one!

**Ray** (*tired*)    Jesus!

**Caz**    There's under-age drinking! Under-age sex. Educational deprivation. Unemployment! Incest! Second-generation apathy!

**Ray**    But Caz . . .

**Caz**    Theft . . . car crime . . .

**Ray**  How bad must it be for these girls even to think that they're gunna have a better life doing sommat like that?

**Caz**  So some of them know what they're letting themselves in for then, is that what you're saying?

**Ray**  As far as I understand it: according to an article in the *Spectator*, some of them know what they're doing.

**Ray** *helps himself to a refill.*

**Caz**  Well, I don't know about that . . .

**Ray**  Presumably they think they can handle it.

**Caz**  Well, tough luck to them then, they had it coming!

*A beat.*

**Ray**  This girl today told me she'd been raped a hundred times, a hundred times, Caz, and that they'd filmed it. She had been raped a hundred times!

**Caz**  I heard you the first time!

**Ray**  How do you ever come back from that?

*A beat.*

**Caz**  You can't save her, Ray.

**Ray**  How do you live with that?

**Caz**  You can't save anybody any more.

**Ray**  They take them to Italy, which must have Mafia involvement, and they are brutalised, and they never come back. And the people behind this know that. And do you know what she told me today . . . She told me she was sold to a woman. She was sold to a woman, who sold her on!

**Caz**  But it's look after number one, Ray, it all changed with Thatcher. We can't have them here, how do we know they're not terrorists?

**Ray**  Oh please!

**Caz**    How do we know for sure though?

**Ray**    That they'd want to submit themselves to that?

**Caz**    How do you know? How do you know she is telling you the truth?

**Ray**    I've been in this game for a long time.

*A beat.*

**Caz** *pours herself another drink, the atmosphere is changing.*

**Caz**    Christ, Ray, it is so depressing.

**Ray**    I know that.

**Caz**    It's so depressing though!

**Ray**    That's the world, that's what's under the radar, Caz, that's the world we're living in! We trot along in our cosy little way complaining about the parking and the council tax and just at the edge of the radar there's a whole world and we don't even want to see it.

*Silence.*

**Caz**    Oh well, another dinner party ruined.

**Ray**    So what?

**Caz**    At least we christened the conservatory!

*A beat.*

**Ray**    I was going to tell you, you know? You're my best mate, how could I not tell you?

*A beat.*

**Caz**    Just finish the article and put it to bed, Ray. I can't stand it, it's horrible! Just finish the article and get it out of the way, and let's get on with our lives! Please!

*Music.*

*Lights.*

**Caz** *exits.*

**Anja** *enters. She is dressed a little bit differently to how we have seen her previously.* **Ray** *sits on one of the four chairs that have been left on stage.* **Anja** *is sitting on a chair and then she becomes animated.* **Ray** *looks at her with a mixture of infatuation and affection. He is becoming fixated by her.*

*Lights.*

*Music fades.*

**Anja**   When I first work in Antwerp they take to clubs to dance. It is okay, but they say I owe money, so I dance for men, for jewels, they have many jewels in Antwerp. At first I think in Italy is mistake, but then they ask for sex. The men I dance for. I think I cannot do this! The sex. The first time is very difficult for me, I feel sick, I am with man in Antwerp and I feel nothing. His hands on me and I feel nothing, I am not there. I am watching! After first time I am sick very bad. After first time is second time in Antwerp, then third time and then so many time in Antwerp is nothing. Some days I am sad! Is good for you, story?

**Ray**   Is it true?

**Anja**   Is good story?

**Ray**   Is it true?

**Anja**   Is true. Hundred pounds! You give I tell very good story.

**Ray**   But is it true?

**Anja**   Is my story!

*A beat.*

**Ray**   Has anyone ever told you that you are very pretty, Anja?

**Anja**   Like your daughter, she is pretty yes?

**Ray**   Yes she is!

**Anja**   You think I am very pretty?

**Ray**   You are!

**Anja**   I don't feel very pretty.

**Ray**   Well you are, very.

**Anja**   You think, maybe is time for sex with you?

*A beat.*

**Ray**   I don't think so.

*A beat.*

**Anja**   So, one hundred pounds for my story.

**Ray**   Of course.

**Ray** *digs into his wallet and produces a hundred pounds in twenty-pound notes. As this transaction takes place* **Kate** *enters.*

**Kate**   How we doing in here? All right, darling?

**Ray**   Yes just . . .

**Kate**   Got to hurry you, darling, we're pushed today. There's a big match on at Wembley, I've got 'em queuing up at the minute. You got everything you need?

**Ray** *stands. It is awkward.*

**Ray**   I think so!

**Kate**   Everything all right with the girl?

**Ray**   Absolutely.

**Kate**   You've not left anything have you?

**Ray** *feels his pockets for his belongings.*

**Ray**   I don't think so!

**Kate**   Yes, we're going to be busy today I should think . . .

**Anja** *seems uncomfortable.*

**Anja**   Is football match?

**Kate** (*to* **Ray**)    She don't like the football!

**Ray**    No?

**Kate**'s *body language is urging* **Ray** *to exit.*

**Kate**    Funny isn't it? I mean the phone's non-stop when there's a match on and she don't like it. She don't want the work I fink, and she's very popular. Right you ready then, darling, see you again shall we?

**Ray**    If I could stay a little bit longer . . . ?

**Kate**    I can't, darling, we got to get sorted today, that phone's been non-stop. You get yourself off, she's got a lot of work on this afternoon. I think Liverpool are playing, I dunno, these lads come down here and they can't get enough.

**Ray**    Can I just . . . ?

**Kate**    What is he like? I've got somebody waiting, darling!

**Ray**    I'm happy to pay . . . I don't mind really. I'm happy to pay!

*A beat.*

**Kate**    What are you like, honestly. All right, darling, but just a quickie eh?

**Kate** *exits.*

**Ray** *is left with* **Anja**.

*Silence. It is sensitive and extremely awkward.*

**Ray**    You okay?

**Anja**    I think.

*A beat.*

**Ray**    The men, the football lads?

**Anja**    I no like.

**Ray**    Me neither.

**Anja**   I no like.

**Ray**   I never have.

**Anja**   I will be busy.

**Ray**   Will they . . . what will they . . . ?

**Anja**   Sometimes one, sometimes two . . .

**Ray**   Will you be okay?

**Anja** *is fairly distant.*

**Anja**   Is all same for me.

**Ray**   Can I help, can I help you?

**Anja**   Is nothing can do. I must pay money.

**Ray**   How much do you owe?

**Anja**   Many thousand, I have to give to men and to rent room. Is many thousand twenty.

**Ray** (*breathless*)   Christ!

**Anja**   Please you must pay now. Or I am bad girl.

**Ray** *looks in his wallet.*

**Ray**   I've only got twenty quid.

**Anja**   I take. I am good girl. Please go . . .

**Ray** *hands over his last twenty-pound note.*

**Ray**   I want to help you.

*A beat.*

**Anja**   Why you think?

**Ray**   Can I try and help you?

*A beat.*

**Anja**   Maybe I think you want to fuck with me?

**Ray**   No, not at all, you are wrong!

**Anja**    Maybe I want to fuck with you? You like I think.

*A beat.*

**Ray**    I dunno, maybe.

*A beat.*

**Anja**    Yes, I think you like.

**Ray**    Maybe I would.

**Anja**    Maybe next time Ray comes it will be good. Yes? Maybe next time.

**Ray** *and* **Anja** *look at each other. She touches him seductively. Lights fade to black.*

# Act Two

**Ray** *and* **Jack** *are revealed in squash kit. Upstage they have squash bags and towels. They are hitting balls against the imaginary fourth wall, as they grunt and groan.*

**Jack**   Agh!

**Ray** *plays a shot.*

**Ray**   Ugh.

**Jack** *plays a shot.*

**Jack**   Ugh.

**Ray** *plays a shot.*

**Ray**   Urgh!

**Jack** *plays a shot.*

**Jack**   Oh . . .

**Ray** *plays a shot.*

**Ray**   Urgh!

**Jack** *plays a shot.*

**Jack**   Urgh!

**Ray** *plays a shot.*

**Ray**   Oh . . . bollocks. What's that?

**Jack**   That's game to me, mate!

**Ray**   I can't concentrate today.

**Jack** *and* **Ray** *stop playing squash and try to get their breath. They are sweltering in the heat.*

**Jack**   I tell you something, I can't wait to hear what Caz has to say about all this. Have you told her?

**Ray**   Not yet.

**Jack**   You are going to tell her, aren't you?

**Ray**   Of course I'm going to tell her but I've got to pick my moment. She'll probably agree with me, but she's stressed out as it is at the minute.

**Jack**   So where is she then?

**Ray**   I've no idea but I've sorted out a bedsit, and introduced her to Amy just so she's got a contact.

**Jack**   Fucking hell, mate!

**Ray**   Hey, don't you start, it's partly your fault. I did it on the spur of the moment, you said get a source! It's just my luck she turned out to be like Anja.

**Jack** *and* **Ray** *towel down.*

**Jack**   I didn't say fall in love with it! You going to introduce me?

**Ray**   Not if I can help it.

**Jack**   Seriously!

**Ray**   What for?

**Jack**   Curiosity.

**Ray**   Hey, this isn't a gimmick, this is somebody's life. This is not a fly-on-the-wall documentary, you know.

**Jack**   It'd be good if it was, I knew you'd got a thing about her!

**Ray**   I haven't got a thing about her, it's not in my nature. Not like you, I'm just trying to be a good bloke.

**Jack**   You are a good bloke, Ray, but I think you've just gone too far!

**Ray**   Hey, she's a human being, you know, not a bloody object.

**Jack**   You can't just leave her though, can you? No job, no passport?

**Ray**    Well, she can't go back, can she? What sort of a life will she have back there?

**Jack**    She's not going to go on the game here, is she? Not in that bedsit?

**Ray**    I bloody hope not. I hope all that's done with.

**Jack**    She's not known anything else though, has she?

**Ray**    Look, I've done my bit, I've made a difference. What's the score?

**Jack** and **Ray** *move downstage and prepare for another game.*

**Jack**    Your serve! Hey, she doesn't think she's still in London, does she? Coz somebody told me of a girl they brought in from Poland and dumped here and she thought she was in London. Apparently she went into Jackson's and asked where the London Eye was. It was only then that she realised.

**Ray** *is keen to continue.*

**Ray**    Are we playing or what?

**Jack**    Well I tell you, all credit to you, mate. I mean, I think you've completely lost the plot but all credit to you.

**Ray**    What would you have done?

**Jack**    Well, I wouldn't have gone into it up to my neck.

**Ray**    I thought you wanted to make a difference?

**Jack**    Up to a point.

**Ray**    Or did you just want to make a film?

**Jack**    Hey. Get a grip.

**Ray**    At least I can stand up and be counted!

**Jack**    Listen, I take my hat off! But will she fit in round here?

**Ray**   She's fine, I've introduced her to Amy and she goes down the Grapes.

**Jack**   Does Amy know what she used to do then?

**Ray**   Talk sense, what do you think I am?

**Jack**   No comment, mate. No comment.

**Ray**   Right my serve is it, come on!

*He hits the ball towards the fourth wall.*

Urgh!

*Music.*

*Lights.*

**Jack** *and* **Ray** *exit, taking their sports bags with them.* **Amy** *enters. They are in the Grapes pub. She places the mike stand downstage and sits on a crate. She is finishing a song as the music fades and* **Anja** *enters up the steep stairs of the pub's attic.*

**Amy**
  Coz everybody wants to be nineteen.
  Do you know what I mean!
  Coz everybody wants to be nineteen.

**Anja** (*breathless*)   I bring drink?

**Amy** *takes the drink.*

**Amy**   Thanks.

**Anja**   Please you are good, sing again.

**Amy**   No, we have to be out of here in half an hour.

**Anja**   I like when you sing.

**Amy**   You're easily pleased!

**Amy** *has a drink and the two girls relax.*

**Anja**   Your father is good man.

**Amy**   Ray?

**Anja**    Is good man.

**Amy**    Oh he's not my dad. Not my real dad anyway. My real dad owned a double-glazing firm, and then Mum married a bloke on supply, but it didn't last too long! She met Ray in here.

**Anja**    In pub?

**Amy**    Yes, I think she was drowning her sorrows. Ray rented a room, when he first came to Hull. My mum and Ray have been together about four years. My dad's been married four times but Ray's okay in small doses.

**Anja**    I think he good man.

**Amy** *is teasing.*

**Amy**    Do you fancy him?

**Anja**    Ray?

**Amy**    Yes!

**Anja**    No!

**Amy** *still teasing.*

**Amy**    You do, don't you?

**Anja**    He is old man.

**Amy**    Don't tell him that, for goodness' sake. That's why he plays squash, he thinks he's still twenty-five. How did you meet him?

**Anja**    In London.

**Amy**    Yes, he said.

**Anja**    In London, I help with his story.

**Amy**    Where are you from?

**Anja**    Moldova. Is poorest country in Europe. Many people leave, many children are left. I wanted to be dancer and sing.

**Amy**   Why can't you?

**Anja**   Too many years.

**Amy**   So what did you do in London?

**Anja**   All questions about me.

**Amy**   Yes, I want to know about you!

**Anja**   What about you, what do you want?

**Amy**   Me? I want to be famous.

**Anja**   Is why you sing?

**Amy**   Everybody wants to be rich and famous here, Anja, it's a way out.

**Anja**   I wish was famous.

**Pat** *enters from upstage. She is clearly worse for drink and breathless from the stairs.*

**Pat** (*breathless*)   Oh hell! You finished?

**Amy**   Yes.

**Pat**   God, them stairs!

**Amy**   Keep you fit, Pat.

**Pat** *notices* **Anja**.

**Pat**   I don't know you, do I, you a student and all then?

**Anja**   Me?

**Pat**   You're not one of these that's tekking uz jobs are you, what are you a Pole? They've all come here since t' floods, mind you we weren't affected but our Sammy was, my son, you ask for somebody to come and do sommat for you and what you get is a load of Poles.

**Anja**   I am not a Pole!

**Pat**  I mean, they're cheap but they're not as good as they say they are. Talk about being European, you can't move for the sods.

**Anja**  I not work here, I do not take jobs.

**Pat**  Well, there's no jobs in here: since t' smoking ban we've been going downhill. 'kinnel you'll not be able to bastard breathe next without somebody being all over you like a bad coat. They'll want to know when you're having a shit next.

**Anja**  I am not Polish.

**Pat**  What are you then?

**Anja**  Moldovian!

**Pat**  Oh bloody hell, where the hell is that?

**Anja**  Is Europe.

**Pat** *addresses* **Amy**.

**Pat**  Hey, I could sing you know.

**Amy**  Really?

**Pat**  Oh aye, I could sing, I could do all that. I loved Paul McCartney and Elvis. Oh what I would've done for Elvis, eh? You wouldn't believe it but I did the circuits.

**Amy**  Singing?

**Pat**  Singing and a bit of stripping, well, more stripping than singing but I've been up there.

**Amy**  Were you a stripper then?

**Anja**  What is?

**Amy**  Pole dancing.

**Anja**  Pole dancing?

**Amy**  Lap dancing . . .

**Pat**   Yes, you name it I've done it! Well, you've got to be broad-minded living with Les. He used to take me from club to club. Six strips a night I'd do sometimes. Couldn't friggin' well do it now like . . . Aye, it's full of fucking foreigners Hull now, mind you I don't mind as long as they're buying beer. Ten minutes girls all right, then the lights are off. Oh these bloody stairs.

**Pat** *makes her way off stage. She is watched by* **Amy** *and* **Anja**.

**Amy**   What?

**Anja**   She is like crazy woman!

**Amy**   I don't think she knows what she's talking about half the time!

**Anja**   Is she always same?

**Amy**   Same or sane?

**Anja**   Please?

**Amy**   I think she's barmy. Ray reckons that they've both got a few tiles loose.

**Anja**   On the roof?

**Amy**   No, on their heads.

**Anja**   Tiles on their heads?

**Amy**   It's a saying.

**Anja**   It's saying on their heads?

**Amy**   They're both a bit cuckoo!

**Anja**   Cuckoo?

**Ray** *enters. He too struggles with the stairs. He has come straight from the squash match.*

**Ray**   Ah all right?

**Anja**   Hello.

**Amy**   You okay?

**Ray**  Just about . . .

**Amy**  They want us out in ten minutes so I'll get this stuff sorted and pay Pat, see if she can string a sentence together.

**Amy** *takes the mike stand and exits.*

*There is an awkward silence between* **Ray** *and* **Anja**.

**Ray**  Okay?

**Anja**  Yes.

*A beat.*

**Ray**  Is everything okay with the flat?

**Anja**  Yes, it is good.

**Ray**  Good.

**Anja**  I must get job. I must get papers.

**Ray**  Yes, I'm working on that.

**Anja**  I must work. I cannot rely on you. Is very kind but I must do something.

**Ray** *is finding it difficult.*

**Ray**  Yes, yes I know, I . . . as long as you are okay.

**Anja**  Have you finished your work?

**Ray**  Yes, I've finished all that.

**Anja**  You look for new story?

**Ray**  Probably! I just hope they still want it that's all.

*A beat.*

**Anja**  It will be a good story?

**Ray**  I hope so!

*A beat.*

**Anja**  Amy I like.

**Ray**    I'm glad.

**Ray** *is struggling to communicate.*

*A beat.*

**Anja**    You must come to apartment.

**Ray**    No, I think I'd better not.

**Anja**    Yes, yes, you must come.

**Ray**    I don't think it would be right.

**Anja**    I will make it nice for you.

**Ray**    I'm sure.

**Anja** *is becoming more confident and effusive.*

**Anja**    Yes, I will make it very nice for you!

**Ray**    You will have to come to supper at my house!

**Anja**    Yes, I will look forward to that!

**Ray**    So would I, Anja, so would I!

**Ray** *looks at* **Anja** *and smiles a warm smile.*

*Music.*

*Lights.*

**Ray**    So let's say I did that, let's say I took a stand and got her out, made a statement. That I stood up to be counted! How many of us would actually do that? We think about it and then it's gone. Let's say that I did that, and let's say that I had to tell Caz, and let's say that I told her down in little Switzerland!

**Ray** *and* **Caz** *are standing with a kite looking out to the audience.* **Caz** *is wearing a light raincoat. Gobos give a sense of place, and we get a suggestion that they are walking through autumn leaves.*

**Caz**    So when's the article going in?

**Ray**    Next month's weekend section.

**Caz**    Of the *Observer*?

**Ray**    The *Yorkshire Post*.

**Caz**    What happened to the *Observer*?

**Ray**    You know what this game's like, don't blink! I was lucky to place it somewhere else.

*A beat.*

**Caz**    At least it's over and done with.

**Ray**    That's right.

*A beat.*

**Caz**    I've invited Jack and Gemma around, by the way.

**Ray**    Oh right!

**Caz**    Try and build bridges. Has he finished his undercover filming?

**Ray**    I think he's going to Turkey next week.

**Caz** *saunters as if through autumn leaves.*

**Caz**    It's lovely down here in the autumn, don't you think?

**Ray**    It is.

**Caz**    The stress just falls off me when I'm down here.

*A beat.*

**Ray**    I think we need to talk.

**Caz**    We are talking, aren't we?

**Ray**    Yes, but we really need to talk.

**Caz**    Oh not this again, Ray, I can't bear it! I can't help the fact that you're nearly fifty, what can I say: get over it, pretend you're not.

**Ray**    Yes well, I think I've made a big mistake.

**Caz**    Oh please.

**Ray**   No, not with us.

**Caz**   I can live without this, you know?

**Ray**   I've . . . erm done something, and I'm not sure it's right.

**Caz**   Why, what is it?

**Ray**   I dunno if I can actually tell you!

**Caz**   Why, what is it?

*A beat.*

**Ray**   I've worked something out with Anja.

**Caz**   Anja?

**Ray**   My contact. The girl.

**Caz**   The brothel girl? Well what have you worked out with her then?

*A beat.*

**Ray**   I've got her out.

**Caz**   Of what?

**Ray**   The massage parlour!

**Caz**   So what's the big deal for us?

*A beat.*

**Ray**   She's here, she's in Hull.

**Caz**   So what?

*A beat.*

**Ray**   Well, it's cost me . . .

**Caz**   Eh?

**Ray**   This is what I'm saying . . .

**Caz**   Well, paying her rail fare is not going to break the bank, is it?

**Ray**  Yes, but now I've got her here I don't know what to do with her.

**Caz**  Well, you've helped her, now leave her.

**Ray**  I feel sorry for her though.

*A beat.*

**Caz**  Did you shag her, Ray?

**Ray**  Wow . . .

**Caz**  Did you . . . ?

**Ray**  What is this?

**Caz**  This is a conversation, Ray, and I want to know the truth.

**Ray**  No, I didn't, it's not in my nature, you know it's not!

**Caz**  So what's the mistake, where is she?

**Ray**  I've put her in a bedsit down Bev Road.

**Caz**  And you're paying for it?

**Ray**  It's next to nothing.

**Caz**  Can't she get a job?

**Ray**  She hasn't got a passport.

**Caz**  Oh bloody great.

**Ray**  She says she's going to help Amy with her songs.

**Caz**  Well, it sounds like she's got a lot to write about.

**Ray**  The thing is she had a load of debt.

**Caz**  I know the feeling.

**Ray**  And that's part of the problem.

**Caz**  Well, would it be rude to ask how much or will I read about that in the paper?

*A beat.*

**Ray**    Twenty thousand.

**Caz**    Wow.

**Ray**    Twenty grand.

**Caz**    That's what she owed?

**Ray**    She was in a debt bondage trap.

**Caz**    So how did you get her out?

*A beat.*

Where did you get the money from?

**Ray**    I borrowed it.

**Caz**    From where?

**Ray**    From the reserves.

**Caz**    What reserves?

**Ray**    In the house!

*A beat.*

**Caz**    What?

**Ray**    This is what I'm saying. I don't know if it's not been a mistake!

**Caz** (*furious*)    I can't . . . a bloody mistake . . .

**Ray**    Hey, hey!

**Caz**    You don't know her, you know sod all about her, apart from the obvious and now this . . .

**Ray**    I know . . . I know.

**Caz**    I'm working in a shit-hole comprehensive to get this slag out of trouble?

**Ray**    Hey!

**Caz**    Don't 'hey' me, this is bloody ridiculous.

**Ray**    Hey!

**Caz**    Bollocks hey!

**Ray** *moves towards* **Caz**.

**Ray**    Caz?

**Caz**    Don't touch me, Jesus Christ!

**Ray**    I just wanted to do something.

**Caz**    And you'll sell the story for what, £500 if you're lucky? We've to find Amy's fees for next term, you take that out and we're in the shit.

**Ray**    I know it looks bad.

**Caz**    How else can it look?

**Ray**    I know but listen to me . . .

**Caz**    You had sex with her, haven't you?

**Ray**    No way!

**Caz**    Yes way, yes way! Well you have made a mistake, Ray, you made a big mistake by telling me anything about her.

**Ray**    This is what I'm saying!

**Caz**    And what do we do now, ask her to supper?

**Ray**    I already have done to be honest!

**Caz**    Do we try and trace her family tree?

**Ray**    Can I explain this?

**Caz**    Where does it end, this?

**Ray**    Can I just . . .

**Caz**    What do I do now, do I go round and make her bed? Wash her sheets? I tell you what we should do, we should get her in to make our beds: she can do some washing.

**Ray**    Don't be funny!

**Caz**   If we've paid for her she might as well come and help clean up. Can she iron? Can she wash? Or are most of her skills to do with being on her back? Or is it on all fours, you'd know wouldn't you?

**Ray**   I just think sometimes you have to make a difference.

**Caz**   Make a difference?

**Ray**   Yes . . . Make a genuine difference, that's why I did it!

**Caz**   She's an illegal former prostitute!

**Ray**   Hey, hey!

**Caz**   And you've paid off her debt bondage to the tune of twenty grand which we're now paying for on our mortgage?

**Ray**   Hey, listen to me!

**Caz** (*angrily*)   Yes, I think we should have her around for supper, it should be frigging illuminating!

*Music.*

*Light.*

**Caz**, **Jack**, **Gemma**, **Amy**, **Anja** and **Ray** *set the conservatory location. The gobos create the atmosphere and the chandelier is flown.* **Caz** *helps issue people with drink.* **Anja** *is dressed in what appears to be second-hand clothes. The atmosphere is tense.*

**Gemma**   Well, that was lovely, Caz!

**Amy**   Just something she always throws together.

**Jack**   I wish I could throw something together like that.

**Caz**   Thanks, Jack, I know you are on your best behaviour!

**Gemma**   Aren't we all?

**Ray**   Did you enjoy that, Anja?

**Anja**   Yes.

*A beat.*

**Gemma**    Good.

**Anja**    You have lovely big house.

**Caz**    Yes, yes, it's not paid for though is it, Ray?

**Ray**    Not yet.

**Jack**    Not like us.

**Ray**    Thanks.

*All laugh.*

**Ray**    But we're trying.

**Gemma**    Do you like Hull, Anja?

**Anja**    What I have seen.

**Gemma**    Good! That's good then!

**Jack**    So what is it like in Moldova?

**Anja**    Bad.

*A beat.*

**Jack**    Yes, right. It must be.

**Gemma**    I bet it's very different.

**Anja**    Yes.

*A beat.*

**Amy**    So what kind of work did you do, Anja, before you came to Hull?

**Anja**    You not know?

**Amy**    No, why?

**Ray**    I don't think we . . .

**Anja**    I work as prostitute in Europe and in London brothel.

*A beat.*

**Amy**    Oh right . . .

**Anja**    Yes . . .

*A beat.*

**Caz**    So . . . coffee anyone?

**Jack**    I think we'd better.

**Caz**    I'll bring a pot.

**Caz** *exits.*

*Silence.*

**Gemma**    So would you ever go back to Moldova?

**Anja**    Is nothing there for me.

**Gemma**    But what about your family?

**Anja**    My family not interest in me.

**Ray**    Anja's cousin sold her.

**Gemma**    Couldn't you go to the police?

**Anja**    My cousin in police.

**Ray**    She sold her, sold her for sex, Gemma.

**Gemma** *is cut.*

**Gemma**    Yes, I'm getting the picture, Ray, thanks!

**Anja**    They make you make sex all time, with period, with no period, it is not matter, they take out some girls' teeth if they have small mouth.

**Gemma**    Oh hell!

**Anja**    One girl is twelve and they sell her much money in Middle East. Turkish men are very bad, they think we are nothing but meat.

**Gemma**    It is just slavery, isn't it?

**Jack**   Christ, well of course it is!

**Amy**   Nothing's changed, not since Wilberforce. I mean there's a lot of flag-waving but what's changed?

**Ray**   How can things change unless we all do something about it?

**Jack**   Meaning what?

**Ray**   Meaning something real!

**Gemma**   It's dreadful, I mean Jack talks about it, but I mean to see one just sitting there in front of you, like a . . . well it's . . .

**Ray**   It's what, Gemma?

**Gemma**   It's heart-breaking.

*A beat.*

**Anja**   I enjoy food thank you!

**Amy**   Yes, but we've got to go now!

**Anja**   Thank you for inviting me to lovely home, it is nice to see where Ray live. Goodbye.

**Amy**   We're going down the Grapes rehearsing!

**Jack**   Bye.

**Ray**   I'll see you later.

**Gemma**   Bye.

**Anja** *and* **Amy** *exit.*

*Silence.*

**Jack**   Mmmm!

**Gemma**   Well, it's not the usual supper chat, is it?

**Ray**   So there we are, that's our new cleaner, by the way!

**Jack**   You are joking?

**Ray**    Two mornings a week: we're paying her, everything's above board.

**Jack**    Cracking shape though.

**Gemma**    What?

**Jack**    I said she's a cracking shape.

**Gemma** *is irritable.*

**Gemma**    I knew he'd have to say something.

**Jack**    I'm only saying.

**Gemma**    You wouldn't have said that if she'd been fat.

**Jack**    Rather obviously.

**Gemma**    I knew he'd have to say something.

**Jack**    I suspect that if she'd been fat she wouldn't have been trafficked. They don't do the fat ones.

**Gemma**    What is this?

**Jack**    I'm simply making a point. There would have been no interest in her if she hadn't been attractive, this is why it's a slave trade, they don't want just anyone. They want ones that they can sell. It's premeditated. It's not an accident that she's fit.

**Gemma**    So now she's fit!

**Jack**    Hey, Caz is the feminist not you, just because she's out of the room you don't have to play her part!

**Gemma**    I can't believe you'd talk about someone like that!

**Jack**    They didn't take any little black slaves, they just wanted the big strong ones, that's the point I'm making, it's selective!

**Gemma**    This is what he does, he has to say something when there's nothing to be said!

**Jack**    I'm trying to make a serious point!

**Gemma**    Drivel comes out of his mouth sometimes, Ray!

**Ray**    I know that!

**Jack**    Hey, I can't help it if she made you feel insecure.

**Jack** *is rising.*

**Ray**    Hey, hey!

**Gemma**    You what?

**Jack**    I'm just saying.

**Gemma**    She didn't make me feel insecure.

**Jack**    Well, you're acting like she did!

**Gemma**    Well, she didn't!

**Jack**    Well, she should do, I mean after all isn't that the point of attraction?

**Gemma**    Shut up you're drunk!

**Jack**    She's dangerous, damaged goods you see, something different: threatening.

**Ray**    Easy, mate!

**Jack**    That's the point, they're different, exotic, that's why it's a slave trade, they're not like us, they do different things, they have different standards! I'm not saying that it's right, I'm not saying that some of the girls don't know what they're doing, some of them clearly think that they can handle it. What I'm saying is we're fascinated by it because basically she's an alien. I mean it literally, she's been to places we can only fantasise about.

**Gemma**    Oh please . . .

**Jack**    Well, she has, at least be honest with yourself. That girl has done things that we can only dream of!

**Gemma**    Jesus!

**Jack**    What have I said now?

**Gemma**    And you're supposed to be right on?

**Ray**    She told me that if you want an operation you pay, if you want a bedpan, you pay, if you want to pass your driving test you take the instructor a pot of coffee. That's the way, you want a degree you sleep with the professor. It's the way things work out there!

**Jack**    Are we any different?

**Gemma**    But she's an immigrant, Ray, she'll get sent back.

**Ray**    She's got thirty days, they're talking about changing the rules anyway.

**Jack**    Not in the next thirty days they're not.

**Ray**    Well, maybe we'll see somebody, maybe somebody will be able to sort it.

**Gemma**    I mean is that right that they can come here and work as illegal sex workers and stay here? I mean is that right?

**Jack**    She could get a job with the Olympics, couldn't she? Will they be bussing 'em in for that? I'm not saying that a few wanks are a bad thing by the way.

**Gemma**    Take no notice, he's drunk.

**Jack**    Thank you!

**Gemma**    Again!

**Jack**    Well, no matter what you both say, she's still got a cracking figure.

**Jack** *finds this amusing.*

**Gemma**    I'll see how Caz is getting on with the coffee.

**Jack**    Yes, make mine a very strong one.

**Gemma** *exits.*

*A beat.*

**Jack**  Bloody hell mate, you've bitten off more than you can chew, haven't you?

**Ray**  Sometimes you have to put your barrow down.

**Jack**  You been there then, have you?

**Ray**  Hey?

**Jack**  Come on?

**Ray**  Are you mad?

**Jack**  Are you?

**Ray**  No way.

**Jack**  It must be killing you, mate.

*A beat.*

There's a line, it's a game, Ray, you don't go over the line.

**Ray**  I do!

**Jack**  What are you trying to prove?

**Ray**  I just wanted to make a difference.

**Jack**  To show us as hypocrites?

**Ray**  Maybe!

**Jack**  Well you've done that all right so now what?

*A beat.*

**Ray**  I want to touch her, Jack . . . I want to hold her and say it's okay! Part of me wants to sing from the rooftops, tell everyone in the world that I've made a difference; part of me is ashamed. I only discovered that this was an issue when I was looking to make money.

**Jack**  Oh aye, there's that!

**Ray**   Last week, I went to see her at the Grapes. They've got a group, it's bollocks but she thinks it great! Her and Amy.

**Jack**   Oh aye?

**Ray**   She seemed so out of place, just here in Hull so bloody lost. So pathetic and all. I nearly touched her then. I nearly held her then.

**Jack**   It wouldn't have been so bad, would it?

**Ray**   I don't know, I just feel like it's out of the box and I don't know what to do with her.

*A beat.*

The strange thing is, sometimes I wish I could just get rid of her. Sometimes I'm so pleased with what I've done and other times I just want to rub her out. Fucking hell, Jack, there are times when I wished that she didn't exist!

*Music.*

*Lights.*

**Jack** *and* **Ray** *exit.*

*Lights come up on* **Amy** *and* **Anja**. *They are rehearsing a song. They have brought on mike stands.*

**Amy**
I wanted to dream in English
Wanted it to be all new
Wanted to find, some peace of mind
Before I grew
Too old . . .

**Anja**
Wanted to dream in English
Wanted to just run away
Wanted to see a world that was free
That's what I'd pray
Each night.

But how do you understand
The rules of a different land
That allows you to just disappear?
Couldn't speak or say
The words anyway
Coz nobody knew I was here
Please don't pretend I'm not here.

**Both**
Wanted to dream in English.
Wanted to come and belong
Wanted to sing of beautiful things
But lost the song
Somewhere.

Wanted to dream in English
Wanted to stay a while
Wanted to be a nice family
A husband, a wife, a child.

But how do you understand
The rules of a different land
That allows you just to disappear
Couldn't speak or say
The words anyway
Coz nobody knew I was here.

**Amy** *and* **Anja** *are left laughing with each other after their song.*

**Amy**    That was good?

**Anja**    Yes?

**Amy**    That was great.

**Anja**    For many years, I am dreaming in English.

*A beat.*

**Amy**    I wish I was like you. You've seen so much of life.

**Anja**    You joke with me.

**Amy**    No, I'm serious. I left school and went straight to university. I've got nothing to write about. We could go all the way with you writing, like the Cheeky Girls.

**Anja**    And we wear costume like Cheeky Girls? I know Cheeky Girls!

**Amy**    Well maybe not the costumes eh?

**Anja**    Yes, I like!

**Amy**    You know Robbie Williams?

**Anja**    Yes I like.

**Amy**    I've seen him at Glasgow.

**Anja**    Oh no!

**Amy**    Yes, fantastic. We went last year me and Mum. Ray hates him, he sat in the car and then drove us back.

**Anja**    Ray did that?

**Amy**    He's not a Robbie fan.

**Anja**    Maybe we go if he come in Hull?

**Les** *stands upstage in one of the portals. He is clearly drunk and as nasty as he can muster, and breathless.*

**Les**    Now then what have we got here? All right? Pat said we'd got another little helper.

**Anja**    Hello.

**Les**    How you doing, darling, all right are you?

**Anja**    I think.

**Les**    You Polish then?

**Anja**    No.

**Les**    Oh aye, they're all Polish in here now, can't move for the fuckers. Bloody hell who would have thought it, Hull the home of continental Europe. You couldn't write it, could you?

**Anja**    Please?

**Les**    You got a flat here then have you, paying rent and all that?

**Anja**    Yes, yes!

**Les**    And you still live at home, do you Amy?

**Amy**    At the moment.

**Les**    At the moment, yes of course you do! And Ray all right is he?

**Amy**    I think.

**Les**    Used to stay here, before him and your mam got together, he was fascinated with my snakes was Ray. Did you know?

**Amy**    How would I know that?

**Les**    Oh aye, he likes a story does Ray. What's her name then?

**Anja**    My name is Anja.

**Les**    Are you looking for part-time work then or what?

**Amy**    Pat said you had no work.

**Les**    Yes, but we could train her up in case, couldn't we? We'd have to put her through a test like but . . .

**Anja**    What is test?

**Les**    You fancy a little job, do you, if one came up?

**Anja**    I can work very hard!

**Les**    Aye, I bet you could! You finished for tonight then? Or are you going sing some more of that bollocks, what was it?

**Anja**    I write.

**Les**    Tell you what, why don't you stay behind one night when Pat's got a karaoke on, I bet you'd like that . . . Be nice that, I'd like to see you both up on t' stage down there. You never know, if I liked you I might sign you up! Drop key behind bar, if I'm in t' cellar will you.

**Les** *exits.*

*Silence.*

**Amy**   Urgh.

**Anja**   What?

**Amy**   Creepy.

**Anja**   You think?

**Amy**   Don't you?

**Anja**   Is okay.

**Amy**   You're kidding!

**Anja**   I think he like all men.

**Amy**   And you should know.

*Both girls laugh.*

**Anja**   I think he follow his dick! And it probably not a nice one.

**Amy** *laughs.*

**Amy**   You?

**Anja**   What?

**Amy**   You make me laugh.

**Anja**   Maybe I write jokes.

*A beat.*

**Amy**   I wish I was like you, Anja.

**Anja**   No way, this is crazy talk.

**Amy**   Yes! I have had no life here!

**Anja**   No, I do not want you be like me. You are somewhere. I am nowhere.

**Amy**   We'd better take this stuff down, before Les has a stroke.

**Amy** *begins to gather the mikes together,* **Anja** *helps but is extremely tearful.*

**Amy**   Are you okay?

**Anja**   Yes, but sometimes I scared. I scared the men who know me know where I am.

**Amy**   That's all over, Anja, that's finished. Ray's seen to that! That's never going to happen to you again!

*Music.*

*Lights. Spotlight on* **Ray** *as he enters.*

**Ray**   Let's say that we could really make a difference if we did something, but how would it be seen, what would people think?

**Amy** *and* **Anja** *strike the mikes and other props, as* **Ray** *watches them.*

*Music fades.*

*Lights.*

**Caz** *enters. She is emotionally stretched. A spotlight picks her out in an upstage portal.*

**Caz**   I mean I wanted to admire him for what he'd done. Even though he'd dropped us in the shit! It was noble, that's the thing he was trying to say, it was noble . . .

**Ray**   Let's say she thought that but . . .

**Caz**   I wanted to admire what he'd done, but I couldn't help but think there was something else.

**Ray**   Suspicion, you see . . .

**Caz**    I could have kicked myself for thinking it, was it me, was it my insecurity?

**Ray**    Let's say it starts to get to you . . .

**Caz**    I wanted to think he was doing the right thing, but I'd been burnt before.

**Ray**    Let's say it was like this every night . . .

**Caz**    How bad has it got to get for you to want to get out? How bad? She was here, you see, she was out of the box! She was real and she was in our house.

*Lights.*

**Anja** *enters. She has a mop and bucket and is about to polish the stage.*

**Caz**    You done the toilet?

**Anja**    Yes.

**Caz**    Have you?

**Anja**    Yes, yes, I do this.

**Caz**    Well, can you do it again?

**Anja**    I already do.

**Caz**    Well, can you do it again because when Ray has a shave he leaves mess all over and I can't stand it being a mess.

**Anja**    But I already do.

**Caz**    Well, can you do it again!

*A beat.*

And then I want to you to take the dog out.

**Anja**    Ray say I clean two hours only. He not want me clean more than two hours.

**Caz**    Well, Ray isn't here, I want you to take the dog out.

**Anja**    Well, Ray say . . .

**Caz**    Just take the dog out and then go to the Tesco's and get me some wine. I haven't got time. We've got an assessment at school.

**Anja**    But I have band rehearsals.

**Caz**    I'm only asking you to do a simple thing, if you can't do that I'll get somebody else. Do you think I'd be better if I got somebody else?

**Anja**    That is for you to say.

**Caz**    You answering back now?

**Anja**    I just say is for you.

**Caz**    Just do it!

**Ray** *enters to witness the tail end of this scene.*

**Ray**    Everything all right?

**Anja**    Yes! Yes!

**Caz**    Oh yes, everything's just great!

**Ray**    Caz, she . . .

**Caz**    She's what?

**Ray**    Nothing!

**Caz**    No, right . . . that's absolutely right.

**Anja**    Maybe I go.

**Ray**    Is this something that we can talk about?

**Caz**    No, Ray, I'm through with talking about it, I've tried and I've tried but I'm through with talking about it, we talk but we never communicate, you're not here, you're not with me, not any more.

**Anja**    I go.

**Ray**    No, please.

**Anja**   Yes, I go . . . I go clean toilet. Sorry.

**Anja** *exits.*

*There is serious tension between* **Ray** *and* **Caz**.

**Ray**   I don't know what to say!

**Caz**   That makes two of us.

**Ray**   I'm trying to make a difference.

**Caz**   Oh grow up.

**Ray**   You grow up . . . she's here, she's doing well . . .

**Caz**   She's all over you like a bad coat.

**Ray**   Eh?

**Caz**   Come on, don't say you can't see it. You save her from herself and the last thing she wants is to be your friend.

**Ray**   What?

**Caz**   You're fooling yourself! If you made it known what you'd really like to do she'd be there for you.

**Ray**   Well, I don't see it like that . . .

**Caz**   Well, I do. I see it like that, what did you think, she was going to come up here and everything was going to be all right? She was going to meet a nice English lad and settle down and you'd be the godfather? You've said it yourself, she's dangerous.

**Ray**   Hang on . . .

**Caz**   She's brutalised and vulnerable, you look into her eyes, you look in her eyes and then tell me that there isn't anything there for you!

**Ray**   You're reading things into it!

**Caz**   Christ, you're a God, you're her saviour!

**Ray**   I can't help that!

**Caz**   We get one life, one go at it! You want to save the world, you go do it. I'm doing what I can, we try and do what we can but there comes a time when we have to leave it at the school gates.

**Ray**   This isn't fair!

**Caz**   There comes a time when we have to say enough is enough!

**Ray**   She's only been here a couple of months, give her a chance.

**Caz**   And you're down the pub every night and it's not because of Amy, is it? You hardly showed any interest in the band, did you? Did you?

**Ray**   No . . . all right I didn't, but Amy treats me like I'm not here. I can't help it that I'm not her dad, Caz. I can't help that, but she treats me like shit. Do this Ray, pick me up Ray, come for me Ray, your tea can wait Ray. Come and get me, I've lost my key, lend 's a few quid Ray, what am I, a bloody servant?

**Caz**   Let her go, Ray . . . Let her go.

**Ray**   I am trying my best here, trying to achieve something. Maybe it's just one little thing. We're such bloody hypocrites, we all nod towards global warming, Save the Whale, Greenpeace, Stop the Trafficking, and yet when anyone actually tries to make a difference it's like they've put their head on back to front. It's like the world can't cope with them.

**Caz**   It's not about all that, it's about her!

**Ray**   What do you want me to do?

**Caz**   I want you to let her go. I want you to come back!

**Ray**   You know what, you know what I wish. I wish I'd never done it. I wish I'd left her to stew in that shit hole, I wish I was like everybody else here, nodding and putting fifty pence in a box and feeling cleansed. Feeling that they'd done their bit and then washing their bloody hands. That's what I wish!

**Caz**    That's what I wish and all.

*Music.*

*Lights.*

**Ray** *moves downstage and sits watching the action.*

**Kate** *is seen in a portal cleaning glasses, moving crates about.*

**Kate**    Funny thing is I thought about that girl, you know what I'm saying? I mean I never thought I'd see her again, I'm mean it was nearly six months. But there's some people you meet and you never forget! It was when I went up to see our Pat, well you could have knocked me over with a fucking feather!

**Les** *enters with a crate. He looks rough as shit.*

**Les**    Kate, your Pat's gone to bed. She says she got a fucking migraine. So it's me and you in the cellar, sweetheart.

**Kate**    I dunno, summing really funny happened.

**Les**    That doesn't surprise me working here.

**Kate**    I dunno, it . . .

**Les**    What?

**Kate**    That girl.

**Les**    Amy, the one in the band, bloody students. I'd kick 'em out but Pat's got a thing about her step-dad. I dunno what she expects like but.

**Kate**    The other girl.

**Les**    Oh her!

**Kate**    I think I've seen her before.

**Les**    Eh?

**Kate**   I've seen her before.

**Les**   How's this then?

**Kate**   In Paddington.

**Les**   What?

**Kate**   Yes, I'm sure it's her, she was there about nine months. She was one of the working girls.

**Les**   You're kidding?

**Kate**   I never forget a face. I'm almost sure of it, never spoke hardly ever, popular and she owed a fortune they said, East European.

**Les**   Well she's that all right.

**Kate**   She'd do anything, they said. I'm sure it's her.

**Anja** *enters.*

**Anja**   Okay, Les, we go now, we have finished, we have turn light off.

**Les**   Have you, that's good then!

**Anja**   Thank you. Good night.

**Anja** *notices* **Kate**.

**Kate**   Hello darling? How're you doing then all right?

**Anja**   Good night!

**Anja** *exits rapidly.*

**Kate**   That is her.

**Les**   Oh aye, we get all the shit up here plagues, floods!

**Kate**   That is her.

**Les**   A bloody hooker in my pub! A filthy piece of shit like that, would you believe it?

**Kate**   That is her, can you believe it?

*A beat.*

**Les**   She a good girl then, did you say?

**Kate**   Cor, a small world innit?

**Les**   It bloody is, Katie girl, it bloody well is, isn't it?

**Les** *and* **Kate** *exit.*

*Music.*

*Lights.*

**Ray**   And let's say that I did visit Anja once in that small flat down Beverley Road. Part of me wishing that she wasn't here, wishing that she was just a story. Wishing that I could put her to bed and pretend she didn't exist, like we all do! And shall we say the flat I had put her in was damp and no better than the basement I met her in, in Paddington. Yes, let's say that there's me and her in this small bedsit, me and her close, and her wanting to make me perogi or pasta, wanting in some way to pay me back.

**Ray** *has taken a candle and candleholder during this speech and lit the candle and placed it centre stage just in front of where he is seated.* **Anja** *enters. She is dressed a little more soberly than previously. She carries a pan of pasta.*

**Anja**   You like pasta, Ray?

**Ray**   I do.

**Anja**   I make very good sauce.

**Ray**   Great.

**Anja**   I like to cook, but afraid not very good.

**Ray**   I'm sure you're absolutely great.

**Anja**   No, Caz is very good cook. I am how you say basic.

**Ray**   Don't put yourself down so much, I'm sure you're better than me, I burn water.

**Anja**   Really?

**Ray**    Well, I'll give it a go.

**Anja**    You make me laugh, Ray.

**Ray**    Do I?

**Anja**    Yes, yes, you make me laugh.

**Ray**    That's good then.

**Anja**    I tell Amy that you make me laugh.

**Ray**    Do you?

**Anja**    Yes, I tell Amy.

**Ray**    I'm afraid I don't make Amy laugh!

**Anja**    I can make her laugh so is okay!

*A beat.*

**Ray**    How's the band doing?

**Anja**    Good, but I think have to finish rehearsing at pub.

**Ray**    Why?

**Anja**    A woman . . . she know me . . . I think is Les relation, she know me.

**Ray**    What woman?

**Anja**    In the pub she know me from London, I think is her very much.

**Ray**    No?

**Anja**    I think.

**Ray**    So what? What's she going to do? Amy says that your songs are good.

**Anja**    I like write songs.

**Ray**    Well, that's good.

**Anja**    You let I will sing to you.

**Ray**    One day eh?

**Anja**   Yes, sure I will sing to you one day eh?

**Ray**   Yes.

**Anja**   Is Caz still mad with me, Ray? I don't like make unhappy.

**Ray**   No, she's not mad with you, Anja, she's mad with me!

**Anja**   We make costume for the band. I make very good costume, you know Cheeky Girls?

**Ray**   Sort of!

**Anja**   Yes, I make very good costume for the band. I think you like, Ray.

**Ray** *laughs.*

**Ray**   Oh dear . . .

**Anja**   What is wrong?

**Ray**   Nothing, Anja . . . nothing, but I'd better go.

**Anja**   Why?

**Ray**   Because this is not right!

**Ray** *prepares to get to his feet.*

**Anja**   No, no is feels right. Is nice pasta, nice apartment!

**Ray**   I think if I stay I may do something that is not right.

**Anja**   Please?

**Ray**   I'm afraid, Anja.

**Anja**   Ray is afraid?

**Ray**   I'm afraid if I stay I may want to . . .

**Anja**   What, Ray? You can do what you feel in my apartment!

**Ray**   I'm afraid that I may want to kiss you, Anja!

*Silence.*

I think that if I stay here I will want to kiss you. And . . .

**Anja**    Oh!

**Ray**    I'm afraid that I might want to hold you, kiss you and hold you.

**Anja**    Is okay!

*A beat.*

**Ray**    No, it's not, Anja, not the way I want to hold you. I want to hold you in a certain way!

**Anja**    Ray!

**Ray**    I'm sorry.

**Anja**    It is okay.

**Ray**    I'm sorry, Anja, I wish I didn't feel like this.

**Anja**    Ray, I like . . . I like.

**Ray**    I know, but I shouldn't have come here.

**Anja**    I don't mind, Ray, hold me! I make feel happy.

**Ray**    I'd love to but . . .

**Anja**    Ray can hold me . . .

**Ray** *is confused and anxious.*

**Ray**    Jesus.

**Anja**    Yes, I owe Ray.

**Ray**    No Anja, you don't owe anybody anything.

**Anja**    Yes, I must pay . . .

**Ray**    I would love to, Anja, believe me, part of me would love to. But you're better than that, you're a lovely person.

**Anja**    I am not person, Ray, I have no papers.

*A beat.*

**Ray**    I can't see you again. I can't see you any more, it's too dangerous!

**Anja**    Dangerous?

**Ray**    For me, for Caz . . . me and you, Anja, do you understand? Do you understand that I'm saying?

**Anja**    Yes, Ray respect me!

**Ray**    Absolutely!

**Anja**    Ray, no sex.

**Ray**    Yes! Sadly.

*They both laugh.*

**Anja**    I understand.

**Ray**    Oh great, thank you!

**Anja**    I like fuck Ray but I no can do because of Caz!

**Ray**    I know, the world's insane!

**Anja**    But Ray can hold me. Ray can cuddle me, I like Ray cuddle me. Okay no sex, but I like if Ray cuddle me, he is my friend! Ray can cuddle Amy, Ray is okay can cuddle me too.

**Ray**    I don't cuddle Amy, Anja, she doesn't let me touch her!

*A beat.*

**Anja**    Ray must stay and have food, he must have wine and taste pasta!

*A beat.*

**Ray**    No, I'd better go, Anja, I'd better go before I make another big mistake!

**Anja**    Why, what is other mistake you have make, Ray?

**Ray**    Trying to save the world, Anja. That's the mistake!

**Anja**    You cannot save world, Ray, but you save me and for that I make pasta. I bring plates, you sit, you eat all pasta and we have wine and I let you cuddle me, no sex real good. Is okay with that, Ray?

**Ray**    I suppose!

**Anja**    Yes, I suppose. I like no sex with Ray. It is best sex I have ever had! I bring plates!

**Ray** *and* **Anja** *laugh.* **Anja** *exits.* **Ray** *remains seated and looks at the candle.*

*Music.*

**Caz** *and* **Amy** *enter at different portals.* **Caz** *seems the worse for drink. She has a wine glass and a bottle with her. An argument rages. Lights pick them out.*

**Amy**    You can't just sell the house, Mother.

**Caz**    Hey, I didn't ask for this.

**Amy**    You can't just sell it though, can you?

**Caz**    How bad it's got to get, Amy?

**Amy**    Ray's all right, what's the problem?

**Caz**    I thought you hated him?

**Amy**    I know but there's the band!

**Caz**    What do you think he's been up to, do you think he hasn't been with her?

**Amy**    What?

**Caz**    Waken up, Amy, he's been laughing at us all the time.

**Amy**    How has he?

**Caz**    I bet he's there now.

**Amy**    He's gone for a meal that's all, she wanted to cook him a meal!

**Caz**    A meal, she's cooking him a meal? And then what?

**Amy**    She's not like that! She's really nice.

**Caz**    She's a bloody hooker, you silly arse!

**Amy**    She was . . . That wasn't her fault, was it? She couldn't help that! She was sold for two hundred and fifty quid, did you know that?

**Caz**    Well, that isn't my fault, is it?

**Amy**    Mother, she's never had anything, she's just getting on her feet and you're treating her like a frigging criminal!

**Caz**    She is a frigging criminal, that's the point.

**Amy**    The men who sold her are the criminals, the men who use her!

**Caz**    Technically, technically she is a criminal and she should be sent back, as far away from me as possible!

**Amy**    To the people who sold her in the first place?

**Caz**    How do we know, how do we know that's true though?

**Amy**    How do we know it's not true?

**Caz**    Oh don't start all that: how do we know anything?

**Amy**    She wants to be here, she's happy here, is that so wrong?

**Caz**    I want her out of this house, I don't want her cleaning here any more!

**Amy**    How's she going to get any cash?

**Caz**    In fact I'll move into a flat, pocket a hundred and fifty thousand and move into a bedsit, that'll sort it!

**Amy**    Ray was just trying to help her, and I'm glad he did, at least he's tried to make a difference.

**Caz** Waken up, Amy. He was using that as a front all the time and I didn't see it! He's had her, first in London and now here; he's had her over and over again.

**Amy** How do you know? How do you really know though?

**Caz** Because that's all she's ever been good for!

*Music.*

*Lights.*

**Ray** *is in another space. He addresses the audience as he dismantles the candle which has been burning through the previous scene.*

**Ray** Let's say it's late. Yes, let's say it's late one night, and let's say that Anja's alone in the attic at the Grapes. Let's say she's going to a club later with Amy and they're going to sing one of her songs. That seems to make sense! And let's say that Amy's late getting there and that Anja's just waiting for her shall we?

**Anja** *begins to sing an acoustic version of 'Dreaming in English'. As she does,* **Les** *enters and watches her. On completion of the song* **Les** *claps sarcastically.* **Ray** *is on stage watching the action.*

**Anja**
    Wanted to dream in English
    Wanted to stay a while
    Wanted to be a nice family
    A husband, a wife, a child.

    But how do you understand
    The rules of a different land?
    That allows you just to disappear
    Couldn't speak or say the words anyway
    Coz nobody knew I was here!

**Les** (*breathless*) Very good.

**Anja** Yes?

**Les** Very good.

**Anja**   Thank you.

**Les**   You got a nice voice there.

**Anja**   It is sometimes not so sweet.

**Les**   So I hear.

**Anja**   Please?

**Les**   I suppose you think you can just come up here and do what you like, don't you?

**Anja**   Please?

**Les**   Well, I thought to myself I thought Les what do you do?

**Anja**   Do?

**Les**   You see I thought shall I throw you out, because I don't want that.

**Anja**   I do not understand, Les!

**Les**   I don't want that, what would people say if they got to know, do you know what I mean?

**Anja**   No?

**Les**   And I thought well maybe there's a way of working it, you know, maybe there's a way of making it work. Coz I mean we could always work something out couldn't we. Because I dare say if you've done it once, you've done it a hundred times.

**Anja**   Please I have to go!

**Les**   You're going nowhere.

**Anja**   Please I must go!

**Les** *blocks the door.*

**Les**   And I'm down there listening to the shite you call music, and I'm thinking well I'm not going to get anything from Amy, am I? I mean I wouldn't mind, you know, just for a change.

**Anja**    Please Les.

**Les**    Because Pat's, you know don't get me wrong, I'm not saying that Pat's not great but you need a change don't you?

**Anja**    Please?

**Les**    You know and I'm in here and Pat's gone to bed, got a fucking migraine and you're just up here aren't you?

**Anja**    Please I am a good girl!

**Les**    Yes I know that and I'm sure we can come to some sort of arrangement.

**Kate** enters. *She too is salacious and oiled, and breathless.*

**Kate**    She is up here then?

**Les**    Oh aye she's here.

**Kate**    I said it was you, funny old world isn't it?

**Anja**    I must go . . .

**Kate**    You're not going yet, is she, Les?

**Anja**    Please?

**Kate**    She ain't going yet, is she?

**Les**    Not until she's got a mouthful of this.

**Anja**    Please?

**Les** *looks at* **Anja**.

**Kate**    You gunna get a gob full of Les then or what?

**Anja**    Please?

**Les**    I think we can come to some arrangement can't we?

**Kate**    Come on, let's have a look then, I always wanted to see what you were up to in that bedsit.

**Anja**   No . . . I not do this any more.

**Kate**   Yes I think you will, because if you don't I know people who'll be interested in you, whether you paid 'em off or not!

**Les**   Come on, get down here!

**Anja**   Please . . .

**Les**   Get your fucking self down here.

**Kate**   Come on girl, what you waiting for?

**Les**   We can call this the rent can't we, and then you can come here and sing your songs as much as you fucking well like!

**Les** *drags* **Anja** *to a chair. He throws* **Anja** *to the ground as he begins to undo his trousers.*

**Kate**   And when you've done Les, you can do me. You hear that, when you done Les, you can get down here and do me . . .

**Les** (*to* **Anja**)   You hear that?

**Anja**   Yes! Yes!

**Kate**   I right fancy that I do! She can do me and all Les, it's only fair innit?

**Les**   And then she can do Pat, she'd like that would Pat, she said that when she first saw her, she said she'd right fancy that! You'll do that won't you, then you and Amy can come in here and sing as much as you like. I mean I've already told Ray that I was thinking about putting the rent up! You'll do that for us won't you?

*A beat.*

**Anja**   Yes!

**Les**   That's good then darling coz we don't want to have a scene do we? We don't want the fucking police here and all that shite do we? Go and get your Pat then Kate, while I get this started.

**Kate** *begins to exit.*

**Kate**    Don't let her go then will you?

**Les**    You think I fucking am?

*A beat.*

You're a good girl aren't you?

**Anja**    Yes, am a good girl!

**Les**    What are you then, Polish?

**Anja**    No!

**Les**    Aye, we get a lot of Poles up here. Right come on, let's get this sorted then shall we?

**Anja** *and* **Les** *freeze. As* **Ray** *addresses the audience* **Kate**, **Amy** *and* **Caz** *enter at upstage portals.*

**Ray**    Let's say that's what happened. Let's say Anja never told Ray how she was paying for her and Amy to rehearse at the Grapes, because she didn't want to let him down. And let's say that after a month of servicing Les and Kate and Pat, one night Les got jealous of Anja's relationship with Ray, lost his temper, threw her down the stairs from the attic and she broke her neck, let's say that!

**Les** *throws* **Anja** *to the ground.*

**Les**    And let's say that she died!

**Caz**    Let's say she died in Hull.

**Kate**    You could say that she'd already died in Moldova.

**Amy**    You could say that she really died in Italy . . .

**Les**    Or in Antwerp!

**Amy**    You could say that she really died in London!

*A beat.*

**Ray**    And I suppose you could say that this was just a play, and that none of it was true!

*A beat.*

**Anja**    Yes, you could say that!

*The ensemble stand and take their bows.*

*Lights fade to black.*

*Curtain.*

Lightning Source UK Ltd.
Milton Keynes UK
UKOW020630070212

186789UK00002B/2/P